The Problem of Pleasure

The tourism and leisure industries are big business. Opportunities for leisure and tourism have escalated as disposable income, technology, travel and education have become increasingly available in recent times. However, this trend has been juxtaposed with an increase in crime, particularly since the early 1950s. Acquisitive crimes have been facilitated with the development of more portable and valuable commodities and some activities, such as drink driving and disorder, have now been socially defined as crimes and are more readily identified through new technology such as the increasing use of CCTV.

The Problem of Pleasure covers them all. The purpose of this book is to inform and enlighten a range of readers, whose interests may be academic or commercial, on possible crime events and modi operandi of criminals. The book has a global perspective, bringing together leading academics from the UK, the USA, South Africa, Ghana, Australia and New Zealand who examine several aspects of leisure that are vulnerable to crime, from illegal hunting to street racing, as well as the impact of crime upon tourists and the tourism industry.

This book will be a key text for students of tourism and leisure as well as criminology and sociology; people working in the tourism and recreation industry; policy makers; and the police.

Carol Jones is a Senior Lecturer in Criminology in the Faculty of Applied Sciences at the University of Gloucestershire, UK. Prior to completing her first degree she worked for many years in the tourism industry in North Wales and Israel, leading to her continued interest in tourism and crime. She also has an interest in victimization, volunteering and crime prevention and community safety.

Elaine Barclay is Senior Lecturer in Criminology, University of New England, Armidale, NSW. For 16 years, she has undertaken rural social research on crime on farms and within rural communities. She co-edited *Crime in Rural Australia* (Federation Press, 2007).

Rob Mawby is Visiting Professor of Criminology and Criminal Justice at the University of Gloucestershire and at University of Wales College, Newport. His interests include crime reduction, policing and victimology, especially in a cross-national context; burglary, tourism and crime; and rural crime and policing. He has published numerous articles and books, including *Burglary* (Ashgate, 2007) and *Rural Policing and Policing the Rural* (with Richard Yarwood) (Ashgate, 2011).

The Problem of Pleasure

Leisure, tourism and crime

**Edited by Carol Jones,
Elaine Barclay and R. I. Mawby**

Routledge
Taylor & Francis Group

LONDON AND NEW YORK

First published 2012
by Routledge
2 Park Square, Milton Park, Abingdon, Oxon, OX14 4RN

Simultaneously published in the USA and Canada
by Routledge
711 Third Avenue, New York, NY 10017

Routledge is an imprint of the Taylor & Francis Group, an informa business

British Library Cataloguing in Publication Data
A catalogue record for this book is available from the British Library

Library of Congress Cataloging in Publication Data
The problem of pleasure : leisure, tourism and crime / edited by Carol Jones, Elaine Barclay and Rob I. Mawby. — 1st ed.
p. cm.
Includes bibliographical references.
1. Tourism—Social aspects. 2. Leisure—Economic aspects. 3. Crime—Economic aspects. 4. Crime and globalization. I. Jones, Carol. II. Barclay, Elaine. III. Mawby, Rob I.
G155.A1P7558 2011
338.4'791—dc23
2011024066

ISBN: 978-0-415-67236-8 (hbk)
ISBN: 978-0-415-67258-0 (pbk)
ISBN: 978-0-203-35740-8 (ebk)

Typeset in Times New Roman by Prepress Projects Ltd, Perth, UK

Contents

PART II

Figures

Tables

Contributor biographies

Elaine Barclay is Senior Lecturer in Criminology, University of New England, Armidale, NSW. For 16 years, she has undertaken rural social research on crime on farms and within rural communities. She co-edited *Crime in Rural Australia* (Federation Press, 2007).

Kwaku Boakye is Senior Lecturer in the Department of Hospitality and Tourism Management at the University of Cape Coast, Ghana. His major interest is tourism security and he has published a number of papers in this area. Other interests include Slave Route development for tourism, host–guest issues, tourism and poverty reduction, and attraction development and management.

John W. Buttle is Senior Lecturer in Criminology in the Department of Social Sciences at Auckland University of Technology (AUT) in New Zealand. His research focuses on matters to do with police reform, accountability, the use of force and non-lethal weapons, as well as public perceptions of the police and crime. John has also conducted research into rural crime and policing in New Zealand and the United Kingdom.

Joseph F. Donnermeyer is Professor in the Rural Sociology program, School of Environment and Natural Resources, Ohio State University. His major field of study is criminology with a special focus on rural and agricultural crime. He is the author or co-author of numerous articles and books on these topics, holds a lifetime Honorary Membership in the Ohio Crime Prevention Association and regularly conducts leadership training on social change and community for police organizations.

Richard George is Senior Lecturer in the School of Management at the University of Cape Town. He holds a PhD in marketing and has written several papers on tourism and crime with specific reference to South Africa. He is the author of *Marketing Tourism in South Africa*, 4th edition (Oxford University Press, 2011).

Zannagh Hatton is based within the Drug and Alcohol Research Unit at the University of Plymouth. Her interests lie in alcohol and opiate abuse, co-existing mental health problems associated with abuse and the differing treatment journeys and pathways to recovery. Her background is predominately psychosocial, as she has worked with young offenders and drug users within mental health and forensic teams and within clinical settings and secure units. Zannagh's overriding interest, however, lies in street car culture, which she has maintained vicariously through association with boy racers across the West Country since completing research for *The Tarmac Cowboys* (unpublished PhD thesis, University of Plymouth, 2007).

Carol Jones is Senior Lecturer in Criminology in the Faculty of Applied Sciences at the University of Gloucestershire, UK. Prior to completing her first degree in criminology and criminal justice at the University of Wales, Bangor, in 2000, Carol worked for many years in the tourism industry in North Wales and Israel, leading to her continued interest in tourism and crime. Carol also has an interest in victimization, volunteering, and crime prevention and community safety.

Alyce McGovern is Lecturer in Criminology in the School of Social Sciences and International Studies and the Program Coordinator for Criminology at the University of New South Wales (UNSW). Alyce teaches across a wide range of courses in the undergraduate criminology program, including Explaining Crime, Crime, Politics and the Media, and Criminology Capstone. Her research explores the relationship between the police and the media. Her current research is looking at the use of social networking and new media technologies by policing organizations as tools for communication with the public. Prior to coming to UNSW Alyce worked at Charles Sturt University as a Lecturer in Justice Studies and Policing, and she has also held numerous research assistant roles researching issues such as fear of crime, policing migration and community engagement.

Rob Mawby is Visiting Professor of Criminology and Criminal Justice at the University of Gloucestershire. He previously worked at the universities of Sheffield, Leeds, Bradford and Plymouth, where he was Professor of Criminology and Criminal Justice for some 15 years. His interests include crime reduction, policing and victimology, especially in a cross-national context, burglary, tourism and crime, and rural crime and policing. He was the UK representative on CEPOL's Special Expert Committee on Police Science in the EU (2005–2007). He is editor of *Crime Prevention and Community Safety: An International Journal*, serves on the editorial board of the *Police Journal* and has published numerous articles and books, the most recent being *Policing across the World: Issues for the Twenty-First Century* (UCL Press, 1999), *Burglary* (Willan Publishing, 2001) and *Burglary* (Ashgate, 2007). He is also co-author of *Police Science Perspectives: Towards a European Approach* (Verlag fuer Polizeiwissenschaft, 2009) and *Rural Policing and Policing the Rural* (Ashgate, 2011).

Fiona Measham is Senior Lecturer in Criminology at Lancaster University. She has 20 years' experience in the drug and alcohol field researching and publishing on licensed leisure and the night-time economy; the regulation and policing of intoxication; gender; electronic dance music scenes and club drugs; and emergent drug trends and policy developments. Co-authored and co-edited works include *Illegal Leisure* (Routledge, 1998), *Illegal Leisure Revisited* (Routledge, 2011), *Dancing on Drugs* (Free Association, 2001) and *Swimming with Crocodiles* (Routledge, 2008).

Jane Monckton Smith is a former police officer who gained her doctorate in criminology from the University of Wales (Cardiff). She came to the University of Gloucestershire from the University of Southampton, where she lectured in Applied Social Science and Criminology. Her doctoral thesis was a Foucauldian discourse analysis focusing on police and press narrative responses to homicide and serious sexual assault. Her current research explores the construction of crime narratives in cases of intimate partner homicide and the primacy of sex in constructing offender, offence and victim identities in cases of homicide. Her book *Narratives of Rape and Murder* has been published by Palgrave.

Karenza Moore is Lecturer in Criminology in the Department of Applied Social Science, Lancaster University, UK. Karenza has published widely on illicit drug use, particularly emergent patterns of drug use in leisure settings. She has also published on social aspects of new media technologies.

Hugh Potter is a sociologist/criminologist currently working at the intersection of criminal justice, public health and the community. His current work focuses on the operations of the criminal justice and community systems, from primary to tertiary prevention of criminal behaviour, injury and infectious diseases. Current research projects include the effectiveness of juvenile justice programmes, local-level re-entry programmes, the impact of criminal justice organizational decision making and processing on service delivery, and developing the Epidemiological Criminology framework. Past research has focused on the production, distribution, regulation and consumption of adult entertainment in Australia. He has worked as a State and Federal researcher and manager; as a manager in the community-based organizational sector; and as an academic at US and Australian universities. He earned his doctorate in Sociology from the University of Florida in 1982.

James Rodgers is a Criminological Researcher for the Department of Social Sciences at Auckland University of Technology (AUT), New Zealand. His research interests focus on media representations and public perceptions of crime and its control.

Rob White is Professor of Criminology in the School of Sociology and Social Work at the University of Tasmania. He has published extensively in criminology and youth studies. Among his recent books are *Youth and Society: Exploring the Dynamics of Youth Experience* (with Johanna Wyn, Oxford University Press, 2008), *Juvenile Justice: Youth and Crime in Australia* (with Chris Cunneen, Oxford University Press Australia, 2011) and *Transnational Environmental Crime: Toward an Eco-Global Criminology* (Routledge, 2011).

Jenny Wise is Lecturer in Criminology within the School of Behavioural, Cognitive and Social Sciences at the University of New England, Armidale, NSW, and the Coordinator of the Bachelor of Criminology course. Jenny's research focuses upon the social impacts of forensic science on the criminal justice system. Her first book was *The New Scientific Eyewitness: The Role of DNA Profiling in Shaping Criminal Justice* (VDM Verlag, 2009), and she is continuing her research in this field.

Ross Wolf is Associate Professor of Criminal Justice at the University of Central Florida, and holds a doctorate degree in Higher Education Administration and Education Leadership. He also has over 20 years of experience as a law enforcement officer, serving as a member of patrol, of criminal investigations and of a plainclothes tactical unit with the Orange County (Florida) Sheriff's Office (OCSO). He continues to serve as a Police Academy Instructor and as Reserve Unit Division Chief. Dr Wolf's research and scholarly activity has focused on police administration and management, reserve and volunteer policing, police use of force and tourism policing.

1 Introduction

The problem of pleasure: theoretical foundations

R. I. Mawby

With chapters featuring the UK, the USA, Australia, New Zealand, Ghana and South Africa, it would be easy to assume that the study of crime, leisure and tourism is both well established and coherent. Such a view would be misleading. Although all the authors here are well-established experts in their own fields, few would associate themselves with 'leisure, tourism and crime' as a specialism. Whether sociologists, criminologists or tourism academics, probably none of the authors would claim that their academic discipline had a holistic take on the subjects covered herein. Indeed, it is noticeable that, whereas sociologists and criminologists have addressed different dimensions of leisure and deviance/crime, few have expressed an interest in tourism and crime. Also, although tourism specialists have embraced crime as a specialism within their discipline, the focus has largely been on tourists and tourist centres as high-risk locations, with less emphasis on the problems caused by tourists, and even less on the relationship between everyday routine (leisure) activities and behaviour when on holiday.

For this reason, this text readily subdivides into two. In the first section, we consider crime, deviance and leisure, what might be termed impermissible or contested pleasures. In the second, we turn to address the relationship between tourism, and the 'pains of pleasure'.

Impermissible or contested pleasures

The following six chapters address the ambiguous relationship between leisure and crime. Again, these may be subdivided into two groups: those that address seemingly passive leisure activities (reading, watching television, computer games, cinema going) and those that concern more active leisure pursuits.

The relationship between crime and the media has an academic pedigree stretching back to labelling theorists in the 1960s who were concerned at the ways in which, *inter alia*, the behaviour of working-class youths was redefined as troublesome and amplified into a social problem (Cohen 1972; Cohen and Young 1973). However, research findings have been littered with contradictions and ambiguities (Jewkes 2004; Leishman and Mason 2003; Reiner 2007). For example, content analysis of both press and TV/film representations of crime suggest that the crimes of the rich, famous and powerful are at least as likely to be the subject of both news reporting and crime fiction. Moreover, the extent to which readers and viewers are influenced into offending as a result of what they read or see is problematic (Reiner 2007), both because of the multitude of other influential factors and because these are passive leisure pursuits that, at least temporarily, keep potential offenders (and, incidentally, potential victims) off the streets.

The two chapters included in this volume consequently reflect a more modest approach to entertainment on the big and small screens. As Jane Monckton Smith notes in Chapter 2, consumption of movies is a key form of leisure-time activity for many people. Focusing on the paradox that the slasher/serial killer film, which is principally dedicated to the violation and abuse of women, is regularly enjoyed by women (Harper 2004), Monckton Smith interviewed teenage female consumers of slasher films. She argues that these young women 'negotiate meaning to their own advantage'. Watching such films was thus a confirmation that their own personal everyday fears were shared by others and were consequently 'normal', and a way of confronting fear in a controlled and supportive way. Nevertheless, consumption of these films has pernicious effects: the female consumer is facing a real-life threat which is being vividly reinforced. In Chapter 3, Jenny Wise and Alyce McGovern shift the emphasis to police procedures and the investigative process on the small screen. They use their own primary research in Australia and secondary sources from North America and the UK to assess the impact of TV police dramas and 'fly-on-the-wall'-style programmes, arguing that the media have a significant influence on community perceptions about the police and the criminal investigative process. Indeed, it is arguable that 'cop shows' and crime scene shows are changing the practices of a range of key players, including offenders, victims, police officers, scene of crime officers and the jury. Some of these themes, interestingly, re-emerge in Part II in the context of how media images of tourist resorts influence holiday-makers' decisions.

Whether or not passive leisure pursuits such as watching films, or indeed their more interactive cousins the computer-generated games, provoke or inspire deviant leisure activities is questionable. However, the remaining four chapters in Part I focus on crime and disorder on the streets rather than cocooned within the cinema 'suites'. In this sense, the deviant leisure pursuits of – particularly – young, working-class males are a core feature of sociological and criminological works stretching back to the Chicago school. Even there, though, the research reflected two complementary perspectives that remain evident today: crime as a reaction to the pressures of growing up in the inner city, later resurrected as strain theory (Agnew 1992); and crime as fun, currently identified with cultural criminology (Presdee 2000). The first of these, fundamental to the zonal theory of urban growth (Shaw and McKay 1969) and epitomized in Merton's (1938) theory of anomie, was translated into the lived reality of inner-city youths through Cloward and Ohlin's (1960) *Delinquency and Opportunity* and, in Britain, Downes's (1966) *The Delinquent Solution*. Confronted by structural impediments to achieving the American dream, working-class youths were seen to adjust by adopting illegal means to economic success, through property crimes. Whereas Cloward and Ohlin suggested that those who failed might also drop out and adopt deviant leisure pursuits, such as drug use, Downes moved anomie theory further into the leisure context by arguing that inner-city youths adopted deviant leisure alternatives when they failed to achieve the leisure-dominated lifestyle portrayed by the media, a point reaffirmed in Cohen's (1972) interpretation of the violent confrontations between Mods and Rockers in British tourist resorts in the 1960s.

Although in no way contradicting this perspective, crime as fun puts the emphasis firmly upon the positive aspects of deviance. It also traces its roots to the Chicago school, where William Whyte's (1964) *Street Corner Society* portrayed youths as embracing the limited opportunities for 'action' in their environment, rather than reacting against failure to achieve societal goals. Cultural criminology embraces this tradition in arguing that youths turn to crime and deviance for the adrenaline and thrills that they get through committing illegal acts such as joy-riding, graffiti artwork, and antisocial behaviour, the thrills that come from what Lyng (1990) calls 'edgework', and then addresses the processes whereby cultural forms and cultural expressions themselves become criminalized (Ferrell 1999; Presdee 2000).

Chapters by Rob White, Zannagh Hatton, and Karenza Moore and Fiona Measham essentially draw on these traditions. In Chapter 4, White considers the 'making, taking and shaping of public spaces'. Although based in Australia, his review provides a general overview of leisure 'on the edge', where deviance offers an alternative to the banal routines of conventional life: where street cultural manifestations such as vandalism, skateboarding, drugs, cruising and peer-group violence provide avenues of expression when other leisure options and facilities are inaccessible, and a means of establishing status through leisure where high rates of unemployment make status through work unobtainable. Nevertheless, as White acknowledges, such group activities may include collective behaviour that is highly threatening and dangerous, leading to moral panics and legislative response. Following Cohen (1972), White argues that many of these groups and their activities may be ostracized and penalized on the basis of their perceived immoral and threatening behaviour and presence.

Hatton's research in the southwest of England focuses on one example of street culture, centred around cars and boy racers. Hatton echoes White in stressing the symbolic importance of the car for young males, whereby 'their cars provide a medium through which they are able to convey a sense of self, of who they are, or who they wish others to believe them to be.' Being involved in the modification and racing of powerful cars is used to confer macho masculinity, something which may have been previously blocked by age, a low economic position or social and spatial isolation.

In Chapter 6, Moore and Measham address more of the 'impermissible pleasures' discussed by White, namely 'immoderate' alcohol consumption and illicit drug use, a subject that has featured regularly in the British (and Australian) press in terms of public disorder and the night-time economy (NTE) (Hayward and Hobbs 2007). Following Measham (2004a), this analysis is also heavily embedded within cultural criminology. The emphasis here, as with White and Hatton, is on youths' behaviour, rather than its impact on the wider community, and indeed they argue that such pleasures 'are ambiguous in terms of the production of harm, the impact on communities and the wider social fabric'. Consequently, they reject a discourse based around drug use as harmful (to both users and society) in favour of one focused on the attractions of 'immoderate consumption' and its minimal consequences for wider society, leading them to question how and why wider social and cultural practices influence whether leisure activities are placed within or outside the realms of acceptability.

This question resonates through Chapter 7, where Elaine Barclay and Joe Donnermeyer review their research on hunting as a popular, if not always legitimate, leisure activity in Australia. Of course hunting, also known as poaching or wildlife offences (Lemieux 2011; Wyatt 2009), may be finance driven rather than a leisure pursuit. Conversely, hunting in Australia bears little similarity to the contested nature of the hunting debate in the UK (Woods 2011). At first sight, Barclay and Donnermeyer's topic also bears little similarity to the preceding three chapters. However, it too covers leisure pursued in public and private space, drawing a distinction between that considered legitimate by landowners and that perceived to be a problem, raising questions about the competing interests of conservation, agriculture and mining as well as leisure and tourism, which are addressed in different contexts in the following section.

Tourism and the 'pains of pleasure'

In contrast to the work on leisure and crime, the research on tourism, crime and disorder has been carried out largely by tourism academics. It has also focused more on local people and them (and tourists) as victims rather than on those responsible for crime in resorts. As a result, there is an established body of research that demonstrates a close association between tourism and crime (Brunt and Hambly 1999; Pizam and Mansfeld 1996; Ryan 1993a). Many tourist areas experience relatively high levels of crime and disorder. Within such areas the routine activities of tourists and seasonal workers may lead to them committing crimes (Bellis *et al*. 2000; Prideaux 1996), tourists and local people becoming the victims of crime (Mawby *et al*. 2010) or both. Equally, residents of many tourist areas express concern at the 'pains of pleasure'. A wide range of studies demonstrates that, irrespective of *actual* changes in levels of crime, local residents *feel* that tourism generates more crime (Davis *et al*. 1988; Haralambopoulos and Pizam 1996; Ross 1992). Of course, not all tourist areas are associated with high levels of crime and disorder. The nature of the tourist area has a direct impact upon crime rates and patterns, with those mass tourism resorts marketed at younger tourists evidencing the greatest public disorder problems. Equally, not all tourists experience the same risk or express concerns.

Unlike tourism researchers, for whom crime and deviance appear to hold considerable attraction, criminologists have, with a few notable exceptions, avoided discussions of tourism as a crime generator. Even studies of antisocial behaviour have tended to focus on the NTE of larger cities and ignore tourists as offenders and tourist resorts as crime and disorder hot spots. This is well illustrated in Rob Mawby's chapter on public disorder, antisocial behaviour and alcohol-related crime in tourist resorts, which offers almost a reverse image of Moore and Measham's chapter. Although with few exceptions (Homel *et al.* 1997) research on alcohol-related disorder has been sited in the metropolis, this problem also confronts many tourist resorts, especially those marketed to young, single tourists. Situating research in southwest England in the context of Australian, Dutch, Greek and English examples, Mawby considers how and why this market is created, its implications for local residents and the difficulty of changing a resort's image.

This focus on the imagery promoted by the tourism industries is taken further in Chapter 9, where Ross Wolf and Hugh Potter contrast two very different US holiday destinations, Las Vegas, Nevada, and Orlando in Florida. Las Vegas is generally known and marketed as a destination for leisure activities aimed at the adult market, a city where gambling, alcohol and sex are central tourist attractions. Orlando, in contrast, is marketed as a family-oriented leisure destination. Wolf and Potter compare the ways in which tourist-oriented policing, criminal law and zoning policies apply in the two areas. However, whereas the overall picture is one of contrasting tourist areas that are policed very differently, a comparison of police crime statistics reveals surprisingly few significant differences.

In Chapter 10, John Buttle and James Rodgers consider imagery in terms of the way crime and insecurity are presented in the media, and speculate on the impact signal crimes (Innes 2004a) have on tourists' perceptions of safety. Unlike most earlier research, which has targeted densely populated sites of mass tourism, they address safety in New Zealand, where tourism promotion of the rural idyll is confronted by press emphasis on sexual and violent crimes, and – as in Australia (Peel and Steen 2007) – media depictions of tourists at risk have proved controversial.

As Richard George also acknowledges in Chapter 11, the image that a resort has *vis-à-vis* its perceived safety is important, since tourists are deterred from visiting unsafe resorts (Brayshaw 1995; Schiebler *et al.* 1996). South Africa is a case in point (George 2001, 2003). Whereas Cape Town is commonly perceived as unsafe, George's chapter focuses upon Table Mountain National Park (TMNP), an urban park on the fringe of the Cape Town metropolis. His findings on concern over safety in both TMNP and Cape Town itself are mixed. However, following Mawby, Brunt and Hambly (2000) and George (2003), even those who perceived TMNP to be unsafe were willing to revisit and recommend the attraction. This was particularly the case for domestic – as opposed to international – visitors, who were both more aware of safety problems and less likely to be affected by them, possibly thanks to their tolerance of higher crime rates in South Africa.

Rural tourism is also a theme in Elaine Barclay and Rob Mawby's chapter on caravan parks in Australia. Partly on account of their rural location and partly, perhaps, owing to the possibility of parks acting like gated communities (Low 2004), park users in general neither perceived crime and disorder to be particular problems nor suffered much crime. However, there were marked differences both between and within different sites, and Barclay and Mawby explain these in terms of guardianship, accessibility and rewards.

In contrast, in Chapter 13 Kwaku Boakye describes the situation in Ghana, where a country dependent upon tourism is bedevilled by crime against international tourists. Although a third of the tourists who were contacted had experienced crime or threatening situations, Boakye suggests, echoing George, that tourists were not deterred from revisiting the country. Following Barclay and Mawby, he also notes differences within his samples, with variations in feeling of safety and experiences of different offence types according to area and the characteristics of the tourists concerned.

Boakye's chapter ends with a review of the response of the Ghanaian police, a topic extended in Carol Jones's concluding chapter. Given the extent of crime against tourists and the distinctive ways in which tourists are affected, Jones looks at the way the police and victim assistance programmes respond to tourism issues, and details dedicated services for tourists in general and tourist victims in particular. Comparing the UK, the Irish Republic and the USA, she looks at the situation in Cornwall, where no specialist services are offered, Florida, where specialist Tourist Police operate, and Dublin, with its Tourist Victim Support service.

Part I clearly focuses on crime, deviance and leisure, with the emphasis on leisure as allegedly problem-generating, albeit many of the contributors reject this perception. From a policy perspective, the emphasis has correspondingly been on policing leisure and especially the NTE. In contrast, Part II, in addressing the relationship between tourism and the 'pains of pleasure', focuses more on tourists and host communities as problem receptors. Consequently, policies address victim services and tourist-related policing as both controlling leisure and providing support to tourists. The distinction is never clear-cut. However, it epitomizes the extent to which a review of leisure, tourism and crime draws together scholarship across a range of disciplines.

This selection of readings on leisure, tourism and crime is, consequently, important for at least two reasons. First, it offers theoretical relevance in adding to criminologists' understanding of the relationship between lifestyle (of leisure-seekers, tourists and local residents) and risk. Second, it has a practical importance in helping to inform the tourist industry of the contested issues surrounding leisure and tourism, and therefore in aiding in the adoption of crime and disorder reduction initiatives that meet the needs of locals and tourists alike.

Part I

2   The paradox of cinematic sexualized violence as entertainment

Jane Monckton Smith

Introduction

Sexual violence is considered one of the most serious of crimes in our society and its potential to cause significant and long-lasting trauma to victims is acknowledged. However, it is also a central theme in various forms of leisure activity from art, exhibitions, theatre, magazines, music video, concerts, literature and true crime books to guided tours and theme park rides. It is also the subject of a highly successful genre in film making – the horror/slasher film – which almost exclusively focuses on the 'serial killer'. The *Saw* franchise, for example, is a series of films described in some film reviews as 'torture porn' and has produced at least three number ones at the box office, with *Saw V* grossing $113 million worldwide (Box Office Mojo 2009), making it the highest-grossing horror franchise in history (Snider 2008). With its own dedicated and named ride and maze at Thorpe Park, an amusement theme park in London, UK, the commodification of sexualized violence is clearly popular and profitable.

This chapter considers what is often popularly represented as a paradox: female consumption and enjoyment of the slasher/horror film, which is principally dedicated to the violation and abuse of women in particular. However, this study is not situated within the framework of film theory, but a feminist concern with violence against women and the narrative conventions which rationalize it. My personal research interest in forensic narrative construction led to my exploring marital narratives in abusive relationships and the way some women can negotiate the meaning within these narratives to diminish the negative impact of the violence. Women use many strategies to deal with violence in their lives and I seek to explore how the conventions of the slasher/horror genre impact on the women and girls who view them, as they are more often than not the victims who are portrayed, and whether or how consumption is a process of negotiation.

The Freudian psychoanalytic position has argued that women may be inherently sexually masochistic, inferring enjoyment of abuse, and this position has entered the cultural imagination as a truth which is used to argue against the harms of sexual violence both real and 'artistic', and explain why women would want to engage with such films (Caplan 2005). In an interview in *The Guardian*, for example, the psychologist Dr Glenn Wilson claims that horror film can facilitate sexual responsiveness in women, but inhibit it in men (Saner 2007). Feminist scholars have argued that this type of approach is an inadequate and prejudicial explanation for women's tolerance or acceptance of violence against them in any form as the inference is that women may enjoy rape or sexual assault (Barter 2009; Caplan 2005; Clover 1992; Dobash and Dobash 2002; Pinedo 1997). There is also an assumption by some writers that the fear created in slasher/horror films is temporary, reversible and suspended as soon as the film is over (Frayling 1986; Jenkins 1994; Pinedo 1997), and this represents the experience as some-what benign. Professor Joanne Cantor reports that horror films have the ability to induce long-term fear by creating an association between a stimulus, such as the shower scene in the film *Psycho*, and a natural fear response in a part of the brain called the amygdala. For example, after seeing *Psycho* many women feared showering for years afterwards (Macrae 2010).

Women's experience and consumption of sexualized violence in this form is complex and I do not pretend to explain it in this chapter; neither do I seek to argue that women do not or should not enjoy serial killer or slasher/horror films, as women are established to be great consumers of this type of entertainment (Harper 2004). What I do argue is that female fears prompted by cinematic images of sexualized fatal violence are overlaid with a lifetime of warnings from loved ones, educators, charities, official institutions and health workers, that women and girls should be particularly afraid of, and avoid, *sexual* assault; not forgetting the routines of feminine security etched on to their social practices or their experi-ences of domestic or other forms of violence and abuse. However, despite or even because of this, women may still negotiate meaning in these films to their own advantage. Drawing from an analysis of sex and gender in slasher/horror films and data from focus group interviews with young women who self-identified as enjoying the genre, I argue that these films embody what is a real and tangible threat for young women and that consumption should not be considered a benign experience or a frivolous paraphilia. When placed in its wider social context the axiomatic narrative is revealed as both insidious and prejudicial, but it is precisely because of this that, far from being paradoxical, enjoyment of or engagement with the genre may be eminently logical for women.

The slasher/horror film

Depictions of female sexual death are part of our cultural landscape, a ubiquitous horror which is exemplified in the violence of the serial killer. Not only is the figure of the serial killer linked to fictional and fantastic characters such as Freddy Krueger from the popular *A Nightmare on Elm Street* franchise (Dir. Wes Craven 1984) or Hannibal Lecter in *The Silence of the Lambs* (Dir. Jonathan Demme 1991), he is also physically extant. Kevin Williamson, the writer of one of the most successful horror/slasher films ever, *Scream* (Dir. Wes Craven 1997), which grossed over $100 million at the box office, said his script was inspired by real-life serial killers such as Ted Bundy and Danny Rolling who exclusively targeted young women (Harper 2004). The highly successful *Saw* franchise has just seen the release of *Saw VI* (Dir. Kevin Greutert 2009), adding to a series described, as noted, in some film reviews as 'torture porn' because of the juxtaposing of sexual imagery with fatal sadistic violence. Perhaps the most enduring serial killer box-office draw, with an impressive merchandising and publication portfolio, is Jack the Ripper. This historically extant character has inspired an ongoing interest in his crimes spawning what Soothill (1993) and Cook (2009) describe as 'the Jack the Ripper Industry'. His instantly recognizable brand has infiltrated British and indeed international folklore to the extent that even police investigations have been influenced and led astray by the apparent veracity of the myths surrounding him, as argued by Nicole Ward Jouve in her analysis of the police investigation of the murders by Peter Sutcliffe, the so-called Yorkshire Ripper, in the 1980s in Bradford, UK (Ward Jouve 1988). The story of Jack the Ripper's crimes has an interesting political history and an enduring pseudo-scientific presence in the literature of criminality, both of which lend credibility to the heavily stylized construction of the discursive object that is the 'serial killer'. Jack the Ripper has appeared in so many factional and fictional representations of his crimes that he has become an intelligible link between real serial killers and the fictional demons of the slasher and horror genres.

The Jack the Ripper and *Saw* franchises, as well as films such as *Scream* and *Nightmare on Elm Street*, are part of the horror genre also fitting neatly into the subgenre that is the 'slasher' film, which focuses exclusively on the serial killer; that is, broadly speaking, an individual or individuals who kill a series of victims sequentially. It is a convention of serial killer and slasher film that the danger is sexualized and the victims will be mainly female – or at the very least, according to Clover (1992), it is females who will spend more screen time being terrorized, injured and killed. The gendered and misogynistic themes which dominate the narratives in these films are well documented (Caputi 1987; Clover 1992; Harper 2004; Haskell 1987; Monckton Smith 2010; Mulvey 1991; Pinedo 1997), but often the narratives go beyond mere misogyny and in Harper's words 'plunge headlong into cruelty against women' (Harper 2004: 17). It is interesting that *Scream*, which is a horror parody, does identify some of these conventions and holds them up for ridicule, but simultaneously fails to openly challenge some of the serial killer/slasher conventions which are included in its narrative, leaving it impossible to tell if they are ironic statements or not.

It is a problem that we fail to acknowledge more widely the conventionality of the dynamics in these films to consider how they might impact on women *in particular*. Frayling (1986: 175) argues of Jack the Ripper films that 'they are frightening but only in the way that a nightmare is frightening. Everything is fine when you wake up', Pinedo (1997: 5) claims that these films are a simulation of horror like a 'roller coaster ride' and Jenkins (1994: 107) sees the fear as 'temporary and reversible'. However, what is missed in these assessments of cinematic sexualized violence is acknowledgement of the narrative as a fundamental part of a discursive construction of sexual murder whereby victimization is not shared across gender. Many considerations of the appeals or repulsions of horror film speak of the audience, and do not address the specific effects of the narratives on women in particular. It seems unlikely that both genders, outside the celluloid buffers of the East End/Ripper simulacrum, experience the (hetero)sexual symbolism and misogynistic violence similarly. Women cannot awake from consumption of such violence as if alighting from a fairground roller coaster – full of adrenaline but otherwise free from any pernicious effects.

The popular cultural belief which suggests that females enjoy violation, or the thought of it, owing to an inherent masochism (Caplan 2005) is deeply damaging but has enjoyed some authority through pseudo-scientific (mis)interpretation of Freudian psychology, and even found its way into the legal system and rape prosecutions (Forrester 1986). It has been suggested that this alleged masochism and desire to be dominated is discursively constructed and that, as Kaplan (2000: 126) argues, 'in practice this is rarely reflected in more than a tendency for women to be passive in sexual relations'. The more sinister interpretation is that women enjoy violence against them and even secretly desire to be raped. There are also the inevitable comparisons with female responses to real-life violence, and similar arguments have been presented to explain why women would remain with abusive or violent partners, or to try to minimize the harm of rape by feeding in to the rape myths. Larcombe (2005) and Clover (1992) argue that women's consumption of entertainment which appears to devalue or violate them is complex and cannot be reduced to simple identification with idealized characters in conventional plots. Clover suggests there are many layers of cross-identification, and Larcombe reminds us that we must consider the complex personhood of the female consumer. Others suggest enjoyment can be derived from the newer horror plots, which often depict stronger intelligent female protagonists who sometimes win in the end (Oliver and Sanders 2004). Some hold that women enjoy narratives of gendered abuse only because they fail to recognize the misogynistic themes – or even that some women are complicit with the sexist regime (Larcombe 2005). Given these arguments it is worth briefly discussing how the serial killer is constructed before considering how he may be received, and placing him in his social context.

Constructing the serial killer

The serial killer narrative is not simply about madmen 'killing'; it has a significant investment in heteronormativity and is very narrowly defined. When making meaning of the serial killer's violence, intelligible links are made between rape, mutilation and death within a dominant discourse of sexual murder (Monckton Smith 2010). The serial killer, broadly speaking, acts on deviant sexual urges in an orgasmic rage and in acts analogous to rape. He is apparently satiated after killing but tension soon builds again leading to another sexualized death. David Schmid (2005: 79) argues that this dominant discourse has constructed an 'extremely limited and distorted image of what serial murder is, who commits it, who is victimized, how they are victimized and why they are victimized'. The narrative of serial killing now offered in popular media is based on interpretation of the crimes of killers such as Jack the Ripper and, as Walkowitz (1992: 3) notes, 'presents a far more stabilized account than media coverage offered at the time'. Similar to Foucault's description of the emergence of the 'homosexual' or the 'criminal' as a 'type' (Foucault 1998), the serial killer, personified in Jack the Ripper, became a 'type'; the characterization and definition of him coming from powerful agencies such as the FBI (Milligen 2006; Schmid 2005; Vronsky 2004) who had their own political agenda. For example, Milligen (2006: 102) claims that the FBI studies used to name and define the serial killer in the late 1970s were based on a specific type of sex crime which updated 'Jack the Ripper for late twentieth century America', promoting a right-wing political morality. The links to heteronormativity are especially clear here because prevailing liberal attitudes to sexuality, especially female or non-standard sexuality, were held to blame for his emergence (Schmid 2005). The political motivations of the FBI in constructing a new domestic enemy in the form of the serial killer are well explicated (Milligen 2006; Schmid 2005; Vronsky 2004) and are relevant in considering the way the narrative has evolved as a moral tale. The threat is highly stylized and drenched in heterosexual meaning and female sexuality is represented as a fragile, dangerous entity in need of control. This has powerful historical antecedents. The gendered characteristics of serial killing translate very well across genres and can be observed in police, news and fictional narratives (Monckton Smith 2010). The 'story' of a serial killing in this sense, and succinctly put, offers 'an awful warning of what happen(s) when the natural order of things is broken' (Emsley 2005: 96).

Narrative conventions in slasher/horror films

The popular slasher/serial killer narrative, which I will focus on, despite some ostensible diversity, is remarkably stable and reliant on dominant gendered subjectivities which polarize men and women. The films in my sample were all, without exception, highly sexualized and the victims were consistently young and attractive. The violence against them was often directly linked to sexual lust with both the rage of the killer and the terror of the victim represented as passionate or even orgasmic. Harper (2004) suggests that the makers of slasher films rely on images of sex and death to tell their stories with a growing concentration on female nudity rather than graphic bloodshed to create spectacle; a feature which he suggests is easier to get past censors than gore and cheaper than special effects. Harper further claims that because of this an increasing number of female roles in these films are given to 'sub playboy, silicone enhanced starlets' (ibid.: 22). Cowan and O'Brien found that female victims in slasher films were significantly more likely than males to be shown as promiscuous, in revealing clothing, as naked, as undressing and/or as using sexual language and engaging in sexual activity (cited in Oliver and Sanders 2004). They conclude that the message conveyed in these films is as pernicious as the message conveyed in pornography: that violence can be fun for women. The ease with which slasher films are able to mix up sex in the form of pornographic images, and death in the form of serial killing, is testament to the way the narrative makes meaning of violence against women. The violence, the motivations and the responses are made coherent through the medium of gender;

it is the intelligible link between offender and victim. Clover's (1992) study of gender in the modern horror film suggests that victimization, though shared to some extent, is different. She claims that men die because of things they have done, but women die because they are women. Women are victimized because of an inherent essence – their very being provokes the actions of the offender. In contrast, males have to actively do something to become victims; they have no inherent power to provoke action. It is this process which more effectively genders, rather than a simple body count of women to men. The motivations written for the violence are the true gendering process; women die because of their sex. In this way *sexual* danger supplants simple physical peril and threats to life. Physical danger becomes sexual danger and for women *sexual* threats are the real threats to their lives.

In my data it was clear that in many films murder and mutilation of women are conflated with rape. The female subjects who endure sexualized deaths are separated from male subjects, who die quicker, more functional deaths. The sexualized murder of women is clearly a stimulant for some: the film director Dario Argento states: 'I like women especially beautiful ones. If they have a good face and figure, I would much prefer to watch them being murdered than an ugly girl or man'; and Schoell, a film historian, notes, 'Other filmmakers figured that the only thing better than one beautiful woman being gruesomely murdered was a whole series of beautiful women being gruesomely murdered' (cited in Clover 1992: 32). Not only do these self-appointed avengers of public morals – as serial killers are often represented – principally target women, according to the definition of serial murder and the narrative conventions of serial killer film; it is in an orgasmic rage: the death of the sexualized victim a metaphor for extreme heterosexual tensions.

Given the strong links to heterosexual practice, female engagement with these narratives will be complex and situated within their lived experience of heterosexuality. Women absorb the same beliefs about themselves as others do about them, so the ways that females negotiate those beliefs in their own interest may be limited. Research into domestic violence has suggested that the violence women endure is sometimes interpreted as a sign of love or passion and the abused female renegotiates its meaning, though not its physical/psychological effects (Borochowitz and Eisikovitz 2002). This linking of love, passion and violence was found to be especially common in teenage dating relationships in which violence or aggression had occurred (Barter 2009), suggesting that women in abusive relationships are negotiating the abuse in their own interests, rewriting it in some cases to represent passion, and to empower rather than disempower themselves. The implication here is that women are accepting that the violence and the threat are not going away, but are a stable part of female life to be dealt with rather than removed; an inevitable threat.

Method and sample

I have deliberately drawn from focus group interviews with teenage girls who self-identified as being consumers of slasher films; my choice was for two reasons.

First, teenage or young girls are often the victims of choice in these films; second, recent research into abusive teenage dating relationships shows a worrying trend for tolerance of male violence, setting in place the potential for lifelong acceptance of abuse (Borochowitz and Eisikovitz 2002). Because slasher/serial killer films frequently include fantastical killers who are more surreal than real, the genre is not always taken seriously as a forum for exploring female reception of male violence. For example, Schlesinger and colleagues rejected such films as *Friday the 13th* (Dir. Sean S. Cunningham 1980) in their study of women viewing violence, claiming that in the pilot study women 'had not taken them seriously' and that they were 'only intended for teenagers' (Schlesinger *et al.* 1992: 19–20). It is precisely because these films are sometimes intended for, and enjoyed by, teenagers that they are the focus in this chapter. Teenage girls are the highest-risk group for sexual victimization and domestic abuse. Most are specifically excluded, however, from the official ACPO (Association of Chief Police Officers) definition of domestic violence, which recognizes victims only over the age of 18; consequently they can become invisible as victims in their own right. These young women also form part of the next generation of adult women and, given the UK government's declaration that a primary rather than tertiary 'after the event' strategy is to be used in combating violence against women (Hansard 2010: 163) – which means educating and changing perceptions in young people – the experiences and perceptions of young women to violence directed against them are particularly relevant, irrespective of genre.

Data were drawn from two sources. First, I drew from an analysis of the gendered aspects of Jack the Ripper films (Monckton Smith 2010) and a similar analysis of slasher films. All slasher films in the sample were suggested by focus group participants. The way the films 'tell' the story was a particular focus; this being the narrative conventions employed. Using the tenets of Foucauldian discourse analysis as a framework for exploring the way that realities are constructed, the film narratives were deconstructed and the commonalities across films identified. In its very simplest terms, discourse, in a Foucauldian sense, is a framework for a way of talking, a way of acting and a way of knowing about something. Different discourses are produced over time, and sexual murder will be constructed differently within different discourses. However, some are more dominant than others and it is the dominant way of 'knowing' about sexual murder represented in slasher/horror film which is the focus for this chapter.

Second, a focus group was put together consisting of 11 girls between the ages of 14 and 16 of varied ethnicity who self-identified as enjoying the genre, and who regularly meet for the specific purpose of watching slasher films. I wanted to explore with them why they watch this type of film in particular and what aspects they identified as particularly compelling. Their comments were analysed, again using the tenets of Foucauldian discourse, to identify how they interpret the danger and the horror presented. A smaller and more informal group of four male viewers was put together to compare some of the more dominant themes which arose from the female group discussion to allow a gendered comparison on those themes only. Some of the key differences are referred to briefly, the main focus being the female interpretation and reception of the themes.

Female consumption of cinematic sexualized danger

We began the focus group discussions by talking about the horror films which the participants had heard of and watched. Largely it was films from the slasher genre that the girls had watched, and especially horror/slasher films that were receiving extensive media hype, such as *Paranormal Activity* (Dir. Oren Peli 2007). When asked which 'killers' they remembered most clearly, all participants named characters that were similar in appearance to ordinary people. In particular the character Jigsaw from the *Saw* franchise was chosen by all the girls as a particularly memorable and frightening character. When asked what he looked like, comments such as 'just an old man' or 'well sort of ordinary' dominated. When pushed to suggest why they remembered him in particular they stated that it was precisely because he was so ordinary that they were frightened of, and so remembered, him. In a similar conversation with male horror viewers when asked what kind of things frightened them most in horror films, after expressing that they did not feel frightened as much as 'thrilled' or 'alarmed', most males agreed that it was films in which a realistic threat occurred, as in *Arachnophobia* (Dir. Frank Marshall 1990) or *Jaws* (Dir. Steven Spielberg 1975), that raised most fear. They did not necessarily consider the fantastical serial killer a real threat. It has been suggested in previous research that men show less arousal and fear than women when viewing slasher films and that perceived realism is important in generating suspense (Oliver and Sanders 2004). Horror films play a role in allowing fears to be faced; Boyanovsky and colleagues found that, during the week following a well-publicized murder of a female student at the University of Wisconsin, attendance of female students on campus for the violent movie *In Cold Blood* rose by 89 per cent (cited in Oliver and Sanders 2004: 249). They argue that individuals will show a preference for a stimulus situation which reflects a real-life fear. It is probable that the threat of the serial killer is more real for women and girls than for heterosexual males.

All female participants agreed that they would watch horror films only if they were with someone else, believing that the best way to watch such films was in a group of close female friends. They said that part of the enjoyment was the shared feelings and the camaraderie; it was a 'safe kind of scared'. Participants also stated that they would consider watching horror with a boyfriend on a date but mainly because the horror format was less embarrassing than a romance format, which may include scenes of consensual sexual activity, and the awkwardness that may initiate. Oliver and Sanders (2004) report that horror films are a popular dating activity, and the girls also stated that one of the reasons for viewing horror on a date would be to encourage some non-sexual physical closeness such as cuddling which would occur if they appeared frightened. In some part then, the display of fear to encourage physical closeness is a tactic to control the date where conventional assertiveness is discouraged in females.

When it came to discussing the particular appeal of slasher films, all the participants agreed that one of the reasons for watching them was to gain credibility with peers:

I can brag at school that I have managed to watch a film that is really gory or scary.
> You can tell everyone that you were brave enough to watch it.
> The worse the film is the more you look like you're really strong.
> I like to let the boys know that I watched a really bad horror film.

From these data it appeared that the girls did not enjoy the films as much as endure them for the kudos they could then claim. The experience, from this perspective, is a form of empowerment and the more films watched the more empowered the watcher.

> Watching the films makes me brave and makes me feel better about myself.
> I don't want to be seen as weak so I watch them.

Here the girls were expressing a wish to distance themselves from perceived feminine weakness and confronting their fears to feel better about themselves. This suggests not comfort with, or enjoyment of, fear or violation, but a desire to demonstrate strength and so boost self-esteem.

When asked which parts of the films they felt were the most scary, as opposed to gory or revolting, the following comments were made:

> It's really scary when you can't see what's going on, like when you know something is there but you can't see it.
> Like when they look in a mirror and they see something in the mirror that wasn't there before, and when they turn round it's gone.

These responses were given far more clarity when conversation turned to their real-life experiences of fear. All the participants agreed that they felt being watched by something invisible or hidden was part of their psychological landscape:

> I am always frightened that there is something there watching me, something I can't see.
> When I'm looking in the mirror I am always worried that someone is watching me, like when I'm putting on my make-up you think you might see them in the mirror.
> I have to close my wardrobe at night because I always have this feeling that there is something in there watching me.
> I hate going anywhere all alone because I always think that someone is watching me.

These comments were spontaneous and all the girls agreed that they felt surveilled in their day-to-day lives; not simply in a sense that they were policed, but that the surveillance was malevolent and of their physicality rather than just their behaviour. It was a feeling that was part of their everyday routines and rituals, part of their lived experience and is an aspect of horror film articulated in Laura

Mulvey's (1991) influential essay which stresses the dominance of the voyeuristic male perspective. In this sense the films present the *real* menace for these young women for they begin to unravel the feelings of a silent invisible presence that stalks them. The spectre has a form and it is gendered. This is not a nightmare that is awoken from; the sexualized threat is omnipresent. Conversely the male group expressed no fear or even suggestion that they were surveilled and when prompted all denied that they ever felt watched. When the girls were asked whether the films had prompted the feeling of surveillance, it was stated that the fear was already there before watching the films, and that it was the realization that they all shared the same fears that was important. However, it was also suggested that the feeling of being watched became more 'real' after watching the films.

The girls were then asked why they would choose to watch a film which played on such real fears and the answer was unequivocal. It was a way of confronting and practicing the fear in a controlled and supportive way, but also and perhaps more importantly, a confirmation that their own personal everyday fears were shared by others, an affirmation of their paranoia as normal:

> It's good watching the way everyone else is scared too, we are all scared together.
> You can check out your mates' reactions.
> I can see I'm not the only one who is scared, it's all of us, we're all the same.

The girls all agreed that there was a feeling of camaraderie, of all facing the same common enemy who scared them all in the same way. It appeared that the feeling of surveillance or 'stalking' was a dominant theme but this had not been necessarily expressed or acknowledged among the group before. It was the focus group discussion which appeared to encourage acknowledgement of the feeling. The girls all seemed to take comfort from the fact that all of them felt stalked or watched and that because of this it gave the feeling less power. Also, when the stalking fear is revealed to be a fantastical serial killer within the films, it is thus somewhat disarmed. However, when the films represent what is in fact a real serial killer, such as the Jack the Ripper films in which women are specifically targeted and surveilled, then this may be entirely different. In summary, it appeared that the girls primarily watched these films as a form of empowerment and exploration. Their everyday gendered fears were temporarily counterbalanced by the extremes of the fantastical killers, their bravery in facing the stalking threat acknowledged and, importantly, their paranoia normalized.

Discussion

The narrative conventions in slasher films are closely related to the practice of hetero/sexuality and rely on gendered subjectivities to tell their stories. In this sense women are stereotypically represented as watched, sexualized, masochistic and weaker than men. They are the natural target or focus for sexual abuse – their relationship with the male killer representing extreme heterosexual tensions and serving as a warning to constrain female sexuality. This narrative convention was clearly part of the lived experience of my focus group participants, who expressed a desire to demonstrate strength and build self-esteem.

The demonstration of strength that they spoke of was clearly tied to their lived experience of feeling a stalking surveillance of their physicality. This aspect to slasher and serial killer films is often explicitly played out and female victims are frequently followed by a voyeuristic camera, as in *Peeping Tom* (Dir. Michael Powell 1960), which exemplifies the technique. These themes cannot be separated from the routine scrutiny of the female body which women experience every day in media images and critique, in stories of hidden cameras, stalkers or pornography, in warnings not to be alone at night in case of waiting strangers or strange followers. Mulvey's (1991) suggestion that women exist only to be looked at gives some clarity to the context of the participants' fear. The conventionality of the sexualized danger in serial killer film translates very well the kind of dangers women perceive to be stalking them. However, acknowledging, sharing and facing that fear, and being seen to face that fear, may be more liberating for women than debilitating. To claim that consumption of these films has no pernicious effects is to fail to recognize that the female consumer is facing a real-life threat which is being vividly reinforced, and to interpret enjoyment of the genre as paradoxical or even masochistic is to disregard the power of sexual threats to women. The young women in the focus groups recognized, even at 15 years, the burdensome omnipresence of their sexuality. It is not the female consumer's enjoyment or engagement with slasher/serial killer films that is paradoxical, but the absurdity of the suggestion that it could be.

3   Crime time

The rise of police programming on television

Jenny Wise and Alyce McGovern

Introduction

As consumers of popular culture and news programming, we are surrounded by images of crime, law enforcement and the criminal justice system on an almost daily basis. Correlating with the emergence of risk societies (Beck 1992; Horsfield 1997; Ungar 2001), public fascination with crime and justice continues to grow. We only need to think about the almost fanatical way in which the Australian public has consumed the television crime series *Underbelly* to see this in action. This fascination has only been compounded by the many changes and developments we have seen in the media in recent years. For example, the arrival of the internet and other new technologies has challenged traditional media formats, such as newspapers, and the demand for immediate news content and the reduction of journalist deadlines mean that we now operate under a 24-hour news cycle (Goldsmith 2010; Lewis *et al.* 2005; R. C. Mawby 2010). Mason (2002) argues that part of the reason we are so fascinated with crime and justice is that most of us have very limited direct contact or experience with these matters, and thus we rely on media reports and representations of them for our knowledge. There is almost a mystique around all things 'crime'. High-profile Australian individuals such as Roger Rogerson, Mark 'Chopper' Read and Carl and Roberta Williams; the UK figure Ronnie Biggs; and those well-known US crime 'heroes' Frank Abagnale Jr. and Al Capone have become popular media figures and household names on the back of their real or imagined criminal statuses, and it is often through such individuals that the public can live vicariously. For most of us who have no desire to become criminals (or victims) ourselves, these mediated representations are as close to the real thing as we will ever get. In this way, the media play an important role in defining our social world, and equally have a significant influence on community perceptions about crime, criminals and the criminal justice system.

It comes as no surprise then that media formats are cashing in on this public fascination with crime. In recent years we have seen an increasing amount of law-and-order-related programming on television, with depictions of crime, criminals and the criminal justice system dominating television screens both locally and globally. Consuming television programmes that depict criminal investigations, whether factual or fictional, has become a significant leisure activity for a large proportion of the population in Western societies. For example, in its second season, *CSI: Crime Scene Investigation* was rated as the second most popular television programme in America, with 23.69 million viewers, and has since remained one of the most popular programmes of the decade (Cole and Dioso-Villa 2007). Along with the numerous *CSI* spinoffs,[1] the popularity of this type of show has also been linked to the explosion in the creation of other television programmes of a similar format, such as *Law and Order SVU: Special Victims Unit*, *NCIS: Naval Criminal Investigation Service* and *Criminal Minds*. In the Australian context, shows such as *City Homicide, Water Rats, Police Rescue* and *Halifax f.p.* have also captured viewers' imaginations.

The popularity of this criminal investigation genre has not been limited to the dramatization of television programmes. Rather, the fascination with police and their crime-solving activities has created an increased public interest in the non-fictional practice of police officers and detectives. As a result, the reality or documentary television format has been flooded with 'fly-on-the-wall'-style programs which aim to give viewers an insight into the 'true' nature of policing. The long-running US series *Cops* pioneered this format, which has similarly been adopted for a number of UK programmes, and in Australia we have seen policing agencies take up this format with gusto in recent times. Shows such as *The Force, Highway Patrol, Missing Persons Unit, Crash Investigation Unit* and *The Recruits* have become staples in Australian television viewing schedules, advancing behind-the-scenes accounts of true policing activities to an audience which seems to have an almost insatiable appetite. Considering the significant role that television plays in the leisure-time activities of contemporary lifestyles, it is important to identify the potential consequences of an increased police profile on television. This chapter will explore some of the many issues raised by these fictional and factual representations of policing, including the effects of these portrayals on audiences and policing agencies alike.

Crime as entertainment

Public interest in law-and-order issues has steadily increased over the past half-century. In particular, the public has become fascinated with factual and fictional accounts of police investigations, the use of forensic evidence and courtroom procedures. Police and criminal investigations are commonly appearing as a central theme in a range of different leisure activities including books, television series, movies, children's *CSI* toys and murder mystery games for adults, and individuals can even participate in crime tours of cities, such as the Jack the Ripper tour of London. Although the focus of this paper will be on police and criminal investigations within television series, we would like to review briefly how the police have been used as a basis for creating leisure activities within these other formats as it provides a valuable insight into the popularity of crime and policing as a source for mass consumption.

One of the most influential modern creators of dramatized investigations and detective novels was Sir Arthur Conan Doyle. Doyle's characters Sherlock

Holmes and Dr Watson became internationally known for their ability to solve crime through deduction and reasoning, often solving crimes that the local police were unable to resolve. Indeed, Sherlock Holmes was often critical of the police officers of Scotland Yard. Even the rare few compliments that Holmes pays to the police are still framed by negative references. For example, in *A Study in Scarlet*, Holmes pays the following weak compliments to two police detectives:

> Gregson is the smartest of the Scotland Yarders . . . he and Lestrade are the pick of a bad lot. They are both quick and energetic, but conventional – shockingly so.

> (Doyle 2006: 29)

Thus, one of the first modern and popular representations that portrayed the activities of police officers was actually quite detrimental to the image of the police officer. Despite this, the reader is still encouraged to believe that investigators, like Sherlock Holmes, and rational crime scene investigations are vital for the safety of society. Numerous authors have since written countless novels that portray police officers and police investigations (Agatha Christie's Miss Marple, P. D. James's Adam Dalgliesh and Ian Rankin's Detective Inspector Rebus, for example). Whether the slant is favourable or detrimental, the use of police officers as key fictitious characters in novels has ensured that there is a continued fascination with police procedures and investigations amongst the general public.

As the previous chapter by Monckton Smith suggests, consumption of movies is a key form of leisure-time activity for many people. It is also a leisure activity that can have a substantial impact on viewers. This is no less true for the television format. The prominence of crime stories in the media has been a focus of much anxiety and debate in academic and other circles. Probably one of the biggest concerns has been around the potentially criminogenic consequences of mass media representations of crime, both fictional and factual representations. For example, shortly after the Columbine High School massacre, it was widely reported that the two gunmen were fans of violent video games, films and music. For many this was seen to signal the deadly impact exposure to violence can lead to. Despite these popular conceptions, however, debates still continue over the links between media and representations of crime and violence, and violent behaviour from consumers of such depictions (Jewkes 2004). Similar fears are reignited whenever a new form of mass media comes to the fore, and we have seen such concerns raised in relation to internet use and crime. For example, the community and authorities have expressed concerns over the link between social networking sites, such as Facebook, and crime (Warren and Palmer 2010). With the lines between work and leisure becoming increasingly eroded by the encroachment of technology into our everyday lives, such concerns presumably will continue to grow.

Crime is also becoming a main theme in children's leisure activities. With the popularity of crime scene shows, such as *CSI: Crime Scene Investigation*, Planet Toys have developed a range of *CSI*-related toys that enable children to become a crime scene investigator and to catch the 'guilty party'. Within the range there are a *CSI* DNA Lab, *CSI* Field Kit, *CSI* Impression Kit, *CSI* Handwriting Kit, *CSI* Facial Reconstruction Kit and a number of others. In addition, toy stores have long sold a range of replica police ID badges and handcuffs. The genre of playing cops and robbers is now far more detailed and 'realistic' for young children who own these accessories. Murder mystery games are no longer just restricted to children either. Adults can organize dinner parties at which they 'host a murder' (Worldwise Imports – *How to Host a Murder*) and the guests become the detectives. Such activities even extend to the internet now, with sites such as Crime Scene (www.crimescene.com) offering visitors the opportunity to 'view the evidence and solve the crime'. Website subscribers can access graphic crime scene photos and other briefs of evidence which they then use to help solve the crimes. The popularity of the *CSI* genre for both adults and children reflects the success of products that focus on criminal activities and, perhaps more importantly, on the successful detection of criminals.

The final crime-related leisure activity that we would like to cover, before moving on to television shows, is that of 'crime scene tourism' or 'dark tourism' (Simic 2009). The popularity of crime scene tourism 'cannot be separated from wider contemporary fascinations with crime scenes' (Wilbert and Hansen 2009: 188). People are fascinated with actual crime scenes to the point that it has become an attraction for tourists. Wilbert and Hansen (2009: 187) compare crime scene walking tours to crime fiction, in which the tour guide is responsible for solving the crime in a form of street theatre. The 'tourists' are taken back to the geographical and cultural space where the murders/crime occurred and police exhibits are shown to the spectators. Crime scene tourism has become a popular form of leisure. In London, for example, there are now several Jack the Ripper walking tours in addition to the Kray Twins tour. In Australia one of the most celebrated criminals, Ned Kelly, has also become a feature of such tourist activities.[2] Together with a government-promoted Ned Kelly Guided Walking Tour, tourists can also purchase their own Ned Kelly GPS Tour, 'an all-in-one audio book, tour guide and GPS navigation system which provides the user with a unique travel experience through Kelly Country' (Ned Kelly GPS Tour website 2010). Crime is big business, and the tourism industry is certainly becoming acutely aware of this.

Police in fact and fiction

The depiction of police officers in fictional accounts has varied considerably over time. In Reiner's seminal work on the politics of police he identified these varying depictions of policing, contending that the lack of analysis of early fictional accounts of policing can be attributed to the absence of television prior to the 1940s. According to Reiner (2000: 160–161) it was not until the 1940s that police narratives in the UK context portrayed policing in a positive light, with heroic, credible and professional policing figures littering television, film and novels of the day. Such depictions, however, were seen to shift by the 1970s, in line with broader community concerns over law and order policies (Reiner 2000). This reflects similar concerns being faced in the Australian context. The

1960s and 1970s marked a period of political and social dissent over matters such as Australia's involvement in the Vietnam War, Aboriginal rights, standards of health and welfare, the equality of women, abortion law reform and censorship matters (Chan 1997; Edwards 2005; Finnane 1987, 1990, 1994a). Civil rights groups, including those representing Indigenous people, women, homosexuals, prisoners and mental patients became increasingly affirmed and their influence grew, leading to important shifts in the balance of power between 'government' and the 'governed' (Garland 2001). This had an effect on policing, as police were increasingly being seen as in alignment with the government and out of touch with the community, the same community whose confidence they relied upon to legitimize the policing role in society. It is little wonder then that fictional representations of the police at this time were less than favourable.

Today what we see is a blurring of these two extremes, with 'bad cop', critical images of the police sitting alongside more positive and often 'nostalgic' (Reiner 2000: 162) depictions of police and the work that they engage in. We also see some more misleading representations of police work in fictional accounts, with an emphasis not only on the 'fun' and 'exciting' nature of policing, but also on the great successes of the police. Like Sir Arthur Conan Doyle's Sherlock Holmes, some of the new television programmes have created an impression of police investigations that is incongruent with reality. According to Nolan (2007: 577) *CSI: Crime Scene Investigation* (*CSI*) has achieved a depiction of crime scene officers and police that 'is completely divergent from the real-life role' of practitioners within the criminal investigative process. In particular, police officers are portrayed in a negative light, while scientists and civilian investigators are seen as the true heroes of criminal investigations:

> In *CSI* it is the civilian investigator who is the dominant and driving force in the criminal investigation. The police officers are depicted as bumbling, clueless functionaries who are barely tolerated by the dedicated, conscientious, and ultimately moral 'scientists' who search for the truth amid the chaotic and gruesome remnants of the violent acts of those soon to be caught.
>
> (Nolan 2007: 55)

As many of those people involved in the criminal investigative process are aware, this is an inaccurate and misleading representation. Although the crime scene examiner does play a large and very important role in the collection of evidence from the crime scene, police officers also have a large role to play in determining what evidence is collected, and in some cases actually conducting a forensic assessment (Green 2007: 352) and collecting the evidence themselves (Wise 2009). This shift in the way that police officers are portrayed (from being the hero in shows such as *The Bill* and *Third Watch* to being portrayed as 'bumbling, clueless functionaries' in *CSI*) may be affecting television watchers who choose to watch *CSI* as a form of leisure. The effects that these types of shows are having will be discussed later in this chapter.

However, it is not only the fictional representations of policing that have come under scrutiny in recent times. According to Mawby (R. C. Mawby 2007: 157), police often engage the media in the investigative process, in both fictional and factual terms. As highlighted earlier, the growth of factual or 'documentary'-style television programming that focuses on the realities of policing has changed the way in which the public engage with, and perceive, police work. Such factual programming exists on a number of levels. For example, factual programming can see police providing the media with information from key investigators in high-profile crime cases. Officers can be questioned about the details of a case or appeal for information, conveying the sound bites we often receive on the nightly news broadcasts. Beyond this, however, factual representations of policing and the criminal justice system have also taken on what is often termed a 'factional' dimension. This style of programming, also dubbed 'reality' television, or infotainment, sees the police engage in 'documentary-style' productions with media networks. According to Mason (2002; see also Doyle 1998), in recent years there has been a blurring of the boundaries between factual and fictional media depictions of policing, which is evident through the emergence of factional programming. He contends that 'the growth of faction or infotainment, through the hybridisation of factual programming, in particular, has significant implications for media constructed images of policing' (Mason 2002: 1; see also Leishman and Mason 2003: 107).

Increasingly, police departments are investing in reality television programmes in an effort to boost their image (R. C. Mawby 2007; Reiner 2000). These shows give 'good copy' or publicity for the police, who have veto over what goes to air and the angles promoted in these programmes (Burton 2007; *Daily Telegraph* 2008; Lawrence and Bissett 2009). They are also good money earners for police agencies and can help mediate public relations budgets, for which police (and governments alike) are often criticized (see, for example, O'Brien 2008). The phenomenon, however, is not unique to Australian police forces. Mawby (2002: 38) has also recognized the growth of police reality television in the United Kingdom, where shows such as *Crimewatch UK*, *Cops with Cameras*, *Police Interceptors* and *Night Cops* are broadcast.

Literature around the Public Relations State (see Deacon and Golding 1994) tells us that this is a common feature of modern-day state institutions such as the police, as governments look towards public relations professionals and opportunities to ensure that the media carry forward their preferred messages to the public, helping to legitimize the role and activities of the police (Reiner 2000: 140). These factual representations, together with more traditional news formats, have presented similar polarized views of the police in much the same way as the fictional representations outlined above have. On the one hand, the news media enthusiastically report on the police successes, whilst on the other hand the police are often maligned when scandal and corruption allegations surface.

Consequences of cops on the box

With the increasing profile of police and police work on television, in both fictional and factual formats, there are a number of issues for consideration in terms of the impact of these media representations on the viewing public. Given that one US study found that over three-quarters of the public form their opinions about crime from what they see or read in the news (Marsh and Melville 2009: 1), let alone the proportion of people who are influenced by dramatic portrayals of policing, it is important to consider exactly what impact the saturation of images of policing in the media may have on police and public alike.

The impact of watching crime series on criminal investigations: the other side of the CSI Effect

One of the most noteworthy consequences of the rise of police television shows as a form of leisure is that it is impacting on various areas of the criminal justice system. In particular, it has been argued that 'cop shows' and crime scene shows are changing the practices of offenders, victims, police officers, scene of crime officers (or crime scene examiners), lawyers, judicial officers and the jury (Huey 2010; Wise 2010).

Police shows using heightened levels of forensic science to investigate and solve criminal cases have come under scrutiny more recently for allegedly changing the practices of those involved in the criminal justice system. Since the early 2000s, there have been an increasing number of television programmes, such as *CSI: Crime Scene Investigation*, that depict crime scene investigations and the use of forensic science to solve heinous crimes. Shortly after these shows became popular, there were complaints from lawyers and judges in America about the perceived changing requirements of juror verdicts (Franzen 2002; Roane 2005; Willing 2004). The term '*CSI* Effect' was quickly coined by journalists to describe instances when jurors convict if forensic evidence is present or refuse to convict if there is an absence of forensic evidence (Franzen 2002; Gonzales 2005; Hooper 2005; Willing 2004).

Since the media started using the term, several studies around the world have looked specifically at the impact that programmes such as *CSI* and *Law & Order* have on potential and real jurors.[3] The findings of the studies vary, with some researchers arguing that there is a *CSI* Effect, and television-watching habits are affecting viewers (Ghoshray 2007; Schweitzer and Saks 2007), while others have argued emphatically that the *CSI* Effect does not exist (Podlas 2006).

In addition to these studies, researchers are now beginning to change the focus of the *CSI* Effect debate away from juries to examine how the alleged *CSI* Effect is affecting practitioners. Huey's (2010) seminal work considers how television portrayals of police investigative work impact upon public expectations of the police investigative role and duties in the field within Canada. Similarly, one of the authors of the present chapter (Wise 2010) has also previously examined the impact of television shows on the work of police officers, scene of crime officers (SOCOs), lawyers and judicial officers within New South Wales, Australia.[4] Findings from these papers, and from anecdotal evidence from within the media, suggest that there are a number of implications for the general public watching crime television shows on how police actually conduct their investigation.

One of the reasons why the *CSI* Effect is impacting on criminal justice practitioners is that shows such as *CSI: Crime Scene Investigation* are inaccurately portraying not only the role of forensic science in investigations, but also the role of police officers within the criminal investigation process. Police investigators are now experiencing queries from victims and citizens about why they are not collecting specific forensic samples, or why they are not processing a crime scene the way investigators do on *CSI* (CBS News 2006; Huey 2010; Lovgren 2004; Wise 2009). One of the first anecdotal documentations of this appeared in a *National Geographic* article on the *CSI* Effect, in which the reporter, Lovgren (2004), reported that:

> A few months ago, a crime scene investigator from the Los Angeles County Sheriff's Department was dusting for fingerprints at the scene of a residential burglary. The victim of the crime was not impressed, however. 'That's not the way they do it on television,' she told the investigator.

Research from Wise's NSW study found similar reports from police officers, with one police officer stating, 'I often get asked by members of the public, "but was there DNA located?"'.

Similarly, Huey (2010) reported that victims and witnesses were routinely questioning both police officers and crime scene examiners in Canada about a range of their duties. For example:

> People start to interview the witnesses themselves, and then saying, 'well, you didn't ask this question.' . . . that has become a real big problem where people don't leave us to do the investigation and they are starting to do investigations on their own.
>
> (Major Crimes Investigator cited in Huey 2010: 57)

> 'Well aren't you going to . . . ?' because that [technique] figured prominently in some episode they saw.
>
> (Forensic Identification Officer cited ibid.)

> I've noticed that since the show [*CSI*] . . . these are the perceptions that people have: I should be walking to the edge of the room, peering in, seeing one hair to the exclusion of all the others that are on the carpet, realize its significance . . . And I do have to explain to people, because if I don't get down on my hands and knees and search for the burglar's hair, then I'm not doing my job!
>
> (Forensic Identification Officer cited in Huey 2010: 58)

As the quotes suggest, forensic officers were more likely to be questioned about their activities than police officers. Despite this, police officers did report that television shows had affected the way they were perceived by the public.

Huey (2010) argues that police television shows are creating a source of occupational role strain for police officers. The glamorization of police work on television has created the 'perception among police officers that the public expects them to perform at near superhuman capacity in order to match the dazzling work of their media "rivals"' (ibid.: 65). This means that when civilians ask police officers to achieve 'superhuman' outcomes they are first asking police to increase their workload and second actually questioning the expertise of the police officer or crime scene investigator. Huey (ibid.) reported that nine of the 31 police detectives interviewed found that the increased workload and the questioning of their expertise led to feelings of frustration or role strain.

In NSW, there was evidence that SOCOs were experiencing more role strain as a result of these television shows, as opposed to police officers. Whereas some police officers did mention that victims had asked them why certain exhibits were not collected, most of the SOCOs reported being pressured by both victims and police officers to collect certain types of evidence, and in particular the types of evidence that appear on television shows such as *CSI*. For example, one SOCO commented:

> because often you'll go to a scene and the detective will be leaning on your SOCOs or me to collect and they'll want door handles swabbed and this swabbed, and that swabbed. And they think it's this magic bullet, you just hold onto the swab and the DNA jumps on it.
>
> (Scene of Crime Officer)

In addition, police officers may want SOCOs to collect more samples from a crime scene than they are actually authorized to collect in order to make a case appear as strong as those on television programmes. For example, SOCOs are often confronted by police officers requesting six or seven samples to be taken from a stolen motor vehicle when they are authorized to collect only one sample (Wise 2009: 131). In the 'interest of harmony' the SOCO will often ignore the one sample policy and collect the extra samples (Scene of Crime Officer). Thus, leisure television shows are impacting on how police officers perceive the role of the crime scene investigation and the types of evidence that are needed to secure a conviction.

It has also been suggested that the popularity of both fictional and reality crime television programmes may be increasing offenders' awareness of what police look for at a crime scene (Goehner *et al.* 2004; Hooper 2005). Although most of the support for this theory is anecdotal, several of the police officers interviewed in NSW reported that some offenders are now wearing gloves as a preventative measure against leaving both fingerprints and DNA evidence where they touch objects (Police Officer 1; Police Officer 2). This can make it more difficult for police officers and scene of crime officers to collect evidence at the crime scene. In addition, when offenders are confronted with forensic evidence in a police interview the offender will try and explain to police why their DNA was at a crime scene innocently, instead of contesting the reliability of the reported DNA match (Defence Lawyer 3). However, others in the study were very sceptical that offenders were changing their behaviour based on what they saw on television about police practices and procedures. For example, one defence lawyer stated, 'a lot of offenders are particularly stupid. They will help themselves to the milk in the fridge and then leave it out . . . even those who have previously been, or had their DNA taken.'[5]

The impact of police reality television: obtaining consent and increasing confidence

One of the other consequences of the increased police profile is the impact of these depictions on the police image. This is particularly important given the active role that police are now playing in their own image management through professionalized media relations units and their engagement in reality-style programming. Police involvement in reality television productions becomes another medium through which the police can try to enlist the media in distributing positive policing messages. Previous research by one of the authors of this chapter[6] (McGovern 2009; McGovern and Lee 2010) has found that the media are often quite aware that they are being used in ways that help police distribute these positive messages out to the public. As one journalist commented in an interview:

> It is always in their interest to publicize police and make them look good, so if there's been a particularly good arrest or something, they're going to want the whole world to know, because it's important for them . . . They want people to know that police are dealing with things out there.
>
> (Journalist 13)

Many journalists, however, feel there is a hidden agenda behind the push for positive policing stories being provided to the media in the form of news briefs or longer reality-style programming, beyond simply assisting the police force itself to look good:

> You've got to keep in mind though that this sort of information is part of an agenda, which may be to create generally a good news story for the police, it may be a story that shows that they're being, you know, tough on crime. It might be a story that shows that the Commissioner was taking a hard line in respect to something. It may be a critic of the police is cast in a bad light, it may be any number of things. But it's got a hidden agenda, and the problem with that is sometimes those stories make good stories, but you get the effect whereby these stories are being spoon fed and you know, I suppose it's open to the idea that this is spin.
>
> (Journalist 5)

This is one of the fundamental concerns when examining police involvement in reality shows. What happens to broadcasting standards when media outlets engage in tabloid, infotainment-style programming (Mason 2002: 3)? When media outlets sign up to deals with policing agencies which give editorial and content control to the police, what questions does this raise about journalistic integrity? When the majority of the public unquestioningly garner their knowledge about the police through media representations (Jiggins 2007) – fictional, factual and reality – concerns need to be addressed in terms of the representations of policing that make it into our media. As Mason (2002: 4) argues, '[t]he reality cop show is another constructed representation of the police', managed by police through their media relations offices. R. C. Mawby (2007) contends that image work is a fundamental goal for the police, and a function of professional media offices operating within policing organizations today.

As we are well aware, the media can greatly influence community perceptions and understandings about police and policing through the representations they broadcast. There is little doubt media coverage plays a significant role in the ways in which the community frames and views issues of crime, law and order, and social control (Chibnall 1977; Hogg and Brown 1998; Lee 2007). For the most part the community gets its information about crime not from personal experience but from the news media. 'Few members of the community have direct interaction with the criminal justice system', so others draw their knowledge about such matters from the media (Jiggins 2007: 203; Mason 2002). Whereas the media often come under fire for misrepresenting crime and policing in a grab for ratings, the trend towards police involvement in infotainment-style programming must lead us to examine the 'aim, nature and role of police cooperation in making such programmes' (Leishman and Mason 2003: 112). With their central role over content and editing, the police are in the position of being able to manage their image in the media in ways which were not previously possible. Not only does this raise questions about the ability of media outlets to critically present such representations, but it also creates concerns about the sort of information being imparted to the public who rely so heavily on media representations to understand matters of crime and policing.

Conclusion

In recent years we have seen an increasing amount of crime-related programming on television, with depictions of crime, criminals and the criminal justice system dominating prime-time television slots across the globe. One of the most prominent criminal justice agencies to capture the attention of broadcasters has been the police, with fictional and factual programs of police work dominating the nightly viewing schedules. This increased police profile on television has resulted in an increased scrutiny of police officers in real life and a growing expectation from victims and the general public that the service they receive from the police will match the services offered in both fictional and reality policing television shows. The glamorization of police work as shown on television portrayals is creating occupation role strain for police officers (Huey 2010) and a change in practitioner behaviour when dealing with victims and other members of the public (Wise 2009). In addition, the use of reality television shows enables the police to portray positive images to the public, which will inevitably change how the public views policing agencies. As already mentioned, both fictional and reality portrayals of policing on television raise questions about the type of information that is being consumed by the public and how this information affects its view of crime and policing. This is of particular concern when these leisure activities are creating role strain for police officers (or even changing the practices of offenders).

Notes

1 *CSI: Miami, CSI: New York* and *CSI: Trilogy*.
2 For an example of such a tour see http://www.jacktheripperwalk.com
3 Examining the decision-making process of jurors is not a new phenomenon. Researchers have been interested in jury decisions for several decades, and a number of studies have focused on the role of forensic science in juror verdicts almost a decade before the term '*CSI* Effect' was coined. For example, Koehler (2001) conducted a study of mock jurors in America in 1995 to examine how jurors viewed forensic evidence. The study found that juries were influenced by forensic evidence, and were more likely to convict where there was strong scientific evidence, including DNA evidence. Studies such as Koehler's have been used as evidence to support the claims of lawyers and the media that dramatized crime scene television programmes, such as *CSI*, affect jurors, despite the fact that Koehler's (2001) study predates the introduction of *CSI*. This suggests that the phenomenon described by the *CSI* Effect is nothing new; it simply has a new name and has been attributed with a greater emphasis in more recent years.
4 As part of this research, criminal justice practitioners within New South Wales, Australia, were asked about the impact of popular television programmes on the way they conducted their jobs. Face-to-face interviews were conducted with 32 NSW criminal justice participants between 2006 and 2007. Of the 32 respondents, 12 criminal justice practitioners openly discussed how they perceived the television shows had affected the execution of their jobs.
5 The defence lawyer is referring to offenders who have had their DNA taken by police in the past and subsequently had that DNA placed on a police database. Once their DNA is on the database, it makes it easier for police to identify repeat offenders.
6 As part of this research, interviews were conducted with NSW Police Media Unit staff and crime reporters from television, radio and newspapers as part of a larger research project. The interviews were conducted with 16 police 'roundsmen' and crime reporters working in radio, television and newspapers in the Sydney metropolitan area, as well as 13 current and former staff members of the NSW Police Media Unit.

4 The making, shaking and taking of public spaces

Rob White

Introduction

Public space is a site for congregations of people to get together and do things. What they do, and how they do it, is intrinsic to the excitement and communal attributes of such spaces. The way they interact with, and in the space, also contribute to the ambiguities of such space: we fear it and are exhilarated by it at the same time.

The aim of this chapter is to explore the myriad ways in which people, especially young people, use public space to entertain themselves, to engage in disreputable pleasures and to assert social identity. The making, taking and shaking of public space is achieved through activities such as swarming, street dancing, making music, hooning, swearing and gang fighting. Transgression takes several different forms and is informed by different motivations and social contexts.

The reshaping of community space (with the advent of the night-time economy), and the redefining of private spaces (through gatecrashing as well as public display of ownership through sheer force of numbers), mark out new dimensions in group leisure that simultaneously pose questions about deviancy, criminality and the boundaries of the conventional. The attractions and discomforts of public space, for tourists and locals alike, are encapsulated in acts and events that simultaneously fascinate and repel – and that keep us coming back for more.

The chapter offers a kaleidoscope of activities and events in order to demonstrate the sheer variety of ways in which public space is utilized and in the process socially transformed. Most of these, at some time and for specific reasons, have generated consternation among authority figures and the public at large. Yet rather than being deviant or problematic many uses of public space are now acknowledged as simply part and parcel of the ordinary urban experience.

As mentioned, this chapter provides a broad overview of activities and behaviours involving young people. More detailed and fine-grained analysis of specific groups and categories of young people feeds into the present descriptions – for example, previous work done on youth gangs (see Hagedorn 2007, 2008) and on Indigenous youth (see White 2002, 2009). How colonialism, immigration and marginalization are linked to particular social constructions of peoples and places is important to understanding why, for example, Indigenous youth and 'ethnic' youth gangs in Australia occupy the social landscape in the ways they do.

Notwithstanding the need for specificity of analysis (which is beyond the scope of the present work), these same groups and categories of street-present young people nonetheless contribute to the general behavioural patterns, cultural atmosphere and social mosaic of contemporary city life. As such, they warrant mention in the discussions of public space issues provided below.

Making space

The form of urban space has fundamentally been shaped by the contours of economic development and class-related social processes over several hundred years (Katznelson 1993; Sassen 1993). The very definition of 'public space' has been the subject of much contestation between different classes, as have the purposes and behaviours deemed to be appropriate within any such space (Worpole and Greenhalgh 1996). In the Australian context, for example, the working-class traditions of using the street as a multi-functional social space have long been a source of middle-class concern (Finch 1993; Murray 1973). The answer then, as now, was often to pursue policies of strong policing and social exclusion for selected groups (Finnane 1994b; White 2007a).

The contemporary period has seen a major reshaping of public street life through the changing political economy of the night-time economy, one result of which is the creation of distinctive mainstream, residual and alternative spaces, practices and identities (see Chatterton and Hollands 2003). The corporate commercial entertainment industries do their best to attract custom in the form of standardized, yet variable, venues and attractions. As Chatterton and Hollands (2003: 93) point out:

> the commercial mainstream is a differentiated 'playground' which offers a number of goods and spaces for the active production and reproduction of social groupings of young people, keen to refashion their night-time consumption identities in relation to their peers and their own labour market positions.

In many places, marginalized youth are not welcome, and they are explicitly and publicly rejected.

Public spaces have changed in concept and design over the years, depending upon the ebbs and flows of economic development and social conflict. In the present era, the social construction of public space is dominated by a series of interrelated developments: the rise of consumerism, the mass privatization of public space, and the intensification of social regulation (White 2007a). Public space is being defined by consumption activities and uses, rather than other sorts of values.

One consequence of these developments is that the shopping centre has evolved to be, for many, the central hub of urban social life. It has assumed a number of symbolic and functional uses, for a diverse range of people. For young people, in particular, it is a major site for meeting together and hanging out. Shopping centres and districts, too, have taken different forms over the years. Sandercock

(1997) comments that recent developments are premised upon providing consumers with a clean, sanitized, attractive and safe environment, but one so highly controlled as to deny the real diversity of the urban environment. As a number of critics have likewise argued, the modern shopping centre or shopping mall has a tendency to be designed, policed and regulated in a manner which is intended to exclude particular groups, such as unemployed and homeless people, from their precincts (Davis 1990; White and Sutton 1995; Worpole and Greenhalgh 1996).

The use of public spaces such as malls, the street and shopping centres is, of course, not entirely consumption oriented (in the strict sense of buying commodities). One of the key thrusts of this chapter is to demonstrate the great diversity of uses, which include subversions of normal use as well as exaggerated consumerism, relating to public space. Indeed, the feeling of connection, the sense of excitement and the exhilaration of being in and around others is not unique to young people – and not everyone is out to shop.

Places and spaces do not simply exist 'out there' as stand-alone socially neutral entities. They are 'made' into something by those who occupy, move through and use them. We make spaces into something specific by 'doing'. We also take existing spaces that are 'unused' and transform them, however temporarily, into something else. Space is also a medium through which we move or travel. Attempts to control space through extensive regulation, intrusive crime prevention and authoritarian rule bring forth a variety of reactions, many of which are embedded in wider cultural aspects of consumer capitalism.

Consider, for example, the subversive element that skateboarding or graffiti represents (Ferrell 1997). The threat is not only to existing institutional regimes of power, but to those wishing to shape cultural spaces in ways which reflect commercial objectives and consumption agendas. Graffiti can be seen to threaten the conventionalized and homogenized ways in which public places are being reconstructed to emphasize managed shopping spaces, where the impetus to act is based upon consumption, not expression; the spending of money, not the spending of energy. Skateboarders likewise assert that this space, this park bench, this railing has different purposes and different meanings for them as compared with the conventional (Snow 1999). Particular use-value is redefined and transformed by the act of skating. Things are no longer what they are officially purported to be (a bench), but are defined in (sub)culturally different terms (a skateboard surface).

The specific content of the action also shapes how space is 'read' and used. Graffiti, for example, takes many different forms, and is associated with different instrumental purposes – from political slogans to gang territoriality to artistic creation to identity tagging (Halsey and Young 2002, 2006; White 2001). For some young people, the graffiti 'gang' is a vital social connection in their lives. The graffiti experience represents an important 'identity-securing form of action', something that confirms who one is and their presence in the urban setting (McDonald 1999). The act of graffiti thus is also about constructing subjectivity that makes sense to the writer.

Graffiti can offer a number of specific benefits to participants (White 2001). Some of these include:

- availability of technologies (e.g., spray paint, textas) which allow *low-cost* ways to make a personal mark on the environment (a form of branding);
- achievement of spiritual wellbeing through actively doing something in which the *meaning* of the action is ostensibly given by the doer;
- the idea of *free expression* and the notion that power is within one's own hands;
- a form of *democratic* expression that is open to anyone regardless of background or skill;
- experiencing it as somehow more *authentic* than either commercial activity or doing something for, or dictated by, someone else;
- the frequent accompaniment of an adrenaline rush and buzz of *excitement* that relates to doing something broadly perceived to be deviant or wrong (but not particularly harmful).

In the view of cultural criminology, ostensibly antisocial behaviour such as doing graffiti is best interpreted as meaningful attempts to 'transgress' the ordinary and the given (Ferrell *et al.* 2008; Presdee 2000). In a world of standardized diversity and global conformities, it is exciting and pleasurable to break the rules, to push the boundaries, to engage in risky and risk-taking activities. Transgressions of this nature are one way in which the marginalized can express a sense of identity and solidarity, in a world that seems to offer them so little. To transgress is to deviate. This does not necessarily mean violence and criminality. For example, street dancers dance in the street for enjoyment and to express their skills and emotions, not to get into a punch-up (Sutton *et al.* 2008; White 1993). However, they are often perceived to be deviant nonetheless.

In this context, deviance offers the perpetrator a means of 'self-transcendence', a way of overcoming the conventionality and mundanity typically associated with the routines and practicalities of everyday 'regular life' (Hayward 2002: 81). For example, the street cultures of youth, such as vandalism, drugs, cruising and peer-group violence, are seen as ways of re-exerting control and providing avenues of expression when traditional avenues of youthful stimulation and endeavour have long since evaporated. In a similar vein, it is argued that graffiti equals pleasure – and pleasure is intrinsically associated with the powerful affective and visceral aspects of graffiti writing (Halsey and Young 2006). At another level, opportunities for young people to further develop themselves and their own relationship with the wider social world are often restricted by the actions of the institutional providers of amenities and public spaces. This takes the form of unnecessarily restrictive rules in the use of some amenities, the presence of security apparatus and personnel, the active intervention of state police and private security guards in their affairs (regardless of whether a criminal act has occurred or not) and general media treatment which suggests that young people have no real value or place in the larger scheme of things (White and Wyn 2008). This can transform general community places into youth-unfriendly spaces.

For some young people, therefore, the illegality of graffiti is precisely the point. The thrill of graffiti work in this instance is premised upon the rush of excitement from 'doing wrong', in breaking the conventions, in sending a message to those in authority that the rules will not be adhered to. We cannot underestimate the emotional attractions of, and exhilarations (and sense of payback) attached to, behaviour that transgresses conventional norms and values.

Young people are not passive users of the street, nor are they reticent about establishing a public presence. In responding to their environments, they have succeeded, as well, in transforming these environments (White and Wyn 2008). Taking and making spaces of their own is never a straightforward or simple social process. It involves adaptation to local conditions and environments, as when skateboarders re-conceptualise the physical landscape of the city to best match their perceptions and uses of street furniture and building architecture (see Snow 1999). Somewhere to sit, a bench, is transformed into that which is skated on, over or along. But this process also involves various types of social exclusion. I sit, therefore, you cannot skate. I skate, therefore, you cannot sit. Transgression is never socially neutral. It involves different understandings of the environment, but it also involves potential conflicts of interest, not only between marginalised youth and powerful adults, but amongst and between young people generally (White and Wyn 2008).

Conflicts between different users of public space also shape how users interpret the actions (for example, youth being noisy and rowdy) and symbols (for example, ways of dress or graffiti) of the other users. For instance, a small number of young people can occupy the local mall in basically anti-social ways. They might be rude to passers-by, sometimes using foul language. They might be aggressive, not only to each other, but to other groups of young people and to the adults around them. They might find it entertaining and funny to provoke the police. They might steal from local shops. They might get stoned. They might hang around, often bored, for hours on end.

A combination of being noisy, being aggro and being out of it brings forth various social responses. Being a nuisance is not, however, a trivial thing. It makes people afraid. It makes people angry. It makes them demand that something be done. Inevitably it leads to a backlash against those perceived to be the problem. Thus, the mall can be a source of fun, excitement and entertainment. Lots of different people, a variety of different shops and cafes, and music from buskers can make it a pleasant place in which to be. Simultaneously the mall can be a site in which there is also considerable fear, trepidation and violence. Public space always has more than one side and it has many different uses and many different users.

The media generally provides a sensationalised account of who is doing what in public spaces – whether this be drunken louts, dangerous driving hoons in the local neighbourhood or violent youth gangs. Graphic depictions of people and events, and the emphasis on stranger-danger, bolster the sense of imminent harm for members of the general public. People of all ages can be affected by such accounts, and may modify their use of public space accordingly. This is especially so in regards to young women, whose actual experiences of harassment on the street may be reinforced by negative media images of violence and alcohol use (White and Wyn 2008).

More often than not, though, young people simply want to 'do their thing' with their friends. This takes a number of different forms (White 2007a):

- youth music scenes that shape cultural and physical spaces (for example, 'hip hop' adaptations around the globe; raves);
- street machiners and car culture (that involve the public parading and showing off of automobiles, and their owners/drivers);
- street dancers and the street as stage (involving public performance and exhibition of skills);
- marking/branding of the public landscape (through graffiti art and other forms of graffiti production).

What characterizes many of these types of activities is that they border on the illegal or are illegal in some way, or they are perceived as antisocial to the extent that they run contrary to the interests and enjoyment of other users of those spaces. Furthermore, while often expressing the creative energies of youth and providing an avenue for artistic, musical and political expression, they may include violent or criminal behaviour (see below). In other cases, however, violence is expressly forbidden by the participants themselves.

Consider 'raves', for example. Raves are essentially dance parties in which a large number of people gather together in one site for the purpose of dancing. They are less prevalent today (in part owing to a shift into commercial clubs) and in some jurisdictions virtually non-existent as a result of extensive legislative and police intervention. Nevertheless, the history of the rave is essentially a history of organized events, outside normal or legal venues, with an emphasis on crowd anonymity, fun, drug taking which is directly related to the dance atmosphere, and non-violence (Chan 1999). The venue and music are 'predetermined' in the sense that considerable organization has to go into planning a rave event. Communication by mobile phone, internet links and friendship networks are essential to the spontaneity of the gathering, since the time and location are usually only shared out at the last moment. The important thing about raves is that they tend to celebrate 'the beat', and violence of any kind is either not tolerated or certainly frowned upon.

Transgression is also evident when it comes to young people and car culture. There are multiple dimensions to young people and car culture, comprising various types of driving behaviour and social events, including street machining, cruising and hooning (Graham and White 2007). The word 'hoon' is a term commonly used in Australian culture to refer to young people, especially young men, who engage in dangerous driving behaviour. It can also refer to those who constantly show off in their cars in public.

Car culture is manifest at the local street level in the form of various activities (Graham and White 2007):

- Street machining: this commonly involves gatherings of car enthusiasts and their vehicles. The key purpose of street machining is display. People do it to show off their usually heavily modified and impressive vehicles, to demonstrate status, material ownership, creativity and craftsmanship.
- Cruising: this can involve doing blockies (driving around the block, over and over again), going for a drive with friends, cruising in certain areas as a potential form of attraction, or driving cars in convoy. Cruising can be quite visible and audible because of hotted-up engines and powerful sound systems, but is generally harmless and legal.
- Hooning: driving that involves risk-taking and danger. Hooning is a crime, and is quite unsafe because of the potential consequences. Hooning involves driving actions such as those listed below, as well as speeding.
    - Burnouts and fishtails: burnout is a sustained loss of traction during acceleration; it involves spinning the wheels, smoking the tires and burning rubber. Fishtails involve driving and burning out in a linear direction punctuated by swerving when the back of the vehicle flicks out to the left or right.
    - Donuts: a sustained loss of traction during acceleration in a circular motion, in other words a burnout in a circle. Also called 'figure of eights' and 'circlework'. It is potentially dangerous.
    - Drifting: this refers to a specific driving technique, as well as a type of motor sport based on that technique. It occurs when the wheels are pointing in a different direction from the direction in which the car is sliding overall. Drifting requires skill, and is growing in popularity. There is potential for harm if the driver loses control of the car.
    - Street racing, time trials, and drag racing: street racing refers to the illegal use of public streets to race against each other. Time trials involve racing against the clock; drivers may compare times after separately racing a set area. Drag racing refers to dragging another vehicle off at the lights. All three are competitive and potentially dangerous.

Hooning, cruising, and street machining demand different physical acts, but the rewards are inherently social. Each one is a form of leisure for some groups within specific youth subcultural contexts (Denholm and Dalton 2005; Forrester 1999; Thomas and Butcher 2003). The activities associated with car culture provide a social alternative for young people with a lot of free time but not necessarily adequate access to other entertainment and recreational options and facilities. For young people who are interested in cars, hooning, cruising and street machining can be seen as an exciting alternative to existing leisure and recreational options.

Walker, Butland and Connell (2000) highlight class issues in relation to car culture and masculinity in Australia. Car culture offers young working-class men 'the building of masculine identity, and thus a sense of dignity and self-worth' when the other approved source of masculine dignity – being a breadwinner – is unavailable on account of high youth unemployment (Walker *et al.* 2000: 156).

For young working-class men, car culture and certain driving behaviour is a form of protest masculinity that cements their manhood and demonstrates rebellion against authorities (Walker *et al*. 2000). Car culture offers a forum of belonging and acceptance for young men who have experienced exclusion from other arenas such as higher education, employment and the leisure market. For young working-class men and also those from minority groups, car culture and certain driving behaviours can give them a sense of being in control of their daily lives, which are probably not marked by feelings of control (Collins *et al*. 2000). Car culture and activities such as hooning and cruising offer autonomy and a way of being noticed amongst peers and in public.

Public space is integral to any discussion of young people and car culture. Cruising, hooning and street machining all involve the social use of public space where young people can exert agency by independently engaging with their surroundings. Young people use public space to meet their needs, and not always in the way a specific space was designed for. One example is that an industrial area may be used as a prime site for hooning and street racers to congregate because it is less frequently under the gaze of authorities. Another example is a beachfront that may become a mecca for cruising and blockies because of its location and potential for seeing and being seen. Public space has a dual function: it is a place where gatherings of young people are visible and anonymous at the same time (White 1990). According to Redshaw, young drivers talk about 'the freedom to go where they want, when they want, which all contribute to a greater sense of control' (2001: 7, cited in Thomas and Butcher 2003). Youth is a time of developing interests and gaining independence, and car culture and the use of public space can meet these needs (Graham and White 2007).

Taking space

Many of these youthful activities can be interpreted as meaningful attempts to 'transgress' the ordinary (see Hayward 2002; Presdee 2000). In a world of standardized diversity and global conformities, it is exciting and pleasurable to break the rules, to push the boundaries, to engage in risky and risk-taking activities. Transgressions of this nature are one way in which youth can assert their identity and solidarity in an atmosphere of competition and fun.

However, group activities based upon transgression can also include collective behaviour that is highly threatening and dangerous – for example, violence that is unpredictable, random and unintelligible (McDonald 1999). This is manifest, for instance, in the phenomenon of swarming: spontaneous gatherings of young people that occasionally result in serious episodes of violence. 'Swarming' refers to the unexpected gathering of large numbers of people in particular public locales (see R. White 2006a). Swarming may or may not feature violence. It does, however, involve large crowds – crowds that may occasionally transform into 'mobs'. The size of the crowd is what transforms a private home or private party into a public event by the spilling out of people onto footpaths and surrounding streets and lawns.

Gatecrashing is one particular form of swarming that can involve events sparked largely by immediate crowd dynamics, rather than intent to harm. The presence of hundreds of gatecrashers at some parties is facilitated by new communication technologies, and the search by some for venues that do not rely upon security guards and bouncers to keep order. Key elements of gatecrashing as a social phenomenon include (Sutton *et al.* 2008):

- What: gatecrashing is attending usually a private party without an invitation.
- When: weekends, usually at someone's special occasion such as an eighteenth or twenty-first birthday party.
- Who: young people between 14 and 25 years of age; active participation of private school students; all classes and ethnic backgrounds.
- Why: demise of school dances and reliance on private parties; availability and costs of the night-time economy for teenagers under 18; thrill of getting past security and/or anticipation of something 'happening' that is different; promise of excitement and stimulation.
- How: large numbers of people (up to several hundred) congregating together; heavy alcohol use; often late arrival (after closing time of pub, club or bottle shop); internet and SMS texting as source of information; sometimes congregate outside premises.
- Doing what: may add to excitement of the party; may be associated with violence (conflict is linked around refused entry or being asked to leave); may involve weapons and at times serious injury or death; may involve police baiting.

Not all gatecrashed parties end in violence. This largely depends upon the atmosphere of the event, who is there, the quantity of alcohol consumed and how order is negotiated by hosts. However, two kinds of violence have been noted. The first involves fights between partygoers (between different groups of gatecrashers, or between the host group and the 'invading' group). The second involves fights against the police, where the 'battle with the cops' can become the objective of the gatecrashing participants (see Toohey, 2003). If police–gatecrasher conflicts occur over time, a pattern of ritual confrontation may develop in which the purpose of taking over the street is less about gatecrashing than about setting up the confrontation to come.

The concept of swarming is generally less relevant in relation to gang violence. Although periodically gang members may amass in numbers, their engagement in street fights, in particular, includes organized battles as well as spur-of-the-moment conflicts. Across the world, gangs vary greatly in the level of organization and group orientation (Hagedorn 2007, 2008). Contemporary gang research emphasizes the fluid nature of youth group formation, while acknowledging the centrality of violence to gang membership compared with those young people who do not identify as gang members (White and Mason 2006; R. White 2006b). Although sometimes involving large numbers of people, gang violence tends to be highly targeted in terms of protagonists. It is rarely random, and occurs on a frequent basis. It is not 'surprising' but is central to the very idea of gang-related behaviour.

Much of the current popular understanding of youth gangs in places such as North America, Europe and Australia is heavily racialized (Hagedorn 2007; White 2008a,b). In part this stems from how the media reports on particular groups, with contemporary media images of ethnic minority communities in different national contexts being generally negative (for example, Lebanese in Australia, northern African in Italy, West Indian in England). This is especially so with respect to recent immigrants and people of colour. It is frequently the case as well that particular events are seized upon by the media to reinforce the 'ethnic' character of deviancy and criminality in ways which stigmatize whole communities (Collins *et al.* 2000; Poynting *et al.* 2004; Poynting and Morgan 2007). As the experience in the United States indicates, immigration is frequently associated with the gang phenomenon. For example, the four major periods of gang presence in the USA – the 1890s, 1920s, 1960s and 1990s – were all linked to significant social changes including increased immigration (see Decker *et al.* 2009; Johnson and Muhlhausen 2005).

Despite first appearances, gang style and gang images are localized in their re-representation and reconstruction. To put it differently, young people appropriate 'universal' images and transform these into their own unique kinds of social practice that give the appearance of 'being the same as elsewhere' but in fact have very different contents and are tailored to their own immediate lived realities and social conditions. For example:

> Despite the similarity in names and gang style, there are important differences between Crips in the USA and Crips in The Netherlands. The latter are far less organized, are not organized around drug sales, are not territorial, and engage in much lower levels of violence. In other words, European Crips have more in common with Crip gang style and affectation than organization or behavior.
>
> (Decker *et al.* 2009: 401)

The terms 'Bloods' and 'Crips' are also used in New Zealand and Australia. Here, however, they are used as essentially ethnic markers: the 'Bloods' refers to Samoan young people, the 'Crips' to Tongan young people (White 2008b). The colours each group wears (Bloods, red, Samoan; Crips, blue, Tongan) are immediate and striking signs of ethnic, and indeed 'home' island, origin. The relationship to US Bloods and Crips is tenuous, and the terms have basically been appropriated less as a gang identifier than for local expressions of ethnicity.

Gang styles and associated cultural forms (such as hip hop) are culturally transmitted, but not necessarily culturally emulated as such. For example, the Australian hip hop scene is dominated by ethnic minority young people whose voices are distinctly (immigrant) Australian and whose cultural content/message is likewise unique to their circumstances (see White 1999). Likewise, Indigenous rappers in Australia have appropriated the form, but use different language (sometimes literally a different language) to express what matters to them in their particular cultural universe (White and Wyn 2008).

Whatever the specific content, the images associated with gangs can have a negative impact on young marginalized people in whichever country they live. The moral panics over youth gangs can lead to the ostracism and penalizing of particular groups on the basis of their presumed immoral and threatening behaviour and presence (e.g. particular migrant or ethnic minority youth). It can involve passing of legislation and stepping up police efforts to prevent or prohibit certain types of activity (e.g. certain types of street use). The persistence of moral panic and crime wave discourses in the media also feeds a more generalized fear of crime, a phenomenon that likewise shapes how people interact and relate to one another as well as to gangs generally.

From the point of view of moral panics over gangs, this usually includes popular representations of stereotypical gang characteristics (e.g. the colour gangs of the USA as dramatized by Hollywood). The circulation of certain material has been enhanced by the advent of the internet and associated technologies such as Facebook and YouTube. The internet, and the many gangs with internet sites, provide a ready forum for transfer of information, images, ideas and attitudes. This last is particularly significant insofar as what is being conveyed includes the usual hyper-masculinity trappings but also affective attributes such as the sense of anger and injustice at being 'on the margins'. Gang membership is an important part of social connection and social belonging, at many different levels. The gang image is seen not necessarily as 'bad', but as something to aspire to or to emulate. Moreover, with the advent of the 'gangs', moral panic itself can serve to amplify the excitement attached to the label. For marginalized and often criminalized young people, transgression can be very appealing, especially as it both inverts the negativity of the label (being instead a sought-after status) and reinforces notoriety (since it feeds back into the very thing that is popularly detested). Street credibility and social respect are fashioned out of precisely the thing that most turns the state against the young people in question: the identification with gang affiliation.

There are complicated intersections between the ongoing projects of the 'self' (i.e. constructions of personal identity), the importance of specific local contexts (i.e. material resources and social histories), and wider global social, economic and cultural processes (i.e. globalization) as these pertain to youth gangs (see Hagedorn 2007; Short and Hughes 2006; van Gemert *et al*. 2008). Group formations such as gangs are located in particular spaces at particular times, and they engage in particular kinds of activities. To understand the fluidity and solidity of identity we need to bear in mind both general ethnic identifications, and the importance of territorial cross-ethnic alliances at the local level – in other words, issues of public space and group ownership. This has been described using the notion of 'defensive localism' (Adamson 2000), in which gangs fight to protect territory. In protecting territory, however, ethnicity and locality combine in ways that sometimes privilege ethnicity, and sometimes territory – depending upon who the protagonists are, and who is defined as an 'outsider' at any given moment (see White 2008b). When all is said and done, the material life and welfare of the gang is basically tied to the local area.

Shaking space

Street violence associated with alcohol use is a major social issue in many Western countries. A leisure culture that links alcohol use with a good time, combined with a general culture of violence as normal, is serving up a social cocktail in which people are getting hurt and, indeed, sometimes killed. Regardless of media hype and distorted images of street violence, the fact is that there is a real problem out there, one that is also affecting the dynamics and nature of public space use.

Much of the media treatment of alcohol-fuelled street violence is informed by certain ideas and images. These include, among others, that alcohol-related violence is increasing and that this increase is primarily due to widespread binge drinking; that female violence is on the rise, driven in part by the 'ladettes' phenomenon (young women who 'get off their face' in most 'unladylike' ways); and street fights and pub brawls, which sometimes include 'glassing' (smashing glasses or bottles into someone's face or head) and other forms of what is seen to be mindless thuggery. These images are sparked by specific incidents that may and quite often do occur on a regular basis. They are the key fodder for the mass-circulation daily newspapers and current affairs television programmes.

It is important, however, to locate alcohol use and violence within the context of very specific sorts of social cultures (Jayne *et al.* 2008). Alcohol is consumed in different ways depending upon the social context. For example, for a number of years at a broad-based cultural level there was an Australian cultural stereotype that suggested 'real' men 'drink heaps' and get into fights. In essence, the problem is not young people as such when it comes to street and other forms of violence. Rather, the key issues pertain to the cultures of violence and of alcohol consumption, within which people, young and old, negotiate their social lives. The fact is that violence of many kinds, including interpersonal violence, is 'normal' within a society such as Australia. We are surrounded by images and incidences of violence. It permeates our entertainment industries, our workplaces, our sporting arenas, our advertising and our street life. Similarly, alcohol consumption and indeed alcohol-related violence are largely considered 'normal' within Australian culture (think here of the pub fight scene in that most archetypal of Aussie films *Australia*, Dir. Baz Luhrmann, 2008). Fighting and drinking go hand in hand, and are integral parts of the existing cultural universe, a social place in which young people are particularly visible (and vulnerable) on account of age, affluence and appearance.

Specific analysis of drinking patterns and cultural contexts, especially in regards to young people, has identified a number of relevant social dynamics. For example, the lack of appropriate leisure options can result in drinking as relief from 'leisure boredom' for some young people (Roche *et al.* 2008). Once they are started on this pathway (to initial use of alcohol), the major issue then becomes how alcohol is actually consumed.

The shift from 'just drinking' to 'risky drinking' has been associated with several different factors. For instance, features of social settings found to encourage risky drinking include, among others, large group size (especially in relation to home parties and gatecrashing), presence of intoxicated people, drinking games (in which the intention is intoxication), and pre-gaming (drinking in order to get 'tipsy' before going to an alcohol-free event or setting where alcohol will be expensive) (Roche *et al.* 2008). Related to these factors, research has found that those young people who drink at their own or at a friend's house prior to attending city nightlife venues reported significantly higher total alcohol consumption over a night out than those not drinking until reaching bars and nightclubs. They are also much more likely to have been involved in a fight in the city's nightlife than those who did not start drinking at home first (Hughes *et al.* 2007). The intensity of access to communication technologies has also been positively correlated with heavy use of alcohol, through for example facilitating the organization of 'big nights out' (Roche *et al.* 2008).

Drinking heavily is socially constructed and very much depends upon the interplay between the individual, culture and society. What to drink, when, how and how much are subjects for deliberation, not simply left to random chance. Cultural explanations point to important shifts in attitudes and thinking about drinking. For example, drinking heavily has been associated with the notion of 'calculated hedonism'; that is, a calculated and planned, rational hedonism in which young people plan to 'let loose' (Brain 2000; Roche *et al.* 2008). Related to this is the idea of a 'culture of intoxication', a culture that is informed by a tradition of 'weekday restraint and weekend excess' (Measham 2006: 258). There is the construction of 'British binge drinking cultures' which reinforce certain styles of drinking, while not precluding the same people, at different times and in different places, from engaging in 'European' forms of drinking based upon restraint (Jayne *et al.* 2008). Other literature also points to the relationship between alcohol use and social constructions of gender, and the specific societal and national contexts within which this relationship is manifested (Gefou-Madianou 1992). For example, the drinking patterns of US male college students have been analysed from the point of view of hegemonic masculinity, in ways that demonstrate how behaviour and expectations are linked to certain gendered cultural norms (Capraro 2000; Peralta 2007).

Culture is influenced by social setting, and vice versa. This is illustrated, for example, in the way in which shots, aftershots or shooters, heavily promoted in bars, became an established and popular part of an evening's drinking during weekend nights out (Measham and Brain 2005). Their consumption is related to consumer objectives of getting drunk quicker and treating friends (since shots are cheaper than other forms of alcoholic beverage). It has also been found that a range of environmental variables associated with the physical aspects of the drinking establishment increase the potential for alcohol-related violence, such as uncleanliness, uncomfortable settings, poorly designed seating and bar access, and poor ventilation (Graham and Homel 2008). Violence around licensed premises is also associated with queues in clubs, pubs and nightclubs, and frustrations associated with patron perceptions of unfair and delaying processes of entry.

The proliferation of vertical drinking establishments has been linked to increased levels of alcohol-related harm. These consist of establishments in which patrons are forced to stand while drinking and have nowhere to place their glasses. This is associated with an increased pace of drinking, and consequential social harms (Nicholas 2008). The type of alcohol served and consumed also has a bearing on alcohol-related assaults, with consumption of cask wine and high-strength beer significantly associated with night-time assaults and alcohol-related harm generally (Briscoe and Donnelly 2001; Chikritzhs *et al*. 2007).

How much alcohol one consumes and the way in which one does so are directly related to the probability of being disorderly across a number of dimensions: drink drive, verbal abuse, creating a public disturbance, stealing property, damaging property and physical abuse (Makkai 1998). Moreover, the frequency of engagement in social disorder increases according to the propensity to drink heavily, to binge drink and to drink in harmful ways.

Importantly, such violence is not class neutral. That is, those who engage in alcohol-related violence tend to be predominantly marginalized and working-class men (see Tomsen 1997a,b), although this, too, depends upon specific local context (Jayne *et al*. 2008). To some degree both the violence and the pattern of drinking are embedded in certain working-class masculine cultures. The fact is that the social context of collective drinking often means that antisocial behaviour is a built-in feature of a 'top night out' for young men. Tomsen (1997b: 29) observes, for example, that 'Rowdy acts of misbehaviour, like pushing, arguing, swearing, loudness and obscenity, are all valued for being part of a continuum of social rule-breaking which heightens the pleasurable experience of drinking as time out'. The normality of both excessive drinking and violence-related drinking cannot be overestimated. Nor can their attractions.

Violence in the media, violence on televisions in licensed premises and violence conveyed through new information technologies are important issues to consider. For example, movies such as *Fight Club* (Dir. David Fincher 1999), television programmes that feature brutal cage fighting, and the circulation of schoolyard violence through YouTube, mobile phones and internet social networks inculcate people with the sense that not only is violence all pervasive, but it is essential, glamorous, fun and an 'ordinary' part of everyday life. Again, the pervasiveness of violent images reinforces the naturalness of violence in practice.

There are other forms of disorder in public space beyond those associated with pub violence, such as situations involving riots and mobs where large numbers of people seem to engage spontaneously in unlawful, antisocial and violent behaviour. Recent riots in Australia have seen hundreds of people take to the streets – generally directing their anger at property, such as cars, and authority figures, such as the police. The riots on Palm Island in Queensland and in the Sydney suburb of Redfern were triggered by the deaths of young Indigenous people in relation to perceived negative police intervention (Cunneen 2007). So too in Macquarie Fields, a western suburb of Sydney, things came to a head after a car chase lead to the death of two young local men (Lee 2005). Longstanding resentments within marginalized communities can suddenly come to the fore when circumstances change quickly. In these particular cases, the riots were purposeful, in that they had specific meaningfulness for the participants, and reflected longstanding antagonisms that find their expression in anti-authority resistance. In other words, there is a social history to each of these events.

Mobs, on the other hand, have a different social dynamic. Although superficially similar to riots, mob violence is not quite the same. Here the key variable is 'the crowd', and the transformation of the crowd into a mob. Consider, for example, the following: a group of school students gather in the Queen Street Mall in Brisbane, and shortly thereafter a brawl breaks out involving dozens of young people; at Skyworks in Perth unchecked alcohol consumption sees extensive street fighting and random assaults skyrocket; at Cronulla beach an ostensible concern to defend the beach against outside 'thugs' is transformed into mob violence that threatens residents and commercial enterprises in the local area (see, for example, Knowles 2004; Noble 2009). In these instances there need not be any 'purpose' or 'intent' to the violence. It happens spontaneously, and grows out of the crowd dynamics themselves. In many cases, mob violence is directly linked to excessive alcohol consumption (White 2007b).

In the context of a large crowd and excessive alcohol use, the rules of engagement between people become even less defined. Mob rule is precisely about lack of restraint, the unbridled use of force against an opponent. In small-scale fight situations a 'ritual mediator' may step in to end the potential escalation of conflict (e.g. a mate who intervenes to cool things down) (see Moore 1994: 76). In mob situations, such mediation is much less likely. Rather, the transformation of the crowd into the mob precludes such mediation and opens the door to unrestrained violence.

The mobilization into crowds simulates the positive experience that young people seek in collective bonding. Periods of boredom and the mundane can be broken by the exciting and the extraordinary. This is the promise of the crowd. Part of the promise of the crowd is the inherent ambiguities of the situation. What will happen next is uncertain. However, the mix of alcohol, adrenaline and alienation certainly provides the volatility required for violence to occur.

The presence of large numbers of people in one place – the formation of crowds – can also shape group behaviour depending upon the purpose of the crowd formation. In some crowd situations, mob-like behaviour may emerge. Being in a crowd seems to offer the opportunity to 'lose one's mind', and thereby to lose the normal social controls that guide human interaction. The so-called mob mentality describes the situation in which the crowd dictates general behaviour over and beyond the individual.

Conclusion

This chapter has demonstrated that people use public spaces in very diverse ways. Importantly, it is the 'doing' that makes the space what it is; public space is a dynamic social achievement in which the unpredictable and the bizarre sit alongside the ordered and the mundane. It is the multi-faceted nature of public space that makes it attractive, compelling and teeming with untold opportunities to get lost in the moment.

Much is said and written about the fear of crime and victimization associated with public incivilities, crime and street violence. However, less is said about how the appearance of some degree of 'social disorganization' is itself a source of pleasure. Indeed, the contrast between highly sanitized, extensively regulated spaces (as in some shopping complexes) and less pristine urban environments with fewer visible social controls makes the latter a more desirable space for many people, at least on an occasional basis. Some public spaces are likely to attract people precisely because of the unstructured, unorganized nature of the space. This is the essence of many tourist hot spots, such as the 'notorious' Kings Cross in Sydney and St Kilda in Melbourne. Much the same can be said of popular drinking spots in Europe, such as Covent Garden in London, Temple Bar in Dublin and the Hackerscher Market in Berlin.

In other words, the use of certain public places carries with it expectations regarding what is likely to occur in those places, and a realistic assessment that street life, to be exciting and interesting, necessarily includes some negative features. The reality is that different people want different things in and from public spaces, at different times of the day and night. This holds true for older people as it does for younger, for the tourist as well as for the local. This is also why the over-regulation of public spaces can put people off, since the safe and the secure is not in fact what we always want or need. Vital space is space with an edge, filled with an energy and excitement of our own collective making.

5 Playgrounds without frontiers

Movin', moddin', pushing the boundaries of pleasure

Zannagh Hatton

Abstract

Using the car to transform behaviour appears to be regarded by some guardians of public and private spaces as an act of deviancy, particularly when such behaviour is accompanied by risky practices or a flagrant disregard for visible symbols of enforcement, local and national legislation. Yet such activities have been attributed in the main to a cohort of young men who subscribe to street car culture and who have been attributed by some media, particularly in the UK, an umbrella term, which is simply 'boy racers'. These young men have been characterized by a history of transforming behaviour in what is experienced as a radical flip from normative behaviours of using the car as a means of transport, to what has come to be regarded as a highly transgressive disorder resulting in a number of performative, risky activities (including extreme modification or 'moddin'' of the car), and where risk appears to have become esteemed. The interactions between the boy racers viewed as potential offenders, the redefined public spaces (public car parks and out-of-town industrial estates) which have become their 'stage' or 'playground' where as they as actors perform, and the guardians of such spaces, which may include the police, local authority and private landowners, present a kind of symbiotic relationship which is shaped by the structure and meanings of the settings in which these activities take place, and where all the actors use their experiences to adjust their behaviour accordingly.

As a means to illustrate this, the ensuing chapter attempts to discuss the extent to which the highly visible symbols of enforcement in place to control and regulate the activities of boy racers are often rendered ineffectual in their purpose, because their interpretation is 'read' by some young men, not as prohibitive, but more as a challenge or obstacle to be overcome, another stage upon which to be visibly heroic and in some cases an opportunity to express self-definition. It discusses the relationship between young men, power, machinery, speed and transcendence and argues that much of their activities is about being 'seen', which is crucial in a place where masculinity is fast becoming invisible and many young men are being deprived of stages for display.

Creating an automotive uniform

Since it was first mass-produced by Henry Ford, the car has symbolized and been conceived as many things including a mode of escape, a way of maintaining freedom of movement and freedom of choice in where we work, live and take our leisure, yet for many it has also become a status symbol expressing style and wealth and an image, sometimes painstakingly constructed, of how the owner wishes others to perceive him (or her). As a commodity, however, the car tends to depreciate rapidly in economic value and thus is no longer something reserved solely for those with a substantial disposable income. Thus, when economic realities force concessions on a young aspiring car owner's dreams, a relatively new model or one slightly older 'but with potential' suddenly becomes an attractive proposition.

Many consumers of such vehicles are young men just starting out, who find these 'with potential' models attractive propositions. A significant number may possess technical abilities, breadth of imagination, ability to barter skills and commodities which far outweigh any barriers a lack of finance is likely to impose. The evidence of their labours is often revealed in a completed and modified car, the likes of which may be found reproduced in a variety of auto-enthusiasts' magazines such as *Max Power*, *Revs* or *Auto-Trader*. This passion and enthusiasm for modification in a variety of guises appears to have been adopted by predominately young working-class males in many areas across the Western world and in many cases car ownership has also provided them with opportunities for varying degrees of excitement and escape from the restrictions and drudgery of their daily lives. Through a deliberate adoption of a type of automotive uniform, they are able to distinguish themselves from peers and indicate membership of, or association with, a particular group. From this, there emerges a kind of distinctive subculture which gives those who subscribe to it a sense of belonging and identity which may be missing from other dimensions of their lives. It can also provide many otherwise disenfranchised young men with some sense of family; of a kind which is of their own choosing and structure as opposed to that which has resulted from a biological process or arrangement over which they have had little or no control.

Over recent decades the occasional performative behaviours in which some young men engage, with and around cars, have attracted regular and lengthy discourses perpetuated by many facets of the media. Many of these appear to address their propensity for redefining public space for their own use, their involvement in road traffic accidents, their disregard for conventional rules and their occasional confrontations with the guardians of public spaces. In brief, the popular media appear to focus mainly on the thrills and spills which can occur when a particular type of young man and his car band together with others, in a kind of impromptu and unofficial yet highly visible automotive gathering.

Media interest in the relationship young men develop with automobiles is not new, and the subject of young men and their passion for cars and risk-taking behaviour has provided the theme for a number of popular films over the years.

Certainly within recent years such films include Bruckheimer's blockbuster movie *Days of Thunder* (1999), *Gone in 60 Seconds* (Dir. Dominic Sena 2000) and *The Fast and the Furious* (Dir. Rob Cohen 2001). Yet, whereas these have succeeded in developing a cult following across the Western world and seemingly provided numerous role models for entrepreneurial followers of street car culture, it would appear that only a limited amount of academic enquiry has been given over to examining the subject of young men and their relationship with the motor car. Some exceptions to this have seen Vaaranen and Wieloch (2002) exploring extensively the young working-class men who subscribe to the Finnish subculture of the *kortteliralli* street racers, whilst Miller (2002) has compiled an interesting collection of global studies which describes the many facets attributed to car ownership by differing cultures. Using Lumsden's (2009) research into the street car culture in Aberdeen and Bengry-Howell and Griffin's (2007) enquiry surrounding the material construction of working-class masculine identities through car modification together with my own ethnographic research into the cultural world of boy racers (Hatton 2007), it is possible to draw parallels with some aspects of the psychosocial line of enquiry employed by Marsh and Collett (1986) in which they explored men's relationships with cars and include reference to many street car cultures, including the *raggare* in Sweden, who have existed since the early 1950s.

This abiding passion for car modification as a practice functions through the active consumption and symbolic manipulation of a standard factory-produced car; a process which has been adopted by many young men across the Western world, who also see the physical manipulation of mechanical and car body parts as contributory and idiosyncratic signifiers of working-class masculine identity. The *raggare* in common with the *kortteliarri* have identified cars as an important part of their subculture, especially V8-powered cars and other large cars through which they repeatedly endorse a much-individualized pathway of consumption. Many *raggare*, for example, adopted and reworked the Volvo 240 and 740 models, which were relatively easy to acquire and, for those who possessed little more than basic mechanical skills, also relatively easy to fix and repair, and the designs of the cars lent themselves to a variety of bodywork embellishment through modification and aggressive colour schemes. Similarly the *bosozoku* from Japan developed a distinct style of car modification which set them apart from other car owners, eponymously called 'Bosozoku style'. This included modifications such as large exhaust pipes, bright paint and large aero kits; many also added oil coolers or less commonly large turbo or supercharger intercoolers with highly polished tubing, usually mounted in a prominent position on the front bumper. With perhaps the exception of the *kortteliarri*, who were predominately interested in thrill-seeking activities, risk-taking, speed and street racing, turning public highways into unofficial race tracks after dark, many of the other car-focused subcultures appeared preoccupied not only with performance but also with the aesthetics of their car's outer shell.

Possibly the forerunner of all this during the 1950s and 1960s was America. During this period there was a rise in those willing to subscribe to the *custom car* and *hot rod* fraternity, the latter focusing on speed and performance whereas the former were more concerned with appearance and external modification. Once again the main proponents were young, predominately working-class men, and all of a sudden, and as if in recognition of the demand for cars which could make a statement, one of America's main car production plants at Detroit became the source of high-performance 'muscle' cars which not only could feed the need for speed, but also had unlimited potential for external modification and embellishment. For those individuals with unprecedented spending who were able to acquire these powerful vehicles and were prepared to extend their own, or even commission somebody else's, imagination and creative abilities to create external modification, it was possible for the cars to make a social statement about their owner. For those with a predilection towards modified cars and thrill-seeking activities, the introduction of drag racing on circuits provided many with an opportunity to make some money (if they won) and to gain an admiring following amongst race track goers. Illegal street racing, however, became *the* source which proffered a real opportunity to gain credibility amongst peers, and the danger and illegality involved in the races provided an edge which the more organized racing did not.

There is a willingness to engage in public displays of performative behaviours in and around cars which appears to have prevailed and spread to other parts of the Western world. In Australia, for example, a moral panic has arguably arisen, at the forefront of which are a group of predominately young male car enthusiasts who reportedly engage in loutish, antisocial behaviour and in particular drive in a manner which is antisocial by the standards of contemporary society; that is, too fast, too noisily or too dangerously. The collective description of those who subscribe to this behaviour is 'hoon'. Their main activities appear to include redefining public space for speeding, street racing, burnouts, doughnuts and screeching tyres. In the UK, Ireland and New Zealand a new stereotype, with characteristics similar to the hoon, has emerged: 'boy racers'. The term 'boy' appears to have been used simply because, although it is acknowledged that a small proportion of females do contribute to the street car scene, young men are the predominate force and the colloquialism or stereotype usually refers to those who are in their late teens or early twenties, who have heavily modified the appearance and performance of what appear to be, in the main, small 'hot hatches'. These vehicles include those manufactured by Peugeot, Vauxhall, Renault, Ford or, for those with a greater disposable income and a preference for a slightly larger vehicle, a variety of Japanese models – or, to use Street Car culture parlance, 'Rice Cars' – which can include the more powerful Mitsubishi 'Evo', the Toyota Supra and the versatile Subaru Imprezza WRX and STI models. In common with the Australian hoons and the *kortteliralli*, boy racers engage in performative activities with their cars, subvert conservative driving norms and rebel against the guardians of public spaces, and it could be argued that these young men have become a contemporary example of Cohen's (2002) 'folk devils'.

A number of the unauthorized cultural gatherings of these young men in their modified cars take place in out-of-town industrial estates. These isolated arenas have become venues where the young car enthusiasts socialize with other like-minded individuals and display their cars and driving skills through a number of performative activities including wheel-spins, handbrake turns, doughnuts, burn-outs, 360s and strip-racing. The open spaces and large expanses of smooth tarmac have facilitated opportunities for the young male drivers to display competitiveness, technical skills and mastery and control; all behaviours which many associate with a particular type of masculinity. Such occasions also provide the young men with an opportunity to express solidarity and belonging and to feel that they are part of, and have a place in, a wider group. Their association with a particular automotive group in many respects becomes a signifier of connection and popularity which on the one hand signifies *belonging to*, yet could also be interpreted as signifying *difference from* other automotive groups who occupy the same geographical space.

For some, however, the performative exhibitionism aspect and the need to show difference through aggressive driving and styles of modification may be less appealing; they prefer to merely display their cars and play their music for wider attention, so they focus upon areas such as town centres, public car parks and long stretches of sea front or promenades where they can cruise up and down in convoy, often late at night, with the intention of seeing and being seen. These young men have become known as 'cruisers'. Yet there is an often espoused distinction between boy racers and cruisers, typically stemming from assorted social stigmas and a related desire to not be associated with the deleterious connotations that the 'boy racer' title can carry. Equally in media reports and conversations conveyed by those with little experience or knowledge of the street car scene, there exists an element of slippage between the terms 'boy racers', 'cruisers' and even 'joy-riders'. Although all these terms have a largely uncharted history, and popular and academic understandings of the labels are often far from clear-cut, 'joy-riding' in the UK at least has been defined by the criminal justice system. It mainly refers to the theft of vehicles for short-term and instrumental use, or to driving performatively (attracting high-speed police chases) and other forms of driving indulged in by what are predominantly young males.

The young men who identify with the *kortteliarri, bosozoku, raggare*, hoons and boy racers, and to a certain extent 'cruisers', have manipulated their cars to represent a badge of nonconformity. They provide an automotive statement which unites them with like-minded individuals who share a passion for the street car genre and for moddin' cars; thus in turn their cars provide a medium through which they are able to convey a sense of self, of who they are, or who they wish others to believe them to be. In simple terms, the car becomes ideally placed to bridge the gap between the real self (who they actually are) and their ideal self (what they would like to be, or aspire to be, or who they would wish others to perceive them to be). Undoubtedly having an impressive or unusual vehicle to drive attracts attention and acknowledgement, albeit in many cases negative. Nonetheless, for those who perhaps are rarely acknowledged in other dimensions of their lives and feel as though they are on the edge of society, their vehicles are a source of pride which demonstrate material ownership and, if the modifications have been carried out by the young owner, they can demonstrate their social capital and they are able to gain kudos for their creativity, personal expression, technical expertise and craftsmanship.

Much public debate surrounding these young men described above, and their driving practices, appears to have been framed around concepts of deviance and youth or indeed a combination of the two. Arguably young males are over-represented in accident statistics and car crime, and the manifestation of their growing association with the varying aspects of street car culture has led to the introduction of legislation which can result in the confiscation of a much-loved car, a court appearance and/or penalty points on a licence, as well as financial penalties in the form of a fine. Yet, far from being prohibitive, for many young men this adds a kind of *frisson* to their car-related activities; for, in addition to the risky practices they seek to undertake through their sometimes extreme forms of car modification and performative exhibitionism to satisfy their own desires or to impress peers, they increase their thrill in risk-taking by pitting their skills and cunning against the guardians of public and private space. The attractions of such risks can be many-fold: for some young males it merely represents a *rite de passage*, the maturational process whereby they approach manhood passing through a phase which inevitably brings with it degrees of delinquency, disenchantment, confusion and rebellion; for others it may be a particular period or critical life event, which could initiate a desire to assert their masculinity through certain macho values such as demonstrations of physical strength, courage, toughness and the ability to survive encounters with those whose role it is to bring about varying degrees of social control.

Manifestations of working-class masculinity through risky driving practices and performative behaviours

Many theoretical statements have been made surrounding the extent to which the life experiences of young people in today's society are significantly differ-ent from the experiences of young people, for example two if not three dec-ades ago. Furlong and Cartmel (1997: 1) have suggested that 'Young people in contemporary industrial societies have to negotiate a set of risks which were largely unknown to their parents . . . irrespective of social background or gender', whereas the contemporary German sociologist Ulrich Beck (1992) has argued that we *all* now live in a risk society and an increasing degree of risk is brought into our daily lives by technology. Undoubtedly one of the greatest feats of tech-nology and engineering readily available to man is the automobile, and in a state of motion it is easily placed to present a daily risk to anyone who may come into contact with it, be it as a pedestrian, passenger, driver or road user per se. Yet for many, and especially young people, quite simply the act of obtaining a driver's licence can symbolize many things, including a coming of age, a point whereby one enters adulthood, when the onset of car ownership or becoming a car driver may be regarded as conferring or suggesting dimensions of citizenship and status, something which may have been previously blocked by age, a low economic position or social isolation brought about by the remote geographical positioning of one's lived environment.

At what stage, however, do some of these young vehicle drivers find themselves being singled out for media and statutory attention and what behaviours or characteristics do they manifest which lead others to judge them? Certainly young adults and particularly young males aged between 17 and 25 have become consistently over-represented among those injured or killed in road traffic accidents or penalized for exhibiting risky driving behaviours such as speeding or dangerous driving. Carrabine and Longhurst (2002) draw attention to the fact that what they perceive to be the more socially deprived and deviant sections of today's youth are also more likely to negotiate consumption of the car through the acts of theft, joy-riding and performative behaviours in and around cars; activities which the media and others attribute to hoons, boy racers and those already described in earlier passages, placing them in an arena which appears to be the preserve of young working-class males. Perhaps one could argue that those who subscribe to the car-based subcultures have come to regard the car rather as others may regard recreational drugs and alcohol: they are ideal vehicles for transforming behaviours in what may be experienced as a radical flip from a highly normative order, to what is regarded by the guardians of public and private spaces as a highly transgressive order.

Using the car to transform behaviour, although potentially regarded as an act of deviancy when the behaviour is accompanied by risky practices or dangerous or careless driving, may be the preserve of those who have more of a predilection towards risk-taking than others, yet a sensation-seeking personality may also contribute to a diverse group of behavioural differences. Social influence too can act as a powerful constraint on rule breaking but conversely it can also encourage it, and when certain types of young men get together with certain types of vehicles the likelihood of risk-taking increases. Indeed the very dimension of thrill and adventure-seeking behaviour, the willingness to take risks and participate in extreme behaviours, is increased when there is the belief that personal status within the hierarchy of the group is under threat or can be escalated to a more significant level through extreme behaviour. Furthermore, someone who is feeling perhaps less masculine or less successful, has a poor self-image and is in need of a bolstered self-evaluation, can go some way in accomplishing this through selective association with peers who appear on the surface to be more accomplished, more daring and thus, more 'real' men.

With the gradual demise of heavy industry, fishing, agriculture and the types of employment associated with an area's metalliferous past, a particular kind of working-class masculinity is fast becoming invisible and many young males are arguably deprived of the more traditional stages for display. Whilst engaged in research into the cultural world of boy racers, I studied the behaviour and lifestyles of a group of young men who appeared to obtain the greatest sense of personal identity, pride, power and self-expression from car ownership, and an enduring passion for cars and car-based activities. Many of them were further bound by other common themes, which included fragmented or fractured family circumstances, an absence of appropriate male role models, relatively poor economic circumstances through limited employment opportunities, an often unproductive period at school or college, and a life lived in a dispersed rural environment with few opportunities to develop broader social networks.

Through their ensuing behaviours in and around their cars, it became apparent that notions of masculinity, the need to portray the characteristics associated with being a 'real' man, were deeply ingrained and an ever-present theme. This tended towards an appreciation for certain macho values such as physical strength, toughness, courage, daring and a predilection for risk-taking and survival. By being involved in the modification and manipulation of powerful cars it became possible for the young men to demonstrate their ideals of macho masculinity of a type that Brandth and Haugen (1995: 379) describe as 'Big, hard and powerful'. The ability to transform abandoned and broken cars, long relegated to the scrap yards, into an efficient and mobile mechanical masterpiece relying on little else other than their own levels of skills, imagination and ingenuity became their cultural capital. The physical labour they engaged in through the modification of their cars often saw them involved in the exertion of extreme physical strength and endurance as they removed and replaced engines and gear boxes with painstaking detail, lifting and welding component parts from which they habitually emerged displaying cuts and abrasions, dirt and grime, proudly bearing such scarifications as evidence of their labours and openly sneering at those less mechanically skilled who were obliged to pay others to carry out such work for them.

Each time they engaged in performative activities with their cars, either alone or with peers, there could be a significant gamble attached. The risk could often be twofold: the level of success of their intended action, against something going wrong with their performance. The thrill gained was not always through competition with one another, but more from the arousal they gained from the actual experience. Yet a significant by-product of their performance, if carried out in the presence of others, was the extent to which their performance was rated by peers. This increased the pressure for them to be seen to do well, or to fail spectacularly. Merely to be regarded as mediocre or second-rate would attract derision from those they sought to impress, and to have their performance considered as less than spectacular was, for many, unthinkable. Driving a car provided many young men with new opportunities for mastery. It allowed them a belief that once behind the steering wheel they would become ostensibly stronger and more powerful than they were ordinarily and the enclosed private space of their car would serve to shield them from the commonplace concerns that beset their daily lives. This search for momentary freedom from the trials and tribulations and what many regard as shortcomings within their existence, such as unemployment, family stresses and concerns about the future, was reinforced for many through the immortal line from the cult film *The Fast and the Furious,* in which the character Toretto, in an attempt to rationalize the excessive speed with which he drove during street car racing, stated that 'I live my life a quarter-mile at a time. For those ten seconds I'm free.' Driving at speed or focusing on performative exhibitionism, the driver appears to become as one with his car and loses himself to the deliberate and calculated movements of gears, accelerator, brake, clutch and steering wheel, swaying in poetic harmony as if engaged in some bizarre dance ritual, during which nothing else matters, and concentration is all-consuming whilst pushing the boundaries of pleasure.

Engaging in performative activities is not always a planned process and spontaneous action is more likely to occur when two or more young men get together and occupy a car. Action can be varied. Inciting another road user to race may be a simple process of driving alongside and staring meaningfully at another driver and overtaking or 'cutting him up', and repeating the process until a response is elicited. An alternative 'game' is to engage in the irritating and dangerous activity of 'tail-gating', which is driving far too close to the vehicle in front, with the prime intention of prompting its driver to quicken their speed. Alternatively positioning alongside a fellow road user at traffic lights and revving the engine, employing once again a 'meaningful stare' whilst moving gradually forward and quickly accelerating away as if on the starting grid at Le Mans, can initiate an impromptu street race. For some boy racers, a relatively common pursuit initiated to relieve boredom, or in response to a wager or bet, has been to bait or goad the occupants of a police vehicle into giving chase, in what has been termed a 'fly-by', necessitating driving at high speeds and engaging in risky manoeuvres in a bid to evade capture or interception. Being victorious in evading the attentions of a pursuing police car or even being apprehended whilst engaging in some performative activity can result in the individual concerned achieving an elevated status amongst peers and an immediate rise within the hierarchy of their group. Ensuing tales of cunning and daring, often interwoven with embellishments about the levels of risks involved, will take pride of place in conversations and successive versions will be trotted out anecdotally for many months to come.

High-speed driving and risk has a long history of being constituted as a source of pleasure, and the thrill experienced by driving fast is one particularly associated with young males. The 'thrill' of speed is something Marsh and Collett have argued as being an inherently corporeal practice which is predicated on the sensations, arousal and physical changes which occur in the body, when acceleration or near misses occur; whereas for some this may evoke fear, others experience a 'sharply tingling experience, which is perceived as intensely pleasurable' (Marsh and Collett 1986: 183). Certainly in many respects it has been possible to draw parallels with the boy racers' performative activities and the arousal theory surrounding gambling (see Brown 1986). In both instances, many individuals concerned lead what they perceived to be insufficiently stimulating lives, so they seek opportunities to take risks to increase their arousal levels to more pleasurable heights, repeatedly seeking the experience and with each successive risk becoming greater than the last.

Many social theorists including Miles (1998) have suggested that the consumption of specific resources can potentially play an important role in who we are and how we construct our social lives. Indeed the process of constructing the identity of a hoon or a boy racer or any of the others described takes more than the mere acquisition of a car; it involves a set of processes which potentially signal to others the level of the individual's self-definitional attainment. Image is all-consuming. If, for example, the boy racers do not possess the correct image in the first place, they seek to adopt a change and many do this through the vehicles they drive, something akin to Marsh and Collett's (1986: 11) suggestion that 'If you are lacking in self-image, one way of making up for it is to drive a particular car which redefines you'. Dittmar (1998) supports this theory and suggests that some individuals may use consumption to create a symbolic identity in order to compensate for perceived inadequacies in certain dimensions of their self-concept, and the car is admirably positioned as a medium through which to do this. If, for example, a man does not feel masculine enough, he may feel that by displaying a widely recognized and accepted masculine symbol, such as driving a fast performance car or piloting a powerful motorcycle, he can change this self-concept and thus create a symbolic identity which suggests to others that he is indeed masculine.

Self-image created by the acquisition of a particular make and model of vehicle and the symbolism associated with cars generally has featured prominently in the advertising and marketing of cars and car accessories since the 1920s. What is shared by these and more modern representations are the messages they convey and the way they pay attention to the anatomical comparisons that, given the evolution of the shape and style of cars, seem to be inescapable. When we drive a car it responds to our physical movements and thus becomes an amplified part of our body; we become 'enhanced humans' (Grey and Mentor 1995: 223). As a result, the car tends to be thought of as part of oneself, both mentally and physically. Those who subscribe to the different forms of street car culture through their process of modification, or moddin', have sought to emphasize the more masculine qualities and characteristics, such as strength, power and aggression. This process of imbuing motor vehicles with the more masculine characteristics is not new. Throughout its history the meaning of the motor car has been contextualized by its strong cultural and discursive link with men and manifestations of masculinity (see Gartman 1994).

Connell (2003) has suggested that masculinity does not exist as an ontological given but comes into being as people act. Boy racers and those who subscribe to the street car culture arguably bring masculinity into existence through performance. Connell's concept of 'hegemonic masculinity' has been particularly influential; it points out the existence of hierarchies of masculinities and reflects the fact that certain masculinities are more dominant and idealized than others. Certainly, for those who identify cars and car-related activities as central domains of meaning within their immediate social network, the abilities of skilful driving, the displays of cunning and daring and the exhibition of resistant practices which cut across other social strata within the normal car-driving scene, together with a propensity to engage in risk-seeking driving behaviours, are idealized and much sought-after masculine characteristics. Having arrived at what they believe to be an ideal self-concept of what it is to be a 'real' man and rich in practical knowledge about their cars, those who subscribe to the street car scene, such as boy racers, become better placed to achieve a level of recognition that elsewhere may have been denied them, and through public displays of performative driving these subordinate young men are able to grab a significant share of public attention.

Blurring the boundaries of public and private space

With expressively loud exhausts, the sound of powerful engines and the loud bass beat of their music which accompanies their journeys, boy racers and others like them manifest their existence. When they grow tired of their chosen playgrounds, such as the isolated or out-of-town industrial estates, they go in pursuit of a wider audience, and drive into town or circumnavigate residential areas with their stereos playing at full decibels and their windows open. The boundaries of public and private space become blurred and many of them use their choice of music to set the mood for the night ahead. One group from my own research did themselves little favour by driving with their windows low and singing loudly as they passed through towns and villages:

> Bad boys, Bad boys what you gonna do?
> What you gonna do when we come for you?
> Bad Boys, Bad Boys what you gonna do?
> What you gonna do when we come drivin' through?

The tone, however, could become too much to bear for some residents, a feeling which revealed itself in subsequent media headlines such as 'Racers Make Life a Misery, Say Residents' (*Western Morning News* 2006). Discouraged and occasionally moved away from the residential areas by an overt police presence, many who ally themselves with the boy racer genre sought to congregate in public car parks, of the type often rendered inaccessible at night, by the placement of barriers across the entrances; much of this being a local authority response to boy racers' pre-existing use of car parks. In implementing these measures, the guardians of public and private spaces were effectively attempting to reduce the boy racers' repertoire of 'playgrounds'. Yet by implementing such installations it could be considered that they underestimated the excitement and challenge such creations could bring, and the destruction or ignoring of such barriers provided an opportunity for individual boy racers to prove their worth in front of peers.

Boy racers through their car-related practices are equally able to present a picture of rebellious young men whose tactics, when faced with obstruction, were extended into action. The obstructions could be perceived or real and could vary from visible symbols of enforcement, such as prohibition notices preventing access to car parks or warnings about speed restrictions, to a belief that certain security measures or rules existed even if, in reality, they did not. Any ensuing action taken accompanied a belief that obstacles were there to be overcome, a venue could be liberated and where, with the right ingredients, an atmosphere could be created, anything could happen and momentarily there could be a freeing of the self to an uncertainty which would be 'new' or 'different' every time.

Gaining access to these prohibited areas opened the way to adventure, where possibility could constitute a kind of grounded aesthetics of risk and risk-taking in circumstances where risk was esteemed. For many participants the unexpected adventures which could follow might be trivial – a bet or a wager about which car can be the fastest between two fixed points or who was to be the most proficient at carrying out common performative activities such as 360-degree turns, doughnuts and handbrake turns within a confined space – or the added *frisson* and heightened atmosphere of possibility created whereby they or peers could be apprehended by the guardians of these public or private spaces and their vehicles confiscated. In many ways it could almost be as if the young men through their performative activities with their cars in regulated public spaces invented their own trials by performance in uncertain situations.

To illustrate this I am able to draw on an example from my own ethnographical account of boy racers in the West Country, when I discovered that locked barriers at the entrance to a multi-storey car park were no deterrent for one group who had travelled 100 miles in one evening to attend a large 'meet' or gathering, only to find access to the sea front had been restricted by a police presence. Undeterred, a breakaway group, led by those familiar with the area, carefully but unlawfully removed the barrier to a multi-storey car park, thus enabling access for all those who wished to join in. Within approximately 40 minutes all storeys of the car park were filled with revellers. The atmosphere was electric and heavy with expecta-tion; almost carnival-like with music being played at full decibels from the major-ity of cars, many of which were equipped with sophisticated and expensive music systems often of greater value than the cars which housed them. All the rhythms being played gradually became fused into one and a few girls who had arrived as passengers danced in groups and swayed to the beat. The young men lounged on their cars chewing gum or smoking and exchanged views on the proceedings of the night so far; ideas for modification were exchanged and cars admired.

From a lower floor the tuneful babble became a roar as two cars raced against one another, competing for supremacy over a short distance. The roars of the watch-ing crowd drowned any mechanical noise and competition to race the winner was fierce. Those drivers who had arrived merely to watch, with no previous notion of competition in mind, were egged on by companions with comments such as 'Get on in there mate . . . you know that you wanna really' or 'You ain't gonna let a weasel like he show us up'. Many, succumbing to pressures from peers, entered the fray. Potential dangers were minimized by careful planning of 'the course' and a number of bystanders acted as 'stewards' to ensure spectators were kept at a safe distance. When all competitive activities had ceased and social exchanges were put aside for the night, all that was left as evidence of the foregoing performance were the scarifications on the surface of the car park resulting from tyre friction against concrete. The dismantling of the car park barrier and ensuing illegal entry into prohibited premises had been carried out in a manner comparable to a true guerrilla infiltration into enemy territory. It afforded those concerned the thrill and excitement of being able to take rebellious action against a system which in their view usually took or expected some form of remuneration or accountability and, when their tactics were successfully accomplished, it marked a temporary vic-tory of cunning and strategic planning over the local authorities, the guardians of public and private spaces, their surveillance resources and associated apparatus;

in fact, a victory over what the young men believed to be all agents of social discipline and repression.

Their clear enjoyment of the evening, the careful organization of both the performative and competitive activities and the successful breaching of prohibitive installations prompted me to ask one of the young men how he thought that the boy racers would justify the initial act of vandalism which effected entry to the venue. His response surprised me as he ignored any reference to the activities which gave rise to the unauthorized access, but rather couched the events in terms of safety, regarding the heightened levels of care and consideration demonstrated by those engaged in the performative displays in a confined area, because the only participants and bystanders were people like themselves.

> In 'ere you can't get up much speed, the revving makes it seem faster what with all the noise an' that so you take more care and no-one's gonna get hurt, or not hurt bad and the cars ain't gonna get too much damage. You might blow a head [gasket] or summat but the energy is contained. We rules out the variables. Nobody's here who ain't caught up an' involved to some extent with moddin' cars. If we was out in the town somewhere there's always a chance somebody's gonna get caught up in it, and that somebody ain't never likely to be one of us lot.
>
> (Jez)

Conclusion

Ultimately what has been covered in this chapter affords only a brief glimpse into the complex cultural world of boy racers and those who subscribe to street car culture. Yet it goes some way to provide a flavour of how some young men have come to view visible symbols of enforcement and the guardians of public and private space not as prohibitive, but rather as obstacles to be overcome and challenges to be undertaken. In some instances, such symbols and guardians become mere resources to be used in the process of demonstrating rebellious action for the benefit of gaining an elevated status amongst peers and an increase of self-worth. It reveals in some small way how the signifiers of masculine identity are revealed through the processes of heavily individualized modification of cars, both visually and performatively, and through risk and risk-taking behaviours. Nonetheless it also uncovers a world largely comprising young working-class men, often unqualified (in academic terms) but not without skill, often inarticulate yet capable of detailed conversation interspersed with technical terms (as long as the subject is mechanical), and often unemployed (and in some cases unemployable). Yet, through their cars and car-related practices, these young men have in many ways been able to maintain a degree of control over their young lives, to identify and use the resources they deem necessary to define who they are *and* to live life as they wish.

It would be easy to dismiss the sets of challenging, rebellious or redefining behaviours by boy racers and the many others who subscribe to the street car genre as being marginal or inconsequential, for this is precisely what the strategies of hegemony would dictate, similar to the way that occupying forces in times of war have dismissed acts of resistance or vandalism as being little more than the product of a handful of troublemakers. Others may view such sets of behaviour as little more than acts or potent signs of nihilistic disaffection, yet I would argue that the young men concerned, and their performative behaviour with their cars, have gained a certain amount of notoriety for what may be regarded by the guardians of public and private spaces as interrelated, deviant, norm-violating and compromising behaviours, and any media-publicized punitive rewards, including court appearances and ensuing fines, or points allocated to a driving licence, far from acting as a deterrent, are regarded by some young men as 'badges' of achievement and masculine identity and examples of honour seeking for being brave whilst challenging rules and pushing boundaries. Such activities have done much to reinforce the iconic allure attached to being a boy racer and has provided those who are part of that subculture with a visibility which other dimensions of their young lives have been unable to.

6 Impermissible pleasures in UK leisure

Exploring policy developments in alcohol and illicit drugs[1]

Karenza Moore and Fiona Measham

Introduction

This chapter examines the regulation and policing of 'impermissible pleasures' across leisure spaces and within the UK's night-time economy (NTE). The official acknowledgement of the social pleasures of drinking by the 'sensible majority' is contrasted with a lack of acknowledgment of the pursuit of intense intoxication as a 'warrantable motive' (O'Malley and Valverde 2004: 25) for both 'immoderate' alcohol consumption and illicit drug use. We draw on the recent emergence of new psychoactive substances or so-called 'legal highs' to explore the notion of 'impermissible pleasures' and to illustrate the bankruptcy of policy responses to leisure-time intoxication, trapped within the discourses of 'addiction' and 'crime and deviance'.

Our concern here is with pleasures that are ambiguous in terms of the production of harm to either the individual or wider society. Pleasure may be conceived of as the product of culturally and historically specific discourses and material practices (Alasuutari 1992) and is the subject of cross-disciplinary consideration (Bendelow and Williams 1998). Considerations of human embodiment and the sensuous, social and poetic dimensions of leisure space production have drawn on geography, sociology and leisure studies (Crouch 2000). The pleasures of consumption practices such as drug use have been usefully examined at the intersection of criminology and tourism studies (Shiner 2010). Research on pleasure ranges from the sociology of the emotions (James and Gabe 1996; Lupton 1998; Williams 2000) to pleasure as interactional and embodied spatially located affect explored within research on emotional geographies (Davidson and Bondi 2004; Davidson and Milligan 2004) and is included in studies on the embodied risks and pleasures of 'going out' (Hubbard 2005) and working in the NTE (Monaghan 2002; Sanders 2005). Within criminology, pleasure is an aspect of both collective experience and individual agency in the performance of crime, as explored by criminologists interested in the emotionality of criminality (Measham 2004a: 213; Presdee 2004: 280–1) and those studying transgression more generally, from Becker (1963), Katz (1988), Hayward (2002) and Presdee (2000, 2004, 2005) to Lyng's (1990, 2005) risk-taking as euphoria-producing 'edgework'. Others characterize pleasure through Foucault's notion of 'losing oneself', being 'swept away' (Robinson 2003), or as 'experiential intensity' (Moore and Measham 2008: 241). Being 'swept away' however, is not necessarily or only framed as nihilistic, escapist or involving a hedonistic loss of self. Intoxicated and intoxicating practices typically entail a 'controlled loss of control' (Measham 2002) or 'controlled pleasure' (Green and Moore 2009) through practices which attempt to produce, optimize and manage pleasure whilst minimizing problems.

Psychoactive substance use is a key site where the potentially pleasurable consumption practices of embodied individuals situated in leisure spaces (house parties, bars, clubs, festivals, parks, the street) become the focus of neo-liberal governance techniques. In such spaces licit and illicit leisure activities combine: electronic dance music (EDM) fans pay entry fees to clubs as legitimate businesses, businesses unlikely to survive without the enthusiastic patronage of their (mostly) illegal drug-taking customers. Given that the use of illicit substances in such circumstances is not for 'medicinal' purposes (prescribed or self-prescribed), pleasure surfaces as a conundrum for 'the State'[2] in relations with primarily economically active citizens who are to be governed at a distance through personal morality within a community setting (Rose 2000). Deliberate immoderate intoxication in leisure settings[3] is thus produced as an immoral and irrational 'choice'. Taking illegal drugs – or more recently 'legal highs' – is produced by official discourses as *inherently* 'dangerous', 'risky' and likely (if not certain) to involve 'harm' to oneself, to others and to communities. Under the current international drug control system, prohibition (by means of criminal sanctions) remains the most usual response to this production of danger, risk and harm, as individuals, communities, even whole nations are encouraged to build resilience to 'the damage drugs cause' (Home Office 2010a: 3). Here pharmacological pleasure has no place; those who pursue pleasure through drug consumption are 'made up' through expert discourses as deviant, self-deluding, pain-seeking addicts (Booth Davies 1997; Hacking 1986; Sparti 2001). Conversely, if drug addiction – conceptualized as a disease which undermines free will – has not compelled users into consumption, then users are framed as innocents compelled into use by unscrupulous Others (such as 'drug pushers' or 'the media') or else simply flawed consumers who lack moral integrity and self-control (Bauman 1998a).

Beyond the prohibitionist position of the UK government and the wider international community, the past 20 years have seen the emergence and maturation of the global harm reduction movement (Stimpson 2007). Concentrating on producing scientific evidence with which to inform policy interventions, the harm reduction movement has attempted to move debate away from its historically moralizing tendencies. In relation to leisure spaces, harm reduction ideas have influenced public health responses to drug and alcohol use and in the sexual health arena, although resources and political acceptability tends to wax and wane. Crucially, harm reduction asserts that some practices are safer than others and so seeks to promote them in recognition that total abstinence from drugs, alcohol or sex may not necessarily be an appropriate, desirable or even feasible goal. However, harm reduction, whilst opening up space for pleasure as a possible if not warrantable motive for certain activities, constructs a neo-liberal, self-regulating subject who rationally assesses risks and possible harms and is impelled to choose to reduce them (Zajdow 2010): refraining, for example, from the practice of 'barebacking'[4] during gay sex parties (Race 2007); from polydrug 'cocktails'; or from consuming illicit drugs outside the confines of weekend leisure (Moore and Measham 2008).

Problematically, public health discourses continue to present pleasure from substance use in leisure settings as mutually exclusive with being a happy, healthy, even hopeful human being: even when causality between substance use and comorbid disorders remains opaque, a 'rational choice' is demanded 'between fun and health' (Sumnall *et al.* 2010). Yet the pleasures of wilful intoxication through alcohol and drug use are increasingly the focus of researchers, from Ettorre (1992) to a special issue of the *International Journal of Drug Policy* (2008). Accounting for pleasure enables a better understanding of user motivations and practices that may otherwise go unnoticed in dramatizations of the 'risks' of drink and drug taking (Race 2009). Furthermore, harm reduction, traditionally premised on changing the 'risky' behaviours of the individual to reduce possible harm, is recognizing the need to move away from individualistic notions of changing a person's behaviour (typically through education programmes) to more holistic considerations of risk and pleasure environments (Duff 2008; Rhodes 2002). This is an appealing development for those concerned with exploring situated leisure, pleasure and criminal/deviant activities, as it can account for the contextual specifics of the pursuit of pleasure within particular cultures, such as the determined yet differentiated intoxication within musical and stylistic 'scenes' (Measham and Moore 2009; Moore 2010). Such an approach begins to acknowledge the ways in which harm reduction possibilities are shaped by the socio-cultural and political contexts in which pleasure is sought: the reluctance of clubs to carry harm reduction material for fear of being identified as a space in which illegal drugs are consumed; the limited acceptability of visible water consumption as a cultural signifier of ecstasy use;[5] or the hurried consumption by a customer of their whole night's drug supply when confronted by security searches, amnesty bins, police and 'sniffer' dogs at a club entrance.

Pleasures which are *visible* in the public domain have been targeted by, and subject to, formal and informal control mechanisms: pertinent examples are outdoor raves, consensual sex in public places with strangers, and urban sports such as skateboarding and free running (Bell 2006a; Measham 2004b). Indeed historically the authorities' concern about pleasure across leisure times and spaces relates to its potential intrusion into work patterns or how it may lead to a 'lack of control', with potential 'disorder' always of paramount concern (Bauman 1998b). In addition, behaviours that do not conform to a broader picture of modernity as a collective aspiration for a cohesive, civil society, even if ostensibly undertaken 'in private', have been regulated and policed by formal means, particularly if groups already deemed to be deviant to the heterosexual norm (i.e. heteronormativity) are involved. Bondage/Discipline/Sadism/Masochism (BDSM) and gay circuit parties are relevant examples here.[6]

Managing pleasurable activities occurs on a spectrum between state regulation (with many variants) and self-regulation. The policing of pleasure and its associated industries may fluctuate according to perceptions of the activities as more or less socially useful or inevitable, warranting more or less formal styles of control. Policing impermissible pleasures across leisure spaces involves not only law enforcement – apprehending and prosecuting offenders – but also 'order maintenance' through, for example, control of crowd flow or surveillance of customers by club toilet attendants. On the other hand, regulatory agencies seek compliance of behaviour as the main objective, with law enforcement remaining an option of last resort. In short, models of regulation and policing may intersect in their social and cultural practices. In contemporary society, this is most noticeable in multi-agency forums and initiatives in which the aims of policing and regulating impermissible pleasures are shared and implemented between agencies and through public/private partnerships (Hadfield and Measham 2010). 'City Safe' in Manchester, for example, includes local authority agencies such as environmental health, licensing and the police, as well as public transport companies, residents' associations, a city centre management company and best practice public/private initiatives (Manchester Pub and Club Network) and awards ('Best Bar None'), as well as the licensees of individual premises.[7]

Whether leisure-pleasure activities are placed within or outside the realms of social acceptability and legal purview changes over time; cigarette smoking in public places is perhaps the clearest example here. Other activities involving 'impermissible pleasures', such as the possession and consumption of cannabis, have changed in relation to social and legal sanctions across relatively short periods (Warburton *et al.* 2005). The efficacy of criminalizing illicit drug users has been the focus of intense debate in the UK. In certain cases the Advisory Council on the Misuse of Drugs (ACMD) has recommended the prioritization of education and health interventions above criminalization of users, in relation to specific ethnic groups (East African khat users, ACMD 2005) and lifestyle groups (non-medical anabolic steroid users, ACMD 2010a), despite the health and social harms associated with non-medical use of steroids and khat recognized in both reports. The Association of Chief Police Officers announced its recommendation not to criminalize users when substituted cathinones became controlled drugs (*Daily Telegraph* 2010), also suggesting that routes other than through the criminal justice system might be more useful for some drug users. However, this belies the fact that the pleasures of intoxication at parties, bars, clubs and festivals across the UK are part of popular leisure activities which routinely come under scrutiny from government, police, private security firms and the media.

Policing and regulating pleasure: still 'dancing on drugs'

The 'official' representation of ecstasy – as a dangerous substance akin to other controlled drugs classified as Class A under the Misuse of Drugs Act 1971, such as heroin and crack cocaine, which are associated with 'addiction' and 'agony' – has been challenged over the past 20 years or so by the mainstreaming, commercialization and enduring popularity of dancing on drugs (e.g. Deehan and Saville 2003; Measham *et al.* 2001) and by a changing assessment of ecstasy's harms

(ACMD 2009; Halpern *et al.* 2011; Sessa and Nutt 2007). 'Official' representations of ecstasy consumption as morally dubious and 'irrational' are undermined by embodied expressions and meaningful lived experiences of pleasure related to dancing on drugs both in local and across global leisure spaces (Hunt *et al.* 2010; Measham 2004c; Shiner 2010). Pleasure is made manifest through the social, cultural, emotional and religio-spiritual embodied practices associated with post-rave EDM cultures (D'Andrea 2007; St John 2004; Moore 2010) and can include sensual and visceral pleasures shared with and intensified by fellow clubbers (Buckland 2002; Jackson 2004; Malbon 1999), driven historically by EDM culture's project of intensifying the sensations of club drugs such as MDMA (Reynolds 1998) through the combined hard repetitive beats and melodies of genres such as trance. Such pharmacological pleasures, rarely explicitly and reflexively explored even within contemporary club studies (Measham and Moore 2006), are further silenced by prohibitionist responses to the 'threat' of popularized illicit leisure, particularly the criminalization of ravers and clubbers as a persistent and visible group of drug-taking risk-takers (France 2007: 134–7; Hill 2002).

Studies of UK clubbers show high levels of club drug use (predominantly ecstasy, cocaine and more recently ketamine and mephedrone) compared with the general population (e.g. Measham *et al.* 2001; Deehan and Saville 2003; Measham and Moore 2009). Club research has consistently demonstrated that clubbers' drug use is aimed at enhancing and prolonging a night out, through the combined pleasures of listening to music, dancing, socializing and, for many, combined legal and illegal drug consumption (Hunt and Evans 2008; Moore and Miles 2004; Pini 2001). There is a growing body of work which recognizes that pharmacological pleasure is an aspect of both drug use within EDM settings (Hunt *et al.* 2007, 2010) and determined drunkenness within the NTE (Measham 2004b), whilst within club settings pleasure itself is symbolically represented through cultural artefacts, most explicitly with the continued widespread use of the 'smiley face' image (Ashton 1992). Such 'smiley faces' have re-emerged as symbols of Nu-Rave and Rock/Rave dance music scenes, reminiscent of the acid house, rave and ecstasy symbolism of the late 1980s and early 1990s EDM scenes (Fitzgerald 2002; Mixmag 2007). The discursive production and symbolic representation of dancing on drugs as a pleasurable and transgressive activity also surfaces in club promotion materials (e.g. advertising straplines on flyers, photographs of club nights) as well as being produced in interactions between clubbers on social networking sites, where anticipation and excitement about forthcoming dance events form part of the processes of elective identity formation, displays of belonging and the successful production of a pleasurable night out.

As noted, harm reduction remains relatively silent on the pleasures of illicit intoxication (Race 2009). This is unsurprising given that harm reduction remains rooted in public health, itself a 'rational enterprise in which "rational" individuals are educated to understand their civic duty to mean self-government through expert discourses' (Zajdow 2010: 220). O'Malley and Valverde (2004: 39) suggest that the regulation of drug consumption in modern liberal societies involves 'a battery of pleasure-denying characterizations . . . each linked with an appropriate set of governing techniques'. Harm reduction activities may be included here. A conundrum arises when the 'rational' subject insists on pursing pleasures in ways that have been represented as irrational or harmful, choosing to 'wilfully' ignore expert advice on health promotion or harm reduction. For example, those who mix gammahydroxybutrate (GHB) or gammabutyrolactone (GBL) with alcohol or consume GHB/GBL without accurate pipette dosage, despite the health warnings regarding overdosing and contra-indicated drugs, illustrate the limits of even resource-intensive and context-specific harm reduction initiatives, such as the presence of dance club paramedics. Indeed, undertaking survey research in south London gay dance clubs during the summer of 2010, we observed multiple instances of the purposeful pursuit of the 'risky' pleasure of combined alcohol/ GHB/GBL intoxication (Measham *et al.* 2011). We abandoned the survey earlier in the evening than planned for both ethical and practical reasons given the 'intense intoxication' of many potential respondents, which produced a club space in which customers were 'swept away' (Robinson 2003: 122) by the pleasures of socializing, dancing and drugs whilst opening up the possibility they would 'go under on G' (the slang phrase for losing consciousness having taken GHB/ GBL). Indeed one respondent did 'go under' whilst being interviewed by one of the authors, to be carried away by security staff to the paramedics' room. In the face of this enduring pursuit of pharmacological pleasure, the UK coalition government has announced a drug strategy which continues the established policy mix of prohibition, enforcement, risk-focused education and prevention strategies (Home Office 2010a), supported by a problematic ABC classification system (House of Commons Science and Technology Committee 2006; Morgan *et al.* 2010; Nutt *et al.* 2010; Royal Society of Arts Drugs Commission 2007).

In seeking to understand alcohol and drug use as cultural practices, interrelated political and media discourses have frequently associated alcohol and drug use with particular 'kinds' of people (e.g. 'clubbers', 'the workshy', 'junkies', 'ladettes') and particular symbolic spaces (e.g. '24-hour party cities', 'sink estates', 'skid row', 'Booze Britain') whilst perceptions and representations of risk and the possibility of pleasure depend partly on who is consuming what, where, when and how (O'Malley 1998). Such people and spaces are typically framed as demanding action, from 'the State', police, parents, schools and communities. Concern coalesces around certain (usually young, possibly gay or minority ethnic) leisure scenes. As O'Malley and Valverde (2004: 39) argue, 'discourses of pleasure would appear to be used governmentally in a selective and directional fashion'. Similarly Race (2009: 14) notes that in relation to drug law enforcement activities, specifically during Australian gay pride dance events in Sydney, 'the drug raid seizes upon and intercepts deviant groups and liminal practices, but, cloaking itself in the generality of drug law, claims not to target them specifically'. In the UK we have witnessed the selective and proactive regulation and policing of British dance music scenes, particularly those involving minority ethnic and lower-income participants (Measham and Hadfield 2009).

What we can see here is that discourses of safety and security in leisure spaces are used to justify increasingly high-profile, targeted policing of specific customers within the NTE (clubbers, bar drinkers) or more generally across leisure spaces (festival-goers), leading to concerns amongst customers about possible arrest or injury regardless of their own individual consumption practices. Although this differential policing within the NTE results in (occasional) instances of protest or resistance to such measures, by and large the random searching of clubbers before entry to dance venues and the high police presence around certain drinking destinations illustrates the relative powerlessness of clubbers and less affluent drinkers within the NTE. Clubbers, without associations with large-scale expenditure on alcohol or high-end consumer goods (particularly within the unregulated free party scene and specific subgenres of dance music), are not considered to be a powerful consumer group by comparison with, for example, higher-spending drinkers (Hadfield 2008) or other consumer interest groups such as motorists.[8]

Continuity and change: exploring pleasure within UK alcohol policy

In relation to alcohol, O'Malley and Valverde (2004: 27) suggest that 'discourses of pleasure as a warrantable motive for action are increasingly suppressed the more problematic that the behaviour appears'. Whereas pleasure is recognized as a possible feature of moderate alcohol consumption (epitomized in recurring advertising and public health messages such as 'enjoy alcohol in moderation' and 'enjoy alcohol responsibly'), no such recognition is afforded immoderate drinking or drug use. A dichotomy is constructed within neo-liberal governance between pleasure, freedom, rationality and normality on the one hand, and compulsion, illness, deviance and disorder on the other. Further, within neo-liberal societies, the so-called sensible majority of citizens are produced in stark contrast to the irresponsible minority (Hall and Winlow 2005), the former presented as needing to be empowered by 'the State' to tackle the latter and mobilized in justification of licensing law liberalization (Measham 2006). The pleasures of the rowdy few are placed in sharp contrast to the stoicism of the silent many, dispersed in long-suffering 'local communities'. Here we can look to the ways in which UK government policy consultations are framed – an important exercise, as 'public engagement' continues to be a maxim for the UK coalition government, as it was for New Labour. The UK coalition's alcohol-licensing consultation document *Rebalancing the Licensing Act* again mobilizes the 'sensible majority' in justification of changes to licensing laws, although this time to rein in the deregulation of the previous Labour government:

> The majority of people drink responsibly but not enough has been done to enable local communities to take action against those that don't. It is vital that local communities – the public and their elected representatives – have the powers they need to tackle alcohol-related crime and anti-social behaviour whilst promoting local business and ensuring that those that drink responsibly are not unduly penalized.
>
> (Home Office 2010b: 5)

Such missives seek to reiterate the broader positive influence of alcohol, not least in terms of urban regeneration, job creation and tax revenue, as the UK coalition government reminds us that:

> Alcohol plays an important part in the cultural life of this country, employing large numbers in production, retail and the hospitality industry. The industry as a whole contributes around £8.5bn to the Exchequer through excise duty alone, and over 200,000 premises have a licence to sell alcohol. Central to this is a system of alcohol licensing that is effective in regulating sales and reflective of local demands.
>
> (Home Office 2010b: 4)

Aside from these economic benefits, the UK government recognizes that responsible consumption of alcohol is pleasurable for the 'vast majority' who participate. Official disapproval of the consequences of immoderate consumption is explicit, with the problem firmly located in those individuals who *choose* to act irresponsibly through their 'determined drunkenness' and expect others to pay for their ignoble pleasures:

> All too often high streets are filled on a Friday and Saturday night with revellers who are not encouraged to take responsibility for their own actions. They drink to excess and expect the taxpayer to meet the cost of their overindulgence. The Government wants a fundamental shift in responsibilities. . . In future, solutions to address alcohol-related problems will be found locally, and by encouraging individuals to take responsibility for their own actions.
>
> (Home Office 2010b: 6)

Multi-level governance structures, with increasing weight given to the 'local' as the site of solutions to crime, antisocial behaviour and policing issues, was a recurrent motif of New Labour (McLaughlin 2005) and looks set to continue within UK coalition government responses. The difficulties arise when citizen-consumers refuse to act (or in this case consume alcohol) responsibly. Norris and Williams (2008) note that this remains one of the contradictions of the liberalization of licensing laws over the past decade. There has been a reluctance on the part of successive UK governments (and also researchers, as noted by O'Malley and Valverde 2004: 32, and Phillips and Lawton 2004) to recognize the pleasures of intoxication per se and to acknowledge that 'extreme drinking' (Martinic and Measham 2008) beyond recommended sensible levels to a state of drunkenness could be enjoyable even if potentially more harmful in terms of health and/or social consequences. Here Anne Milton MP, Parliamentary Under Secretary of State for Public Health, speaking to the Westminster Health Forum on Alcohol in July 2010, considers which motivations might lead people, particularly young people, to drink 'too much'. The pleasure of intoxication is notably absent; instead compulsion, 'peer pressure' and youthful disregard for the future feature heavily:

We need to better understand what makes people drink too much. We need to better measure success in helping them drink less. And we need to better commission services to help people when drink becomes a problem . . . That means focusing on the evidence for behaviour change. It means going beyond passively providing information, and looking actively at the question of motivation . . . If we take young people at school, how we give them the skills to make decisions about the huge range of difficult choices they come up against. How, when they are revelling in their immortality between the ages of 14–24, do we get them to behave responsibly?

(Department of Health 2010)

With personal responsibility uncritically championed by the UK coalition government, little sympathy remains for those 'revelling in their immortality' who persist in acting irresponsibly. Promises to 'ban the sale of alcohol at cost price' and to 'review alcohol taxation and pricing' remain qualified with commitments that such formal controls should not 'unfairly penalize responsible drinkers, pubs and important local industries' (Cabinet Office 2010: 14). Thus, the polarization of the sensible majority permitted to pursue pleasure in moderation against a persistently irresponsible minority intent on intense intoxication looks set to continue in the new UK coalition era. An even stronger case is then built for justifying punitive measures against those individuals, cultural groupings or 'scenes' that insist on continuing to pursue their 'impermissible pleasures'.

The challenge for the government, public health and alcohol industries in their promotion of sensible drinking is the evidence that a considerable number of drinkers *do* find drunkenness in itself a pleasurable state to be actively pursued and that this is not necessarily a pleasure reserved for the young (Measham and Østergaard 2009). Describing it as 'determined drunkenness' (Measham 2004b), 'intense intoxication' (Hayward and Hobbs 2007) and 'calculated hedonism' (Szmigin *et al.* 2008), a range of studies including government-funded research (e.g. Engineer *et al.* 2003; Richardson and Budd 2003) suggest that drunkenness, for young and not so young drinkers in the UK and elsewhere, is considered both a motivation for consumption and a *positive* outcome in some societies (Martinic and Measham 2008; Measham 2010). However, in UK alcohol policy documents, the pleasures of immoderate consumption through alcohol are as impermissible as the pleasures of altered states of consciousness by illicit means, discussed below in relation to illegal drugs and recent policy developments regarding emergent psychoactive substances, the so-called 'legal highs'.

Prohibition, pleasure and leisure: the 'legal high' conundrum

Prevention of drug use is an absolutely important element of the coalition Government's approach to drugs. Young people need to be empowered to make the right decisions and we all have a role to play in helping them to do that by changing attitudes towards any drug use.

(James Brokenshire, Parliamentary Under Secretary of State for the Home Department, House of Commons 2010: column 152, lines 106–9)

Following a six-week consultation period (Home Office 2010c), the UK coalition government published its Drug Strategy in December 2010 (Home Office 2010a). Given the swift reiteration of the new government's opposition to decriminalization (Home Office 2010d) in the face of high-profile calls for a rethink with regards to drug policy from, among others, Ainsworth (former Home Office drugs minister), Godlee (editor, *British Medical Journal*) and Gilmore (former president of the Royal College of Physicians), it is unsurprising that prohibition continues to dominate government drug strategy, enhanced by a greater emphasis on abstinence-based treatment programmes for 'problem drug users' (Home Office 2010a). The tensions between a less centralist approach to governance and the continued criminalization of drug users is evident in the Home Secretary's introduction to the *Drug Strategy 2010*, which claims that 'gone are the days when central Government tells . . . the public what to do' (Home Office 2010a: 2) followed by the strategy declaration that 'people should not start taking drugs and those who do should stop' (ibid.: 9).

Successive UK governments have publicly acknowledged clear evidence of harm to individuals from alcohol and tobacco, through the UK government ban on smoking in public places, for example, but have remained reluctant to classify either of these substances under the Misuse of Drugs Act (MDA) 1971. This reluctance differs markedly from the wave of classification and reclassification in the last decade of other recreational intoxicants with far lower levels of prevalence, physical or social harm, including cannabis, psychedelic 'magic' mushrooms, GHB, GBL, ketamine, methamphetamine, synthetic cannabinoids, substituted cathinones (such as mephedrone) and naphyrone. The rapid emergence of mephedrone highlighted both the continued strength of demand for intoxicating substances in the UK and the now familiar official responses to the non-medical consumption of psychoactive drugs. The unprecedented speed of criminalization of substituted cathinones, from their emergence and growing popularity amongst clubbers, weekend recreational users and teenagers (Measham *et al.* 2010; Mixmag 2009), through to the ACMD's recommendations and – 18 days later – legislation, was in part due to the rapid crystallization of support for a ban amongst all three main political parties, united in their faith in the deterrent value of classification just weeks before a general election. However, there remains a lack of robust evidence on the deterrent principle both in the UK (HMSO 2006; MacCoun and Reuter 2001; Police Foundation 1999; Royal Society of Arts Drugs Commission 2007) and elsewhere (e.g. Reinarman *et al.* 2004). In the case of cocaine, use did not decline in the 2000s, despite a prohibition regime which includes severe maximum penalties for Class A possession (seven years' imprisonment) and supply (life imprisonment) (Hoare and Moon 2010). In the case of mephedrone, initial research suggests that the 2010 ban has had a mixed response (e.g. Winstock *et al.* 2010; Measham *et al.* 2011). Although some users have stopped taking mephedrone on account of its illegality and resulting reduced availability, others have been displaced to more familiar illegal drugs or to second-generation 'legal highs'. Nevertheless, the emergence of a street trade in south London's NTE was witnessed by the authors less than three months after the ban, with mephedrone rising in price from £10/g purchased legally and online before April to £20/g from club dealers by July 2010. By contrast, in the case of ketamine, criminalization appears to have had little effect on availability, price or use (Curran and Morgan 2011); in the case of GHB, its criminalization appears to have merely created confusion regarding the legal status of GHB and its precursors GBL and 1,4-butanediol (1,4BD), which subsequently replaced the banned GHB (Wood *et al*. 2008).

'Mephedrone madness' unfolded across a 12-month period in the UK, from early reports of use in the spring of 2009, to the intense media and political scrutiny afforded 'legal highs' by the spring of 2010 (Measham *et al*. 2010) and the resultant banning of substituted cathinones on 16 April 2010. Concern about mephedrone resulted from a coalescence of fears around purposeful intoxication, vulnerable youth, the seemingly ungovernable realm of the internet and, in echoes of earlier drug panics (Kohn 1997), the threat of a mysterious white powder imported from China. The ease of access to 'legal highs' contrasted with the subcultural capital typically required to obtain illegal substances (knowing a dealer/friend; being part of a particular music scene). Suddenly pharmacological pleasure was available to anyone at the click of a mouse, including young people with little or no previous experience of psychoactive drugs. Yet ease of access was only part of the story. Pursuing pleasure through drugs that 'worked' (i.e. produced desired effects), in the wake of falling purity levels of popular illegal drugs such as ecstasy and cocaine, proved to have a particular attraction for experienced drug users (Measham *et al*. 2010). Banning substituted cathinones surfaced as the purported solution to the emergent use, harms and casualty rate that appeared to be associated with mephedrone; the familiar policy response of the 'criminalization of intoxication' (Measham and Moore 2008), yet to an unfamiliar substance for which the research literature was virtually non-existent (ACMD 2010b). Since the 'mephedrone madness', a number of other substances emerged as possible successors, resulting in the banning of naphyrone in July 2010 and the importation ban of 2-DPMP in November 2010, sometimes sold under the brand name 'Ivory Wave'. It is perhaps Ivory Wave rather than mephedrone which illustrates the challenges now facing policymakers aiming to control 'legal highs': originally containing methylenedioxypyrovalerone (MDPV) and by mid-2010 the much more potent desoxypipradol (2-DPMP), it was the drug 2-DPMP rather than the branded product Ivory Wave which was specified in the importation ban, thereby facilitating a possible future third incarnation of the product. Whereas the first generation of 'legal highs' were low-priced, high-purity amphetamine-type chemicals characterized as doing 'exactly what it says on the tin' (Lifeline 2010: 1), second-generation 'legal highs' by contrast contain a wider variety of chemicals, of variable purity and psychoactive effect, inaccurately labelled, mixed together and often containing old stocks of the now illegal substituted cathinones (Brandt *et al*. 2010, 2011). Perversely, these second-generation 'legal highs' – possibly without the knowledge of users, internet/head shop retailers or police struggling with limited resources and outdated testing facilities – are as likely to contain *illegal* highs. The challenge of identifying the chemical composition, effects and consequences of these emergent drugs, both individually and in combination, illustrates the constraints for policymakers, the academic community and harm reduction advocates when faced with a rapidly developing, internet-based, illicit consumer market and continued demand from apparently 'irrational' consumers who may purposefully disregard harm reduction advice even if it were able to stay abreast of the shifting chemical compositions of second-generation 'legal highs'.

Criticism of the length of the review and classification process under the MDA 1971 for the substituted cathinones (*Daily Express* 2010) – whilst new 'research chemicals' and 'bath salts' of unknown effects appear by the dozen online – led to the introduction by the UK coalition government of Temporary Class Drug Orders (TCDOs), a flagship policy in the Coalition Agreement (Cabinet Office 2010) included in the Police Reform and Social Responsibility Act 2011. TCDOs facilitate the rapid banning of importation and supply (but not possession) of a psychoactive substance of unknown harm as a precautionary measure whilst the ACMD review process occurs. One concern is that, in the unlikely event of an ACMD recommendation against permanent control leading to the lifting of a TCDO, indirect official sanction could be considered to be bestowed upon a new psychoactive drug which has not received the level of regulatory scrutiny required of medicines and other products sold for human consumption. The greater danger, however, is that ongoing criticism of the laborious process of individual review of emergent drugs by (unpaid) ACMD experts in their 'spare time' would increase rather than be abated by TCDOs and, alongside the logistical problems of operating such bans, might push the UK authorities away from individual review and towards broad-brush legislation like that currently on the US statute books.

In the United States, such 'cat and mouse' responses to individual drugs of concern are sidestepped altogether with the US Controlled Substance Analogue Enforcement Act 1986, which outlaws the supply of drugs which are 'substantially similar' in chemical structure or effect to stimulant, depressant or hallucinogenic drugs that are already controlled. By criminalizing all drugs considered 'similar' to those already controlled, the Analogue Act does not review the possible harms (or lack of harms) associated with any individual emergent drug, which in effect results in the criminalization of the activity of recreational drug taking rather than individual drugs. In the UK, the rapidity of the emergence and escalation in popularity of 'legal highs' since 2009, the growing role of the internet in marketing and purchasing drugs in a globalized drug trade, and criticism of the creaky 40-year-old review process enshrined in legislation passed in a pre-internet/globalization age may not be solved simply by the introduction of TCDOs. Analogue legislation could be considered the logical conclusion in the regulation and policing of the impermissible pleasures of intoxication: it extends the long arm of criminalization to potentially *all* stimulant, depressant and hallucinogenic drugs *regardless* of their individual potential for harm and *before* any problems emerge, specifically because the motivation for use is recreational rather than medical.

Discussion

In this chapter we have explored the 'impermissible pleasures' of immoderate drinking and illicit drug use in any form, enacted within and across diverse leisure spaces. We have argued that harm reduction may be viewed as a compelling response to the contradiction at the heart of UK government policy on drugs, alcohol and consensual sexual practices, embodied by the rational consumer able to purchase pleasure in a free market. Responsible citizens must fulfil their role as non-flawed consumers, pursuing permissible pleasures in moderation in appropriate leisure spaces (the restaurant, the gastropub, the dinner party, the theatre). Flawed, visible pleasure-seekers who prefer local drinking 'dives', outdoor raves, unknown new 'legal highs' or dogging are deemed wholly 'irresponsible' and irrational in their risk taking by political, media and medical discourses, which ignore the possibilities of localized practices of self-regulation even in these supposedly most 'uncontrolled' and 'hedonistic' of spaces (Race 2009).

The pursuit of such pleasures presents a problem to neo-liberal democracies. As we have noted, despite compelling evidence that the pleasure of intoxication is a significant motivation for both drinking (Engineer *et al.* 2003; Measham 2004b; Measham and Brain 2005; Richardson and Budd 2003) and drug use (Coffield and Gofton 1994; Moore and Measham 2008; Parker *et al.* 1998), there is a denial or at least an absence of recognition of the pharmacological pleasures of intoxication as a warrantable motive within discourses on alcohol and drug use, including those of the harm reduction community (Measham 2006; Moore 2008). Where pleasure *is* discussed (for example, in the case of 'sensible' drinking), it is in relation to not the pharmacological effects of alcohol itself but the social context of consumption, the pleasures of being with family and friends at social events (HM Government 2007). Yet people do pursue the pleasures of intoxication, and more prosaically are able to discuss its pursuit. In light of the relative neglect of musical, stylistic and pharmacological 'scenes' within harm reduction public health provision – with no national organization, helpline or policy provision for adult polydrug use currently in the UK – 'lay' or what Friedman and colleagues (2007) term 'micro-social' harm minimization has developed in online (e.g. drugs-forum.com) and offline friendship groups and 'expert user' networks which do acknowledge possible pleasure from drug use (Perrone 2006; Tackett-Gibson 2008). Lay harm minimization, pleasure maximization and sometimes simply being 'swept away' by an altered state of consciousness fill the void left by the dominant systems of thought and of action (Rose and Miller 2010) around the framing of immoderate drinking and illegal drug use, characterized as involving addiction, compulsion, risk, harm and uncertainty.

The US Controlled Substance Analogue Enforcement Act 1986 in a sense 'solves' the problem of the pursuit of pleasure through intoxication by a fast-track criminalization of all emergent psychoactive drugs, regardless of harm. Its translation into UK law would ensure the formal and direct prohibition of intoxication per se rather than its indirect prohibition through the review and classification of individual drugs under the MDA 1971. Any acknowledgement of a leisure-pleasure demand for illicit drugs is framed as 'sending the wrong message'.[9] Yet without a full and frank consideration of the pleasures of these transgressive leisure practices and an exclusive focus instead on danger, risk and harm, we risk uncritically replicating the language and dictates of 'moral entrepreneurs' (Becker 1963), whilst denying the agency of those who seek impermissible pleasures and undermining the possibility of micro-social harm minimization practices.

Notes

1 We would like to thank Teela Sanders and Keith Soothill for their early contributions and their kind support in the writing of this chapter.

2 It is worth noting here that the notion of 'the State' as a unified actor acting with autonomy and purpose ('the media' are also typically conceptualized in this way) is challenged by writers within Foucauldian traditions, who suggest instead that distributed or non-unitary activities of government better articulate 'the State'. In this sense there is no 'power of the State', but rather 'relations . . . established between political and other authorities', which leads us to ask 'what funds, forces, persons, knowledge or legitimacy are utilised: and by means of what devices and techniques are these different tactics made operable' (Rose and Miller 2010: 275). Such a framing of 'the State' interrogates both the systems of thought (responsibilization, moderation) and the systems of action (multiagency partnerships, public–private finance initiatives) that make up state–citizen relations in neo-liberal societies.

3 Leisure settings may include domestic spaces. Studies of illicit/illegal leisure have tended to neglect certain domestic settings such as house parties, dinner parties, gaming parties and private gay sex parties. Further, there is growing interest in the practice of 'preloading' alcohol and/or drugs at home or at friends' houses prior to attending bars, pubs or clubs.

4 'Barebacking' refers to the practice of having penetrative sex without using a condom, although it is used more often to denote men who have anal sex with men without a condom.

5 This is especially the case when under the watchful eye of private security firms who threaten to eject patrons 'if I see you in the dance tent with a water bottle'. This was said by private security personnel to one of our respondents at an independent music festival in the summer of 2010. Thus clutching a water bottle is seen by some security personnel in itself as a potent symbol of ecstasy consumption.

6 BDSM activity amounts to an illegal assault if it results in marks or injuries which are more than transient and trifling, such as bites or bruises. Following the infamous Spanner Trials, in which a group of homosexual men were charged in Manchester Crown Court with actual bodily harm despite indicating that the acts they performed on one another were consensual, there has been ongoing controversy regarding the position of the law with regards to consensual BDSM acts (C. White 2006). Some have noted the differential application of the law to homosexual participants as compared with heterosexual participants. Those interested in BDSM (slightly more likely to be amongst the gay and lesbian population) have been medicalized, stigmatized and criminalized, that is framed as in need of therapy and/or social and legal sanction.

7 See http://www.cityco.com/, http://www.manchesterpubandclub.co.uk and http://www.bestbarnone.com for more details.

8 Roadside drug testing of motorists suspected of being under the influence of drugs was delayed again in the UK (House of Commons Transport Committee 2010), despite the estimate that one in five road traffic accidents involve drivers who have consumed illegal drugs. The authors would suggest that driving under the influence is of greater

concern in terms of potential harm to both the individual and wider society than dancing under the influence.

9 This notion of 'sending the wrong message' and the repetition of the purported deterrent effect of criminalization was recently reiterated by the coalition government's Crime Prevention Minister, James Brokenshire, who, on speaking to the British press regarding the 'Ivory Wave/Vanilla Sky' importation ban, stated 'The ban will send a clear message to users that these substances carry a risk and will prevent new chemicals becoming widely available' (Mail Online 2010).

7 The problem of access

Outdoor leisure activities and access to private rural land[1]

Elaine Barclay and Joseph F. Donnermeyer

Introduction

In much of the developed world, participation in outdoor leisure pursuits, such as bushwalking, camping, hunting, fishing, horse or trail-bike riding and four-wheel-driving has increased rapidly in modern life. This is largely because of greater leisure time, higher disposable incomes, increased mobility of people through improved transportation, growing international and domestic tourism, developing commercial interests, the promotion of high-risk activities, emphasis on health and fitness, and greater environmental awareness (Campion and Stephenson 2010; Pigram and Jenkins 1999: 1). However, outdoor leisure activities require access to open spaces, which is not always possible. Public spaces where people can undertake such activities, such as national parks or state forests, are in limited supply and are not always open to the general public, and those that are accessible are often subject to fees, permits and other limitations. Access to privately owned space is also limited largely by the restrictive attitudes of landowners (Pigram and Jenkins 1999: 161). The problem of pleasure as discussed in this chapter is therefore the problem of attaining access to private rural land for outdoor leisure. The discussion draws upon the findings of an Australian study which compared landholders' attitudes towards the issue of property rights and access rights to private land for leisure pursuits with those of hunters and other recreationists.

Rules and norms concerning access

Attitudes and informal social norms regarding access to public and private land for outdoor leisure activities vary around the world. These variations relate to different historical developments in public policy and private development, government initiatives or lack thereof, and informal and formal laws and regulations regarding property rights and access rights (Pigram 1981). For example, variations of a *right to roam* or *'everyman's right'* exist in many parts of Europe. In the Nordic and Baltic countries, the right to roam is a cultural norm (sometimes codified in law) that is founded upon a historical socio-cultural necessity for access through private land (Campion and Stephenson 2010). In Sweden and Norway, *Allemansretten* is the right of access to most private land to hike, ski, cycle or camp, fish or boat, or pick flowers, mushrooms and berries, although there are obligations to respect wildlife, property, crops and livestock. Hunting rights belong to the landowner, and therefore are not a part of access rights (Swedish Environmental Protection Agency 2010). Countries such as Germany, Denmark and Switzerland allow access to only specific areas such as forests, unenclosed land and alpine pastures (Campion and Stephenson 2010).

In the United Kingdom following a polarized debate about access, the government introduced the *Countryside and Rights of Way Act* in 2000 to give the general public a conditional right to walk in certain areas of the English and Welsh countryside without compensation for landholders. Access is confined to uncultivated areas namely mountains, downs, moors, heath and coastal land. There is an expectation that recreationists will protect the natural environment and respect landowners' rights to manage their land (DEFRA 2010). This move was followed in Scotland with the Land Reform (Scotland) Act 2003, which codified the ancient tradition of the right to universal access to rural land similar to rights established in Scandinavian countries (Campion and Stephenson 2010).

In the USA, more than 66 per cent of the land is privately owned, and many states have implemented programmes to encourage landholders to improve fish and wildlife habitat and maintain hunter access. However, increasing urbanization has reduced the amount of available space for recreation, which has placed greater pressure on private landholders, who have responded by closing their properties, particularly to hunters (Benson 2001).

In New Zealand, 31 per cent of the surface area is preserved as national conservation area to be both a recreational and a spiritual resource for all residents. There has also been a tradition of rural landholders granting public access to private land with permission. However, as in the USA, this tradition is waning with changing patterns in land ownership and use (Campion and Stephenson 2010).

Australia is experiencing similar pressures. Many areas are environmentally fragile or unique, which has encouraged a strong conservation ethic. Coastal areas are highly urbanized. Farming activities occupy 60 per cent of the surface area (ABS 2006). Consequently, there is potential for conflict over land use between the competing interests of conservation, agricultural and mining as well as leisure and tourism (Pigram and Jenkins 1999: 12–14).

In Australia there are tight restrictions on access to national parks for four-wheel-drive and other off-road vehicles, and access to wilderness areas is forbidden. Hunting on crown land, in state forests or on private land is subject to permission by landholders. Hunting is also forbidden in national parks and wilderness areas. Authorities are concerned about damage to vegetation and wildlife, biosecurity, soil erosion, bushfires and thoughtless or deliberate acts by visitors. These concerns have placed greater pressure upon those recreational spaces that remain available and attention has turned to private land as a possible option for leisure opportunities (Pigram and Jenkins 1999: 208).

Many Australian landholders regard access to private land for sport or leisure as a privilege that may be earned by good behaviour and responsibility (Pigram 1981). From the onset of European settlement in Australia, a traditional or *absolutist* concept of total control over land ownership has pervaded national consciousness (Reeve 2002). This attitude to property rights evolved from a history of class struggle that centred around land and capital. The privileged classes were the free settlers who had the capital and influence to obtain large acreages of land for grazing while the emancipist settlers who struggled to purchase or lease small selections for farming formed a disadvantaged class (Lees 1997: 8). There are still remnants of this distinction between graziers and farmers today but the notion of absolute property rights has endured (Lees 1997: 2–9).

Some landholders will act with almost feudalistic zeal to maintain exclusive use of space on their properties. It is common to see 'No Trespass' signs at property boundaries, and warning notices in the rural press advising that access to a property is denied and trespassers will be prosecuted (Pigram 1981). Yet other landholders will be open and receptive to requests for access from the public. On properties where large numbers of pest animals such as feral pigs and rabbits or kangaroos need to be controlled, hunters may be welcomed, particularly if they are known to the landowner, seek permission to hunt on the property, and show respect for the infrastructure, crops and livestock. Problems arise when hunters disregard this protocol (Pigram 1981).

Trespass and illegal hunting in Australia

In Australia, statutes proscribe the unlawful entry of persons onto private property. It is also an offence to deliberately leave a gate open, or cut or damage a fence to allow animals to escape (Barclay *et al.* 2001). A study of property crime victimization on farms in New South Wales (NSW) (Barclay *et al.* 2001; Barclay and Donnermeyer 2002) found that trespassing and unauthorized hunting were the most common problems, being experienced by 40 per cent of landholders. Holiday seasons and weekends were the times that offences most often occurred. The main offenders were from metropolitan or regional city areas. Landholders and police believed offenders were responsible for damage to crops and vegetation, arson, vandalism, littering, failure to shut gates, disturbance or shooting of stock and for having dogs that attack livestock. They also believed that offenders were responsible for the theft of fuel, tools and other small equipment. As a consequence, many landholders have closed their properties to all but trusted family and friends. Others expressed helplessness about their inability to secure their properties. They reported experiencing considerable anxiety because many unauthorized hunters were armed, owned savage dogs and frequently ignored their requests to enter their property only with permission. One family reported that they sometimes left fuel out in a paddock that they knew would be taken by hunters that they had warned off the property. They would rather sacrifice fuel than have a tractor vandalized (Barclay *et al.* 2001).

Social norms defining access to private land

Clearly landholders' attitudes are fundamental to the provision of access to private land for leisure activities. These attitudes are a function of historical precedents and landowners' personal values and beliefs; legal, economic, social and ecological concerns; national, local and family traditions and social norms; government incentives; the type and volume of leisure activities; and past experiences of granting access (Pigram 1981; Pigram and Jenkins 1999).

Barclay and colleagues (2004) in a study of crime on Australian farms identified several social norms prescribing access to private land. A widespread adherence to the absolute property rights of landholders meant that people who wished to access private farmland were expected to seek the landowner's permission, abide by the conditions of entry and show respect for the property. Absolute ownership also means that landholders are ultimately responsible for the management of their land and farm operation. Landholders were expected to be good neighbours, watch for each other, cooperate in establishing and maintaining fences, and inform their neighbours of any activities that might impact on their farm operation.

However, to be effective, social norms need to be legitimized and understood by everyone whose behaviour they must influence. Newcomers to a district and visitors from city areas seeking outdoor leisure may be unaware of the rules of good conduct and unwittingly breach social norms (Hall and Pretty 2008). Some people believe they have a right to enjoy nature irrespective of land ownership and can come into conflict with landholders who are keen to protect their property and their privacy. Conflicts arise because the landowner is only one individual among several groups with an interest in how rural lands can be utilized and managed (Pigram 1981).

The study

The aim of the study was to compare attitudes towards public access to private rural lands for outdoor leisure from the perspectives of landholders as well as the hunters and other recreationists who desire access to private land. The study was conducted in three inland regions in northern New South Wales (NSW) and southern Queensland (see Figure 7.1). The southern Queensland region is between 200 and 300 km inland from the city of Brisbane. The northwest plains in NSW lie a further 200 to 300 km southwest. These regions were selected because they experience significant problems with pest animals such as kangaroos, feral pigs and goats and are therefore likely to be targeted by unauthorized hunters. The area is remote and properties are large. The terrain is flat with many areas of scrub or bushland and several watercourses which harbour pest animals. Beef and sheep grazing plus cotton, wheat and barley production are common. The third area, the northern NSW tablelands, is situated approximately 300 km to the east of the northwest plains. Properties are smaller and the main production is grazing and wool. The terrain is hilly to rugged with areas of thick vegetation. There are a number of world heritage national parks that attract many visitors.

Focus groups were the primary means of data collection because the target populations were small in number and scattered across a vast and remote area. The study was designed as a follow-up to the earlier research (Barclay *et al.* 2001), which had quantified the extent of trespassing and unauthorized hunting on farms. Nine focus groups were conducted, with a landholders' organization, a

Figure 7.1 The study area. 1, southern Queensland; 2, NSW northwest plains; 3, northern tablelands.

hunters' club and a four-wheel-drive club in each of the three case study areas. There was only one type of each organization in each area and members were representative of the target populations living within each district. The focus groups were conducted at the commencement of general meetings of the clubs or organizations where the target population was gathered together at one time. Table 7.1 displays the numbers of participants in each focus group. The hunters were all male, but landowners and four-wheel-drive groups included males and females. Ages ranged between 21 and 65.

The organizations were approached initially with a letter outlining the purposes of the study and requesting time with members for discussion. Arrangements were then made with club presidents to set a time and date for the focus groups. All participants were provided with a statement outlining the aims and objectives of the study, assurance of the confidentiality of the information they provided,

Table 7.1 Number of participants in focus groups

	Landholders	Hunters	Four-wheel-drive clubs
Northern tablelands of NSW	15	32	15
Northwest NSW	14	30	16
Southern Queensland	8	8	34

and their right to choose not to participate. The discussions were guided by a structured questionnaire tailored to each group to allow comparisons between case study areas.

All groups included discussion on property rights and access. Landholders were asked about pest management on their land, whether they dealt with the problem themselves or engaged professional hunters, if they allowed recreational hunters onto their property, and whether they had any particular conditions regarding access. They were also asked about problems with unauthorized hunters and trespassers and what measures they took to prevent the problem, whether they reported any incidents to police and the outcomes of that action. Landholders were asked who they thought was responsible for trespassing and unauthorized hunting in their district.

Hunters and members of four-wheel-drive clubs were asked if they had arrangements with private property owners for access, whether they thought property owners worry unnecessarily about recreationists/hunters on their land, whom they blamed for trespassing or unauthorized hunting on rural lands, and whether they had any suggestions for property owners for managing trespassing or unauthorized hunting.

Twelve key informants in the selected areas were also interviewed either face-to-face or by telephone to gather additional information to clarify and support some of the findings of the focus groups. Those interviewed included police officers in each region, professional hunters, hunting safari operators and representatives of government agencies. With participants' permission, all focus group discussions and interviews were recorded and the tapes transcribed and analysed.

The study was limited by the inability to identify and include hunters and recreationists who trespass or hunt illegally. However, it was possible to assess the nature and extent of victimization experiences among landholders and discuss problems of access with hunters and recreationists. Hunting organization members are bound to a strict ethics code guiding their sport, and provide education and training for hunters in weapons safety and handling and ethical hunting practices, and are therefore unlikely to commit offences of unethical or unauthorized hunting. Similarly, four-wheel-drive clubs promote responsible off-road touring, environmental awareness and driver education, and are actively involved in volunteer maintenance of tracks in public forests, public recreation areas and historical sites (Four Wheel Drive NSW and ACT 2010). Yet participants' knowledge and understanding of their respective leisure activities provided valuable insights into the reasons why some people may not abide by the rules.

Results

The landholders

Landowner concerns about trespassing and unauthorized hunting differed greatly between the three study areas. In the northwestern NSW plains and parts of southern Queensland, where there are significant problems with pest animals, landholders' negative experiences with trespassers and unauthorized hunters had led them to restrict access to their land to only trusted professional hunters and family and friends. Some landholders would not leave their properties over long weekends or the Easter holidays, as those were the times that people come out from the cities to hunt illegally. As one participant stated:

> We have one professional hunter and my husband won't allow anybody else on the place. If you do it for one, you have to do it for everyone. He did let these guys on once – told them where they could and could not go. But they set fire to 1000 acres of wheat stubble. So that's it now – never again.

Trespassers were also concern for these landholders. One participant maintained:

> A lot of people think that landholders have a lot of land and that it won't hurt to drive around on a little bit. They have no respect.

Rubbish left at campsites was particularly offensive:

> They mow down trees, start fires and leave so many bottles and rubbish you wouldn't believe it.

Some people boat up a river to access fishing areas on private land. Sometimes, the impact of trespassers was not discovered for some time. One participant explained:

> Some things you don't always see immediately. We had a crop of organic wheat – and if you have people driving around at certain times of the year with dirty vehicles that have been in other crops with turnip for example – it's surprising how much seed can be spread from a vehicle. Then you have a lot of weeds come up and you can't spray organic wheat. So we have to pull up the weeds by hand.

Landholders were also concerned about public liability and having to pay a large sum in compensation to a person who was injured while illegally on their land. Landholders are legally liable as part of their 'duty of care' and, although they are covered against such events under their public liability insurance policy, premiums would escalate following a major compensation payout. One participant had visitors sign a waiver against legal liability in the event of any mishap even though such a document would not be legally valid in a court of law.

In the more rugged terrain of the northern NSW tablelands and the more remote part of southern Queensland, participants acknowledged experiences with tres-passers and unauthorized hunters, but were less concerned and appeared to have more control over what occurred on their land than participants in the other areas. They believed that people needed to escape the pressures of city life; hence pro-viding them with opportunities for recreation was a positive thing for landholders to do. Typical of positive comments was the explanation of one landowner:

> If they are genuine campers, they ask permission and will ask where they can camp. These are the ones you really enjoy having on the place. We encourage people to come out and camp for weekends. It's important for city people to be more aware of what's happening in the bush. They also spend money in the town and it's good for local businesses.

In all three regions it was common practice for landholders to grant access to their land only provided visitors complied with specified conditions, such as shutting gates, notification of arrival, only one hunting group at any one time on a property, no rubbish and no dogs. The failure to shut gates was the most frequently occurring and annoying problem. One farmer stated:

> Probably if they shut the gates you wouldn't even know they were there. But you find the gates open and you have to spend the next three days sorting the cattle out.

To address these problems, most landholders provide specific instructions for people accessing their land. As one explained:

> We give our hunters a topographic map with areas shaded and all the build-ings marked on it so they know where they can go.

Landholders were grateful if hunters reported back on the location and size of feral animal populations on the property and also information on anything out of order, such as injured stock or damaged fences. Such behaviour ensured ongoing access to the property.

Overall, participants believed that there was little they could do to prevent trespass and unauthorized hunting occurring apart from placing warning signs on property boundaries and locking gates and farmhouses and participating in *Rural Watch*, a type of Neighbourhood Watch. Few participants had bothered to report incidences of trespassing and unauthorized hunting to police, owing to their inability to find sufficient proof and a common belief that there was little the police could do to prevent these activities.

However, many participants reported that regular visits by trusted hunters to control feral animals on their properties seemed to deter unauthorized hunters. All participants reported that they relied on professional and recreational hunters for pest management on their land, as their farming commitments left them little time to control the problem themselves. Participants reported that these trusted hunters were keen to guard their hunting territory against unauthorized hunters. Similarly, trusted fishermen also guarded their fishing areas against unwanted intruders.

The hunters

The hunters in all three focus groups were passionate about their sport and clearly invested a lot of time and money in hunting activities and participating in voluntary environmental conservation projects. In all regions, hunters were able to hunt on their own properties or had private access arrangements with landholders for hunting. They emphasized that members of hunting associations abide by a strict code of ethics for hunting or otherwise face disciplinary action imposed by their association or lose their firearm licence. Participants distanced themselves from people who hunted illegally or unethically. They resented the fact that deviant hunters damaged the reputation of legitimate hunting associations. As one stated:

> We get really upset when hunters generally are blamed for problems on the land. All of us here who are members of the club have had to pass stringent requirements to gain their shooters licence. As far as we are concerned, we have too much to lose by doing the wrong thing. You forfeit your firearms; you lose your licence and get a fine.

Some participants had been refused hunting access because of previous poor behaviour by unauthorized hunters. The participants offered several reasons for why this behaviour occurred. First, the social and physical distance between city-based hunters and rural communities limits their contact with farmers and consequently opportunities for hunting. Further, increasing restriction of access frustrates hunters and encourages unauthorized access. One participant explained:

> Often the problems arise when young blokes go out west hunting and they go to one property and ask permission to hunt and are told no, they go to the next and ask and they are told no and so on, and they say 'well we haven't come all this way for nothing'. An intelligent management system by property owners may lessen the problem – but that is their prerogative and it is their private land.

Second, the negative attitudes held by the general public towards firearms and hunting practices, as well as the activities of the animal welfare movement in Australia, discourages young people from joining hunters' associations and the opportunities to learn about correct hunting practices, which incorporate respect for property rights. Third, strict regulations governing firearm ownership discourage people from obtaining a licence and hunting legally.

Fourth, some participants maintained that the current generation of landholders take a more businesslike approach to farming and are therefore less tolerant of trespassing and unauthorized hunting than were their predecessors. One participant added that few landholders consider the benefits recreational hunting provides for landowners and communities against the costs of the damage to properties and to the environment caused by feral animals. Yet, regardless of these complaints regarding landholders, hunters strongly advocated the rights of landholders to control access to their property and to set conditions by which people may enter their land.

There was a general view that the size of the feral animal problem meant there was a place for both professional and recreational hunters. Hunters were strongly opposed to the current pest management policies that support costly baiting programmes to eradicate feral animals rather than allowing people to hunt. They believe these policies have been influenced by animal welfare groups. Such policies ignore the economic benefits for rural communities from hunting. There was also strong disapproval of government bounty systems for feral animal control. Bounty hunters were not considered to be 'real hunters', because they are more interested in the money than in hunting as a sport. Participants claimed some landholders restrict hunting access so that they can monopolize the rewards from bounty hunting. One group suggested that, rather than providing bounties, rural communities could sponsor hunting clubs to control feral animals. One of the most positive arrangements cited by focus group participants was the agreement between the Sporting Shooters' Association and National Parks and Wildlife in Queensland, where hunters assisted National Parks and Wildlife with conservation programmes and occasionally conducted supervised feral animal control.

Some participants maintained that a commercialized hunting industry was an excellent means of providing opportunities for recreational hunters while subsidizing income for landholders and in the process reducing the problems associated with unauthorized hunting on farms. Safari tour operators interviewed maintained that landholders could earn significant returns by hosting safaris. There is increasing demand for access to properties for this type of tourism and the regular presence of hunting groups on private properties can deter trespassers and unauthorized hunters.

The four-wheel-drive clubs

Like the hunters, the four-wheel-drive club members also conform to a strict code of ethics for touring in rural areas and resented being associated with people who trespass. Some participants believed trespassing occurred because people were unaware that they had entered private property. They called for better signposts on public roads and more detailed and current maps for the touring public. One participant explained:

> The problem is that you don't always find out that there is a locked gate somewhere until you actually run into it and you may have come miles and

miles through someone's property. The difficulty is finding out who owns the land to ask for access or having to go all the way back around because you come to a locked gate and it's not sign posted or marked on the map.

Participants in all three groups had established arrangements with landholders for access to their properties. None of the participants reported being denied access to private land as a result of landholders' negative experiences with trespassers but they had observed the growing numbers of private properties that had 'No Trespass' signs. One stated:

You can go out west along the South Australian border and you can drive for 500 km and every property you come to will have signs on their boundary 'No Shooting', 'No Hunting', 'No Fishing', 'No Camping' – all the way along. It's rare to see a property without signs on the gate.

Nevertheless, participants strongly advocated the rights of landholders to control access to their land and appreciated the problems some landholders experience with trespassers. One woman stated:

I think it's the same as having a house block in town – you wouldn't want people driving on your front lawn. Just because you have a big property, if you own it, people shouldn't be going on there without your permission.

Few approved of landholders who blocked designated public access roads that traverse their properties or restricted public access to fishing areas on their land. Participants called for legislation to ensure that public access roads remain established rights of way. The practice of some landholders requesting fees for use of private roads on their properties was accepted by the participants as probably being necessary to cover the costs of maintaining the roads. Participants believed there was a need for governments to provide support to landholders for road maintenance and fencing, as well as public liability insurance to accommodate public access to heritage sites situated on private land.

Participants were concerned about the increasing restriction of access to national parks and state forests for four-wheel-drive touring. More areas are being turned over to national parks and more park areas are being declared wilderness areas where access to four-wheel-drive vehicles is denied. Consequently, there are fewer and fewer areas where people can legitimately tour.

Land-cruiser parks, which are becoming more common in Australia, do provide opportunities for four-wheel-drive enthusiasts and offer driver competitions and skills improvement, but many participants claimed these parks fail to provide for those who prefer to tour in open areas.

Land-cruiser parks cater for the extreme sports. It attracts a lot of people because you can do what you like. It's all right for those who like to go around in circles, but we would rather do a scenic tour in a forest or national park.

A memorandum of understanding between four-wheel-drive groups and National Parks in New South Wales has provided a solution to these concerns. The agreement allows club members to pursue their recreation while providing voluntary support services for National Parks, such as monitoring and maintaining park trails. The participants suggested that similar cooperative arrangements could be made with organizations such as fire brigades to check firebreaks across a community, which would allow members to enjoy touring while building up trust and positive relationships with landholders. Agreements between clubs and farmer organizations could also provide access to private property and, in return, members could provide a voluntary service for landholders. A register of legitimate four-wheel-drive clubs could be provided to landholders and both National Parks and State Forests to validate requests for access to private land.

Discussion

From a labelling perspective (Becker 1997), legitimate outdoor leisure activities such as bushwalking, touring or hunting may be redefined as deviant by some sections of the community when they violate social norms and negatively impact on the lives of others. Elsewhere in this volume, Rob White and Zannagh Hatton similarly report on the leisure activities of young people within public spaces, such as swarming, dancing, making music, hooning or boy racing, that are often defined as deviant by other groups of people who hold different expectations of the same public space. Yet the pleasure in these leisure activities for young people is the ability to conduct them within the exciting and dynamic environment of public space. Similarly, the attraction of outdoor leisure activities for enthusiasts is the ability to conduct these pursuits in wide open spaces. Conflicts arise when diverse groups (including landholders) hold different values and expectations about how rural lands should be utilized and managed (Pigram 1981).

Hardin's (1968) article 'The Tragedy of the Commons' highlighted the way open access resources are subject to collective action dilemmas: rational self-interest can lead individuals to outcomes that are inferior to those they could achieve if they worked together. Given the prevailing acceptance of landholders' absolute property rights in Australia, is it possible to find a way forward to accommodate the needs of all stakeholders?

The study found there was significant variation in landholders' attitudes towards granting access to the land and their perceptions of trespassing and unauthorized hunting as deviant between the three study areas. Landholders who were the least anxious about trespassers and unauthorized hunters in their district talked about their communities as places where neighbours were concerned and interested in each other and were aware of any suspicious activities. These landholders demonstrated high levels of social capital to informally maintain control over access and the kinds of people they allow on their land.

In contrast, participants who were more anxious had locked gates and farmhouses and placed 'no trespass' signs on property boundaries, although many believed their efforts were in vain. The only fruitful preventative action was to ensure regular visits by trusted hunters to control pest animals, which seemed to deter unauthorized hunters from entering a property. Furthermore, landholders believed that trusted hunters (and fishermen as well) tended to guard their hunting territory against unauthorized hunters and trespassers. Here there was widespread acknowledgement of social norms defining informal rights of access to trusted recreationists. The findings suggest that landholders who establish arrangements with professional hunting safaris could gain an added source of income while ensuring pest management on farms and, at the same time, deter trespassers and unauthorized hunters from entering the property because of the presence of regular hunting parties, something that has been proven in the United States (Jordan and Workman 1990).

A lack of awareness by users of social norms denoting the protocol for seeking permission to enter private rural lands or to act responsibly and respect the farming operation facilitated trespassing and unauthorized hunting. Hall and Pretty (2008) note that visitors to a district seeking outdoor leisure activities may be unaware of prevailing norms regarding access and responsibility, and, even if they are aware, visitors are not subject to the same social pressure to adhere to social norms and support each other as more permanent residents. There is a need for more public awareness of the formal and informal rules regarding access to private land as well as ethical hunting practices. Continued government support and promotion of courses for prospective hunters offered by hunting associations on best-practice hunting and weapons safety and handling is recommended. It was evident that memorandums of understanding between farmer organizations, National Parks and State Forests and various recreation groups had positive outcomes for all stakeholders and this can guide future policies.

One limitation of this research was that only one farmers', one hunters' and one four-wheel-drive group from each of the three areas was surveyed. Therefore the findings cannot be generalized beyond these regions in Australia. Not included were the very hunters and recreationists that all participants identified as problems. Hence, further research could greatly improve understanding by incorporating individuals without organized club affiliation and especially those who have been detained or arrested for trespassing or unauthorized hunting. Research comparing the practices of hunters who grew up on farms, in small towns and in large cities would allow for a more specific assessment of how lifestyle influences hunter attitudes and behaviours. Further research could include a wider range of leisure activities to identify specific needs for access. Finally, research in other localities, with differing typologies, environmental conditions and localized norms about property, may reveal more nuanced regional variations in the ways that landowners, hunters and recreational users of land express these issues.

The findings cannot be generalized to other countries given the unique nature of Australia's climate, land mass, property size and pest animal management. However, other countries appear to experience many of the same concerns about property rights and the increasing restrictions on access rights for leisure pursuits. As urban populations and the demand for outdoor leisure activities increase, many of the issues identified in this study may be observable in other countries. How these conflicts are resolved will be determined by how countries define property rights and access rights.

Conclusion

Outdoor leisure activities are a vital and necessary part of modern life. However, outdoor leisure opportunities are very much dependent on the amount of available space. The available space is dependent upon government policies regarding public access to national parks and forests and upon the attitudes of landholders towards public access to their private land. The Australian experience reflects those of other Western countries. The study has shown that even in developed countries informal customary rights remain critical to certain access rights and these rights are sustained by local expressions of social relations and norms. As countries increasingly urbanize and greater pressure is placed upon access to natural environments there will be a need to seek ways to nurture relationships between rural landholders and recreationists. Such arrangements will require landholders to appreciate the necessity to provide public access to their land for leisure opportunities and for the public to understand that conditions of access must be guided by a 'do not disturb, do not destroy' principle (Campion and Stephenson 2010).

However, in Australia, the problem of trespass and unauthorized hunting on farms is one that needs to be addressed before any change can be expected in the attitudes of some landholders towards opening their properties to the public. More research into the whole question of property rights, public access and rights of way would provide a greater understanding of these issues in planning future policies and programs for leisure opportunities in rural areas.

Note

1 The research that forms the subject of this chapter was supported by a grant from the Rural Industries Research and Development Corporation, Canberra, Australia.

Part II

8 Public disorder, antisocial behaviour and alcohol-related crime

From the metropolis to the tourist resort

R. I. Mawby

Introduction

Public disorder is a key component of feelings of insecurity in postmodern societies. Just as crimes such as burglary threaten the security of private space, so public disorder threatens use of public space, allegedly imprisoning more vulnerable groups within their own homes, particularly after dark. Although there are subtle differences between public disorder, antisocial behaviour and alcohol-related crime, in the UK much of this public concern has been over drunken behaviour, allegedly encouraged by liberalized licensing regulations. In the light of this, the finding from the British Crime Survey (BCS) that 16 per cent of those surveyed perceived there to be a high level of antisocial behaviour in their area suggests that a significant minority of citizens are concerned about levels of disorder on the streets (Walker *et al.* 2009). Specifically:

- 30 per cent considered teenagers hanging around on the streets to be a problem;
- 28 per cent considered people using or dealing drugs a problem;
- 26 per cent considered people being drunk or rowdy in public places a problem;
- 10 per cent considered noisy neighbours or loud parties a problem.

Interestingly, though, with notable exceptions British government thinking has tended to see both antisocial behaviour in general and alcohol/drug misuse as particularly urban problems, associated with the night-time economy of city centres in the largest metropolitan areas. This was evident during recent debates over more flexible licensing arrangements, when the focus was almost exclusively on metropolitan locations (see *Crime Prevention and Community Safety: An International Journal* 2009). The main exception to this has been (local and national) government response to publicity surrounding alcohol-fuelled disorder in Newquay, a tourist resort in the southwest of England. This chapter addresses the issues faced in Newquay, drawing on research conducted in Cornwall for the

2004 Crime and Disorder Audits. Before focusing on that, however, the following section locates the debate in an international context, by using four examples from the academic and wider literature:

- the policing of street disturbances between 'Mods' and 'Rockers' in 1960s Brighton;
- policing the 'schoolies' holidaying on Australia's Gold Coast;
- responding to Amsterdam's reputation as a centre of drugs and sex tourism;
- Faliraki revealed as the sex, drugs and alcohol destination for young people from Britain.

Public disorder and tourist resorts in international context

'Mods' and 'Rockers' in 1960s Brighton

Stan Cohen's (1980) seminal work on the 'Mods and Rockers' conflicts in England described the convergence on south and east coast resorts in the 1960s of groups of working-class youths, whose behaviour was perceived as a threat to the established social order. However, the research does not focus on tourism; rather, the example of public disorder, what Cohen (1980: 180) calls 'expressive fringe delinquency' at seaside resorts, is coincidental; any other example of reactions to youth cultures might have been taken.

According to Cohen, the resorts at the centre of the Mods and Rockers drama had been traditional bank holiday resorts for London's working classes. They also shared a certain shabbiness, having lost their traditional family holidaymakers to the Spanish costas. Their facilities were meagre and overpriced and the youths went with the hope, rather than the expectation, that they would experience some excitement, whether this involved sex, drugs or 'aggro'. Following Downes (1966), Cohen saw their reaction as in part a response to the disjuncture between the leisure opportunities promised in the media and the reality of their situation as impoverished working-class youths in dead-end and unrewarding jobs.

However, Cohen's work emphasized societal reaction rather than explaining primary deviance. This was done in terms of concepts such as 'moral panic' and 'deviation amplification'. For example, the concept 'deviation amplification' was used to explain 'how the societal reaction may in fact *increase* rather than decrease or keep in check the amount of deviance' (ibid.: 18). Reaction to local conflict in resorts such as Brighton in part reflected concern over the changing nature of tourism in the area and a forlorn hope for a return to the past. However, a localized conflict became redefined as a major social problem through sensitization, the social control culture and exploitation. 'Sensitization' refers to the way in which subsequent acts were interpreted and defined as further examples of the phenomenon; thus all resort conflicts and many examples of adolescent hooliganism were reclassified as Mods' and/or Rockers' activities. 'The social control culture' referred to political and penal response, with tougher policing, harsher sentences and disregard for due process, and clamours for draconian measures to stamp out the 'evil'. 'Exploitation' referred to the ways in which various agencies used the inventory for their own ends; for example, by claiming more resources or promoting the moral values of their own organization.

Although Cohen's work allows us to appreciate that disorder in seaside resorts is not a modern invention, it focuses on failed policy responses rather than successful intervention by tourist and criminal justice bodies. In contrast, the 'invasion of the schoolies' demonstrates that public disorder in tourist areas is not just a British issue, and identifies successful disorder reduction strategies.

Invasion of the schoolies

In Australia, the end of the school year regularly sees thousands of school leavers ('schoolies') descend on coastal resorts to celebrate, a rite de passage evident since the 1980s.[1] Gold Coast resorts such as Surfers Paradise are particularly favoured and indeed to a large extent promote themselves as catering for young singles. In late November and early December each year a succession of schoolies from Queensland, New South Wales and Victoria take over resorts such as Surfers Paradise, resulting in drink-related public disorder problems that spill over into vandalism and violence. This provokes concern among locals and other holiday-makers, with claims that films such as the hit teen movie *Blurred* had encouraged the behaviour, and has led to calls for the tourist industry that actively promoted the resorts to school leavers to fund crime reduction initiatives.

One early initiative is described by Homel and colleagues (1997). According to Homel and his colleagues, acceptance that different constituencies have different perceptions of risk is fundamental to the situation. Local residents were concerned about public disorder, but owners of the pubs and clubs in the area saw the image of Surfers Paradise as the night-time leisure capital of Queensland as crucial to their success. The initiative therefore aimed to draw these various constituencies into an alliance, whereby a reduction in antisocial behaviour would be seen to benefit all those concerned. The mechanism whereby this was to be achieved involved the creation of a multagency partnership incorporating licensees, local government, police, health and the public. The partnership therefore addressed:

> the way licensed venues are managed (particularly those that cater to large numbers of young people); the 're-education' of patrons concerning their role as consumers of 'quality hospitality'; and attention to situational factors, including serving practices, that promote intoxication and violent confrontations.
>
> (Homel *et al*. 1997: 266).

These initiatives sat alongside increased security measures that included the registration and training of security personnel, joint patrols by police and private security and the introduction of neighbourhood watch.

Homel and colleagues (1997) reported an impressive short-term impact for the initiative, in terms of both outputs and outcomes. Licensees were assessed as

operating according to the new standards, and the extent of alcohol-related disorder reduced appreciably in the first year of the initiative. However, a year later,
problems were resurfacing, as individual licensees began to flout the rules in the
interests of short-term profits. As a result, by 2010 local people were once again
calling on the police to win back the streets, and the government was promising a
new initiative in 2010.[2]

Responding to Amsterdam's liberal identity

The questions raised for public order by Amsterdam's reputation as the European
capital of sex and drugs tourism, on the face of it, appear somewhat different.
However, when the result is that young males are attracted to the streets of the
Netherlands' capital city, similar problems arise.

The expansion of foreign tourism and increased migration of impoverished
women from poorer to more affluent societies have combined to fuel an expansion in sex tourism and tourist destinations defined by sex tourism. Amsterdam
is a case in point. Although prostitution in the city is long established (Boutellier
1991; Brants 1998) and has been encouraged by what Brants calls the 'fine art of
regulated tolerance', sex tourism is a comparatively recent phenomenon (Nijman
1999) but one that is crucial to Amsterdam's (and the Netherlands') income from
tourism (Carter 2000; Dahles 1998; Wonders and Michalowski 2001).

Although drug tourism is also associated with South America and Asia (Uriely
and Belhassen 2005; Valdez and Sifaneck 1997), nowhere is the association
between drugs and tourism more evident than in the Netherlands. As Nijman
(1999) explains, this is relatively recent and somewhat contrived, with Amsterdam
now holding many of the characteristics of an alternative lifestyle theme park.

Drug use is illegal in the Netherlands, but the policy of 'expediency' allows
key players in the local law enforcement system to enforce the laws differently.
In Amsterdam and other larger cities, this has resulted in the condoning of the
sale of soft drugs in the 'coffee shops'. Jansen (1994) reported that in the early
1990s some 1,000 coffee shops in the Netherlands, and about 300 in Amsterdam,
were openly selling hashish. Many of these specialized in providing marijuana
for tourists. In particular, the Damstraat district, at the heart of tourism in the city,
became established as the main location for purchasing hashish and the centre of
the coffee shop phenomenon (Gemert and Verbraeck 1994). Nevertheless, hard
drugs had become increasingly available in the area, with tourists creating much
of the demand.

More recently, however, the impact of drug (and possibly sex) tourism on
public order has provoked a reaction to this tourism-generated identity from
Amsterdammers (Nijman 1999). This was illustrated in the web page of one
local resident, Joanne Kearins,[3] paralleling a move, in recent years, towards less
liberal criminal justice policies. This incorporates the partial abandonment of
'limitless tolerance' towards a 'two track policy' in which the interests of society
are considered alongside those of the drug user (Horstink-von Meyenfeldt 1996;
Lemmens and Garretsen 1998; Leuw and Marshall 1994). Current discussions

involve restricting coffee shop drug sales to nationals in an attempt to curtail drug tourism.[4] It may thus be that the nature of drug tourism in Amsterdam will change. The challenge will come when this impacts on the tourist industry. A similar situation applies to the sex industry.

Faliraki as the sex, drugs and alcohol destination for young people from Britain

Faliraki, a small town in the northeast of Rhodes, developed into a resort appealing to young single holidaymakers looking for a holiday based around alcohol and sex. Young tourists were attracted by advertisements by such organizations as Club Med, with an emphasis on alcohol and casual sex.[5]

The ITV *Club Reps* feature in January 2002 that associated Faliraki with binge drinking and unlimited opportunities for sex accelerated the expansion in numbers of (young British) tourists and shifted the definitions of normal and acceptable behaviour. Later that year *The Guardian* featured a story about the risk of rape in Faliraki, repeating a Home Office warning to females holidaying there alone (Gillan 2002). The *Evening Standard* on 28 June 2002 then reported 'a record number of arrests for "advanced sexual activity".'

However, 2003 was the year in which Faliraki appeared to monopolize the British news. Following the death of 17-year-old Patrick Doran, stabbed with a broken bottle in a nightclub brawl, the British press directed its attention at the problems of violence, public disorder, drunkenness and overt sexual behaviour in the resort. Reports included accounts of local police attempts to clamp down on deviant incidents, local reactions to the problems, the involvement of senior police officers from Blackpool in attempts to restore order and – ultimately – attempts to rebrand the resort.

On one level, the problem in Faliraki is described in terms of the public nuisance resulting from drunken holidaymakers annoying local people, creating excessive noise and defacing the environment with the flotsam of their nights' revelry: litter, vandalism and the least palatable residues of urine and vomit. Such public disorder issues were accentuated by drug dealing that occurred openly in the pubs and clubs. On another level, this drunkenness resulted in more serious offences, when it increased aggression and reduced inhibitions among potential offenders and diluted any security concerns potential victims might have held. Pub brawls were a nightly feature, albeit they rarely had such tragic consequences as the death of Patrick Doran. Rapes, involving both British and Greek perpetrators, also appeared relatively common, if rarely reported and even less often recorded (Gillan 2002; McVeigh 2003).

Although explanations for the public disorder situation in Faliraki include discussions of poor management of the night-time economy and the inappropriateness of the Greek paramilitary style of policing, the main focus of criticism has been the way that Faliraki has been marketed. As tourism developed on Rhodes, Faliraki repositioned itself as a destination for mass tourism, especially marketed at younger British holidaymakers attracted by its promise of hedonistic heaven.

This suited both the British travel industry and local tourism entrepreneurs. As Jeannette Hyde (2003) observed in a short but perceptive piece in *The Observer*:

> The Greek authorities should be doing some real soul searching right now. Rather than flinging in jail or fining every girl who flashes her breasts, they should be asking themselves how they can destroy the monster of Faliraki in Rhodes that they have created.
>
> If the Greeks had not marketed Faliraki as a 'yoof' destination, they wouldn't have the problems they have today. You can't say 'Let's bring lots of youngsters to our shores to spend like crazy in clubs and bars making the owners handsome profits' then complain about the type of business you have created. It's like a lap-dancing club complaining about too many lairy drunken men on the premises.

This message strikes particular resonance in the context of Newquay.

Newquay as Cornwall's Faliraki?

The research in context

Cornwall, in the far southwest of England, is a county that has long been reliant on the tourist industry (Jones 2008). The 2001 census indicated that in each district in Cornwall the numbers employed in hotels and catering alone exceeded the combined total in agriculture and fishing, the two traditional employment sectors. At the peak of the season there are over 270,000 visitors to the county, which adds more than 50 per cent to the all-year population. London and Devon are the only areas in the UK that attract more visitors. Tourism accounts for at least 30,000 jobs, with many more at the peak of the season.

However, the extent of and nature of tourism vary markedly across the county. Newquay, a town of some 20,000 people, is both the most popular place for tourists to stay and the centre of mass youth tourism. It is allegedly the most common place for young British tourists to spend their first holiday away from their parents. Describing the annual 'Run to the Sun' festival, during which the town is 'invaded' by car enthusiasts intent on a boisterous weekend, Barton and James (2003) argued that the hostility displayed by local residents towards such events contrasted with the tolerant attitude of the local tourist industry that promoted such events to extend the tourist season. Problems of crime and disorder in Newquay are, however, not confined to the 'Run to the Sun' weekend, and have been identified by both academics (Brunt and Hooton 2010; R. I. Mawby 2007) and journalists (Hattersley 2004),[6] culminating, in 2009, in street protests and a call for action to reclaim the resort for local people and 'responsible' tourists.

The remainder of this section locates this ongoing conflict between local residents and young tourists 'hellbent' on a good time in the context of research conducted as part of the 2004 Crime and Disorder Audits in Cornwall, which included surveys completed by local residents,[7] business representatives[8] and (in

2005) maingrade police officers,[9] before returning to recent developments. Local people were asked a series of questions about the area where they lived and the town they most frequented; businesspeople were asked about the town in which their business was located; and the police were asked about where they were stationed.

Tourism as trouble: local people's perceptions of Newquay

Local people were given a checklist and asked how much of a problem some 19 issues were. Unlike the British Crime Survey (BCS), though, we distinguished between where people lived and the town centre they most often visited. In each case, they were presented with a list and asked 'How much of a problem would you say the following were?'

Ten of these issues referred to potential public disorder situations:

- children/teenagers hanging around
- people using/dealing in drugs
- drunken people in public places
- noisy neighbours/loud parties (local area only)
- assaults
- tourists/visitors as a nuisance
- muggings or robbery
- people begging on the streets (town centre only)
- tourists/visitors as victims
- racial minorities as victims

As Table 8.1 illustrates, children/teenagers hanging around, people using/dealing in drugs and public drunkenness were the most common public disorder situations

Table 8.1 Percentage of residents who felt the following were either a very or fairly big problem in their most used town centre or home area

	Town centre	Home area
Children/teenagers hanging around	60.1	29.1
People using/dealing in drugs	52.4	15.4
Drunken people in public places	47.8	17.0
People begging on the streets	26.5	n/a
Assaults	25.9	4.5
Muggings or robbery	20.8	4.2
Tourists/visitors as a nuisance	13.5	7.4
Tourists/visitors as victims	6.9	1.3
Racial minorities as victims	5.8	1.3
Noisy neighbours/loud parties	n/a	11.2

considered problems by Cornwall residents. However, what is most striking about Table 8.1 is the disparity between local area and town centre. In the eyes of local residents, public disorder is a town centre problem rather than one associated with residential areas.

For residents of the county as a whole, three towns/cities were particularly associated with crime and disorder problems: Plymouth, locally the only 'real' city, albeit in neighbouring Devon, with a population of about 250,000; Penzance, a tourist town in the west of the county that has, according to the 2001 census, the highest rates of deprivation in the county; and Newquay, with lower levels of deprivation but – as already noted – with a distinctive tourist industry. In identifying the issues surrounding the relationship between tourism and public disorder, it is instructive to compare citizens' perceptions of these three urban areas and the remainder of the towns covered. Two points should be stressed before drawing these comparisons. First, respondents were asked about only their 'most used' town, so that, for example, different people are evaluating Newquay and Penzance. Second, views are likely to be positively skewed because respondents in many cases are evaluating the place they *choose* to go. For example, some whose closest town is in fact Newquay may have chosen to frequent another town because they perceived Newquay to be an unsafe place.

Table 8.2 illustrates that, on various indicators of public disorder, people who frequented Newquay indeed saw it as evidencing considerable problems. Although, in line with police and drug agency data, Penzance was more likely to be seen as having a drug problem, Newquay still ranked above Plymouth and was over 50 per cent above the Cornwall average. In terms of assaults, Newquay

Table 8.2 Percentage of those who felt that the following were either very or fairly big problems in different towns

	Newquay	Penzance	Plymouth	Elsewhere	Total
Children/teenagers hanging around	66.7	63.4	67.8	59.0	60.1
People using or dealing in drugs	79.2	86.2	73.1	45.5	52.4
Assaults	60.3	44.6	52.7	20.8	25.9
Drunken people on the streets/in public places	97.5	66.4	58.9	42.3	47.8
Tourists/visitors causing a nuisance	84.0	14.3	12.5	9.8	13.6
Tourists/visitors being victimized/picked on	18.8	15.1	17.0	4.9	6.9
Muggings or robbery	48.7	44.4	40.0	15.5	20.8
People begging on the streets	44.7	65.4	42.9	19.7	26.5
Racial minorities as victims	2.7	9.5	18.9	5.0	5.8

ranked first, with 60.3 per cent considering these a problem in the town, over double the Cornwall average. However, it is in terms of perceptions of public drunkenness that Newquay stands out, with an incredible 97.5 per cent considering this a problem, again double the Cornwall average. The extent to which such problems are identified with tourism is implied in the finding that no fewer than 84.0 per cent felt that there was a problem with tourists in the town causing a nuisance. In no other urban centre did more than 15 per cent feel this! Although far fewer felt that tourists tended to be picked on, again Newquay ranked first on this indicator.

In order to provide an overview, a scale was constructed based on the nine items, in each case scoring a 'problem' as 1 and 'small/no problem' as 0. This gave an antisocial behaviour score ranging from 0 to 9. Overall, residents of Cornwall scored relatively low on the scale, with a mean of 2.55. However, those who cited Newquay as their most used town scored significantly higher, with a mean of 5.02; Penzance was scored at 3.98 and Plymouth at 3.82.

Two other sets of questions further indicate the perceived relationship between tourism and public disorder in different parts of the area. First, Table 8.3 illustrates

Table 8.3 Perceptions of the impact of tourism on the following

	Newquay	Penzance	Plymouth	Elsewhere	Total
Income and standard of living	0.65	0.73	0.78	0.70	0.70
Employment opportunities	0.65	0.74	0.61	0.64	0.65
Area's overall prosperity	0.63	0.72	0.68	0.63	0.64
Availability of leisure facilities	0.29	0.43	0.26	0.41	0.40
Quality of life in general	−0.01	0.21	0.26	0.16	0.16
Noise	−0.87	−0.50	−0.50	−0.50	−0.52
Violent crime	−0.56	−0.16	−0.19	−0.23	−0.24
Property crime	−0.58	−0.21	−0.15	−0.24	−0.25
Litter, vandalism etc.	−0.80	−0.56	−0.39	−0.50	−0.52
Disturbances/public disorder	−0.79	−0.32	−0.23	−0.34	−0.36
Alcohol abuse	−0.83	−0.33	−0.32	−0.38	−0.39
Drug abuse	−0.71	−0.21	−0.18	−0.28	−0.29
Amount of affordable housing	−0.55	−0.62	−0.63	−0.59	−0.59
Traffic congestion	−0.82	−0.78	−0.71	−0.76	−0.76

1, positive response ; −1, negative response; 0, 'no difference'.

that, when local people were asked how they felt tourism affected different aspects of life, those who associated themselves with Newquay tended to be least positive about the advantages tourism brought and most negative about its disadvantages, especially those reflecting crime and disorder issues. For example, noise, violent crime, disturbances/public disorder, alcohol abuse and drug abuse were all more likely to be listed as negative effects of tourism by those frequenting Newquay than by those frequenting any other towns or cities. The last example is particularly instructive. Although Penzance was, as already noted, seen as the Cornish town with the greatest drug problem, in Newquay drug misuse was far more likely to be considered a *side effect of tourism.*

Tables 8.4 and 8.5 illustrate a slightly different take on the impact of tourism on public disorder. Local people were asked who they felt was 'mainly responsible' for 'property crimes such as burglaries or thefts', 'crimes of violence or threats' and 'drunken behaviour or other disorderly conduct . . . experienced by local people', in each case being allowed to opt for two answers. Overall, they felt that local residents were primarily responsible, especially for property crime, although a significant minority felt that outside casual workers, who are generally attracted to the region by the tourist industry, were responsible for violence (28.4 per cent) and tourists were responsible for drunken or disorderly behaviour (27.5 per cent). However, crime and disorder problems in Newquay were significantly more likely to be blamed on both outside casual workers *and* tourists. Table 8.4

Table 8.4 Percentage of those who attributed 'violence or threats . . . experienced by local people' to the following

	Newquay	Penzance	Plymouth	Elsewhere	Total
Local residents	33.0	58.2	54.8	51.4	51.5
Tourists	36.3	5.5	9.7	11.2	11.6
Local casual labour	19.8	17.7	14.5	14.4	15.0
Outside casual labour	50.5	28.7	21.0	27.5	28.4

Table 8.5 Percentage of those centres who attributed 'drunken behaviour or other disorderly conduct . . . experienced by local people' to the following

	Newquay	Penzance	Plymouth	Elsewhere	Total
Local residents	39.6	68.8	58.1	65.4	64.5
Tourists	68.1	22.4	16.1	26.5	27.5
Local casual labour	15.4	17.7	17.7	11.8	12.8
Outside casual labour	35.2	21.5	14.5	15.5	16.9

indicates that half felt that outside casual workers were responsible for violence, and Table 8.5 shows that over two-thirds associated tourists with 'drunken behaviour or other disorderly conduct'.

These are, of course, only respondents' *perceptions.* We have no direct evidence that outside casual workers or tourists do actually contribute to this extent to Newquay's public disorder problem (Mawby 2008). Nevertheless, the perception of local people is that tourism, particularly the specific nature of the local tourist industry, explains much of Newquay's public disorder problem. Although respondents identified some 'conventional' crime problems, such as burglary, with Newquay, the main crime and disorder problems associated with the town were public disorder problems, for which tourism was blamed. Respondents correspondingly focused on street crime, violence and antisocial behaviour, particularly associated with alcohol misuse, as endemic to the town. Newquay also ranked highest in the county for a range of more minor examples of antisocial behaviour (e.g. litter and being bothered in the streets by young people or drunks). In contrast, local people frequenting Penzance were far less likely to consider public disorder, as opposed to other examples of crime, a problem (the exception being drug misuse), and far less likely to identify tourism as a generator, and other areas of the county were seen as benefiting from – rather than blighted by – tourism.

Conflicting discourses: the business sector and the police

Earlier research on the negative impact of tourism has illustrated the extent to which local people's views may conflict with those with a stake in the industry (Haralambopoulos and Pizam 1996), a point reiterated by Barton and James (2003). The findings from the CBCS well illustrate this. Whereas businesspeople's ranking of area problems almost exactly corresponded with local people's perceptions, they identified public disorder as less of a problem locally than did residents, albeit they were more likely to express concern about the impact of public disorder on their businesses. Nor did businesspeople based in Newquay stand out from those elsewhere in seeing Newquay as a hot spot for antisocial behaviour. Indeed, only in the case of tourists as a nuisance did Newquay rank top, with 21.4 per cent seeing this as a problem in the area where their business was located and 37.5 per cent being concerned about the impact it was having on their business. The difference here was, however, far less evident than among local people. Newquay businesspeople were also far less likely to say that violence or drunken behaviour was characteristic of the area. This apparent denial of a local problem is made more notable by clear evidence from police statistics that violence in the centre of Newquay was common, and that the night-time economy provided a clear focal point for disturbances (R. I. Mawby 2007). Those businesspeople based in Newquay were generally slightly most likely to associate antisocial behaviour with tourists or tourism, but there was a marked difference between their perceptions of the local situation and those of the Newquay public.

This adds fuel to the argument that the business community, which is significantly reliant on the tourism industry, is at least ambivalent in its acknowledgement of the extent to which tourism affects alcohol-related disorder.

In complete contrast, police officers' views were largely in accord with those of local people. Asked to assess problems in the town where they worked, children/teenagers hanging around, people using/dealing in drugs and public drunkenness were commonly cited, although assault was mentioned as a problem at least as frequently. In each case, indeed, a higher proportion of officers saw these four public order scenarios as a problem locally than did residents or businesspeople. There was also, for the police, clear water between these public order problems and the others listed, suggesting that the latter were considered uncommon (e.g. robbery) or inconsequential (e.g. begging). Interestingly, 19.4 per cent of police officers and 13.5 per cent of local residents but only 7.9 per cent of businesspeople perceived tourists as a nuisance.

Moreover, it was also clear that from a police perspective Newquay was associated with public disorder, especially linked to tourism. Table 8.6 illustrates that, on various indicators of public disorder, police who were based in Newquay and Penzance[10] were more likely to identify problems there than were those stationed elsewhere. As for the public, drug misuse was particularly associated with Penzance, although in the case of the police so were muggings and begging. Again, Newquay was associated with alcohol-related disorder and tourists/visitors causing problems, and to a lesser extent tourists/visitors being targeted. Using

Table 8.6 Percentage of police officers based in Newquay, Penzance and other urban centres who felt that the following were either very or fairly big problems

	Newquay	*Penzance*	*Elsewhere*	*Total*
Children/teenagers hanging around	89.3	77.8	75.6	77.1
People using or dealing in drugs	85.7	96.3	75.6	78.6
Assaults	89.3	77.8	72.6	74.7
Drunken people on the streets/in public places	96.4	85.2	66.7	71.4
Tourists/visitors causing a nuisance	89.3	19.2	10.3	19.1
Tourists/visitors being victimized/picked on	32.1	14.8	4.9	8.6
Muggings or robbery	17.9	40.7	3.6	8.6
People begging on the streets	35.7	55.6	15.6	21.4
Racial minorities as victims	7.1	7.4	5.4	5.8

the same disorder scale as for the public, police from Newquay averaged 5.43, those from Penzance 4.77 and those from elsewhere in Cornwall 3.29.

Newquay police were also more likely than those based in Penzance or elsewhere to consider that tourism had an unfavourable impact on disturbances/public disorder, alcohol abuse and drug abuse, and were the only subgroup in which a majority felt that tourism overall had a detrimental effect on quality of life. Like local people, the police sample felt that local residents were primarily responsible for 'violence or threats' and 'drunken behaviour or other disorderly conduct' that was 'experienced by local people'. However, 72.4 per cent and 89.7 per cent of the Newquay subsample, respectively, named tourists as responsible.

Recent developments

In 2009, the public disorder problems in Newquay again made national headlines when two young tourists, 18-year-old Andrew Curwell and 16-year-old Paddy Higgins, died in alcohol-related cliff-fall accidents.[11] Initial criticism involved parents blaming the resort for its poor supervision of alcohol use and dangerous clifftop footpaths, local agencies blaming parents for condoning their teenage children's alcohol misuse, and local residents blaming local agencies for destroying the town's image as a family-friendly resort. Public hostility to tourists' antisocial behaviour was reflected in a widely publicized march through the town, with residents calling on local politicians to help them reclaim their streets and reconstitute Newquay as a safe and peaceful family holiday resort.[12] Local politicians and the tourism industry then criticized protesters for further threatening the resort's image.

However, reflecting the views of local people and the police captured in the 2004/5 surveys, the protest led to a public acceptance of the need for action. A multi-agency partnership was established, incorporating police, local councils, licensees, the National Health Service and residents. Under a 'designated public spaces' order, police in the town now have the power to confiscate alcohol and stop on-street drinking. The partnership has similarly tackled the issue of underage drinking, with pubs and clubs signing up to the 'Challenge 21' protocol on identification. The police have also dealt with young tourists found drunk or incapable by detaining them and contacting their parents to come and remove them from the area. Alongside such law-and-order measures, the partnership has also promoted alcohol-free club nights.[13]

It is too soon to evaluate the success of the partnership. The fact that the numbers of young holidaymakers coming to Newquay fell in 2010 may well threaten the new aura of multi-agency cooperation. However, the scheme has received national recognition, being named as one of the government's 12 'Pathfinders' to show other towns how agencies can work together to provide community safety, and receiving the endorsement of the new coalition government during a well-publicized visit by the new Home Office Minister for Crime Prevention, James Brokenshire.[14]

Conclusions: conflicting discourses and partners singing from different hymn sheets?

As Cohen's seminal work reminds us, alcohol and public disorder problems are not a recent invention. Nor are they restricted to the UK, or to British tourists abroad. However, the contrasting examples of Amsterdam, Faliraki and Newquay illustrate conflicting discourses: one person's (the local resident's) problem is another person's (the tourist industry's) profit.

The findings from our 2004/5 surveys in Cornwall indicate a clear difference between the police and public on the one hand and the business sector on the other. The public, and to an even greater extent the police, saw some aspects of crime and disorder as a problem in their local towns; businesspeople were rather less likely to identify local problems, but did acknowledge the detrimental effect of social disorder on their businesses. Additionally, whereas both the public who frequented Newquay and the police who worked there identified it as a hot spot for disorder and antisocial behaviour, businesspeople from Newquay did not stand out in the same way. This disjuncture between the different local constituencies raises questions for crime reduction partnership working in areas such as Newquay.

The importance of involving the public and other local agencies in the policing process was acknowledged in the 1998 Crime and Disorder Act. The Act required local authorities, the police, health authorities, police authorities and probation to work together to address crime and disorder problems in their area through Crime and Disorder Reduction Partnerships. The benefits of such a partnership approach in tourist areas is well illustrated in Homel and colleagues' (1997) Australian research. However, the Gold Coast initiative seems to have had a limited long-term effect, with partners from the private sector reluctant to turn away from the lucrative alcohol-fuelled leisure market. Equally, in Faliraki, reactions to the problems of public disorder may be short-term. In Newquay the success of the new partnership arrangements crucially depends on whether alternative lucrative tourist markets can be mined, a questionable scenario in the wake of the recession, which has, for example, impacted on luxury second-home developments.

More generally, however, I am suggesting that it is unfair to focus criticism on young tourists for public order problems in resorts such as Faliraki or Newquay. Key players in the tourist industry create resorts that benefit themselves and market the resorts accordingly. Tourists who arrive to 'live the dream' that has been commodified can scarcely be blamed. Nor can the police, caught between the interests of local residents and those of tourism's infrastructure, often with their own agendas to balance alongside these, but in Newquay at least clearly aligned with local residents. Maintaining public order in tourist areas is not solely the responsibility of the police. It involves the parents of the young tourists and key local agencies. Among these, the role of the tourist industry is paramount, since it is the discourse that it has created that defines the nature of the tourism/ crime relationship.

Notes

1 See, for example, http://www.buzzle.com/editorials/11-28-2003-48074.asp; http://www.goldcoast.qld.gov.au/t_news_item.asp?PID=2303&status=Archived; Fickling (2003).

2 http://www.brisbanetimes.com.au/queensland/violence-crackdown-valley-to-be-treated-like-schoolies-20100830-13xtu.html

3 http://travel.nzoom.com/travel_detail/0,1940,194816-136-147,00.html

4 http://www.dailysmoker.com/amsterdam-cannabis-drug-policy-netherlands

5 http://www.club18-30.co.uk

6 See also http://www.telegraph.co.uk/travel/familyholidays/2080090/Newquay-The-teenage-invasion.html; http://www.guardian.co.uk/alcoholandyoungpeople/waves-of-partying

7 The Cornwall Crime Survey (CCS): 2,214 questionnaires were completed with a response rate of 30.5 per cent (see R. I. Mawby 2007, 2008).

8 The Cornwall Business Crime Survey (CBSC): 618 were completed, a response rate of 39.4 per cent.

9 The Cornwall Police Survey (CPS): 283 responses, a response rate of 31.7 per cent (see Mawby 2009).

10 Plymouth is not included here since by definition none of the police sample were stationed there.

11 http://www.thisiscornwall.co.uk/news/Hours-picture-taken-Paddy-16-plunged-70ft-death-grieving-stepmother-asks-served-alcohol/article-1151281-detail/article.html

12 See, for example, www.thisiscornwall.co.uk/news/Flat-leaves-owner-hospital/article-1203253-detail/article.html; www.thisiscornwall.co.uk/newquayguardian/safe-responsible-behaviour/article-1243658-detail/article.html; http://news.bbc.co.uk/1/hi/england/cornwall/8186024.stm; http://www.guardian.co.uk/society/2009/jul/12/alcohol-binge-drinking-underage-newquay; http://news.bbc.co.uk/1/hi/england/cornwall/8553408.stm

13 http://www.cornwall.gov.uk/Default.aspx?page=24605; http://www.cornwall.gov.uk/default.aspx?page=24927; http://neighbourhoodpolicing.devon-cornwall.police.uk/BCU-1558/Sector-1628/Pages/NewquaySafe.aspx

14 http://www.homeoffice.gov.uk/media-centre/press-releases/newquay-safe-partnership

9 Sin City v. Fantasyland

Crime, legislation, and policing in two different tourism environments

Ross Wolf and Hugh Potter

Introduction

Tourism destinations can have a multitude of interesting features that people find attractive when planning their vacations or holidays. Many locations market to a particular subset of society in order to promote their amenities to families, singles, couples, college-aged vacationers or seniors. Examples of this can be found in the two tourism destinations of Orlando, Florida, and Las Vegas, Nevada, which market to specific types of recreational consumers. The city of Orlando is located in the central Florida area within Orange County, and Las Vegas is located in Clark County, Nevada. Orlando has been dubbed by its city leaders as "The City Beautiful" but uses the family-friendly phrase created by tourism marketers "Orlando makes me smile" (Orlando/Orange County Convention and Visitor's Bureau 2010a). With its theme parks, nearby beaches, resorts, and family-centered activities, Orlando markets itself as wholesome, safe, and peaceful. Las Vegas promotes itself very differently. "What happens in Vegas, stays in Vegas" is arguably one of the most famous tourism slogans ever constructed. Las Vegas advertises to the world as a city where the sinful activities of gluttony, gambling, alcohol, and sex are rampant, appealing to an entirely different crowd from those who may be interested in visiting Orlando.

Nicknamed "Sin City," Las Vegas is the most populous city in the state of Nevada. The notion of rampant sin is supported by the city's tolerance for gambling, adult entertainment, and all-you-can-eat buffets, combined with the proximity of legalized houses of prostitution. The Orlando area, on the other hand, is home to Disney World®, Universal Studios®, Sea World®, and other family-style resorts. The only professional sports franchise in the city of Orlando, the Orlando Magic basketball team, gets its name from the city's retired tourism slogan "Go for the Magic." As we will develop further, the imageries promoted by the tourism industries in the two cities are quite distinct.

At first glance, travelers worried about crime might be apprehensive about traveling to Las Vegas because of the type of clientele the city is likely to attract and the potential for "shady characters", and Orlando might appear to be a safer vacation destination. One might also expect lower rates of reported crime in the Orlando/Orange County area than in the Las Vegas/Clark County area. Our hypothesis for this review is that an area that openly promotes "adult entertainment," especially sexually oriented adult entertainment (prostitution, exotic dancing, etc.) will have higher recorded criminal activity than an area that is focused on promoting "family entertainment." This chapter will examine the legal structures, tourism promotion efforts, local regulations concerning the adult entertainment sector, policing efforts and methodologies, and the resultant comparative crime rates. We will focus on the relationship between the way in which the broad category of "adult entertainment" fits into the criminal codes of these two areas, the local structuring of policing such entertainment, and their relationship to recorded criminal activity in general.

Literature review

"Fear of crime," or the fear of becoming a victim of a crime, may cause people to restrict their behavior to "safe places or safe times or avoid certain activities they perceive to be dangerous" (Pantazis 2000: 432). It can be argued that there actually exists a "fear–victimization paradox" (Meadows 2001: 5), which suggests that those who have never been victims are the most fearful, and this paradox may have a marked influence on the tourism industry (Wolf 2002, 2008). Potential tourists who have never been victims of a crime may hear or read of crime in other countries, states, or cities, and decide not to travel. Often fueled by the news media, reports that crime "is pervasive" may incite an irrational fear (Meadows 2001: 5) that can drive potential travelers from one vacation destination to another.

Popular media also adds to these perceptions. For the Las Vegas area, there is the arguably most-popular television series *CSI*, which weekly dramatizes crime in that area. The equivalent show for Florida is set 250 miles (400 km) south of Orlando – *CSI: Miami*. In fact, almost all crime dramas set in Florida are set in the southeast corner of the peninsula, commonly known as the "Gold Coast," not the Orlando area. Almost all crime dramas set in Nevada focus on Las Vegas; only a comedy, *Reno 9-1-1*, is set outside the city. Thus, from a popular media perspective, crime is an accepted part of Las Vegas, but not of Orlando.

Criminal justice literature is full of theories and practices to combat crime. These theories can also be related to the tourism environment and may help form theories on policing methodologies. Community policing developed from the urban foot-patrol beat officer, who communicated with all the residents in his area and developed local solutions to local problems to maintain order. Greatly expanded in its use today, community policing relies heavily on the "broken windows theory" of Wilson and Kelling (1982), which posits that the deterioration of an area and the apathy of its citizens lead to an increase in criminal offenses. Community policing is an attempt to remedy this situation through cooperation between police and citizens. In a much broader context, however, community policing is a change of philosophy in the way in which police services are provided (Purpura 2001).

Research on the effectiveness of community policing has yielded mixed results. Cordner and Sheehan (1999: 411) reported that, whereas this model of policing may tend to make citizens feel safer, "it may not have much of an effect on the amount of crime". Glensnor, Correia, and Peak (2000) point out there have been varying degrees of success with community policing, despite the acceptance of the model by academicians and police practitioners. However, Cordner and Sheehan (1999: 413) also reported that community-oriented policing (COP) can be much more effective if it also incorporates "a greater utilization of other government agencies and private resources to solve community problems," or the problem-oriented approach to policing. Nolan, Conti, and McDevitt (2005: 9) point out that there is a "philosophical gap between traditional law enforcement and community policing" that can benefit from situational policing, which applies knowledge of group and social processes to neighborhoods. Community-oriented policing and situational policing can be combined in a newer, more targeted approach to policing in tourism areas called tourism-oriented policing (Wolf 2002, 2008).

Tourism-oriented policing

Tourists can easily fall prey to crime as they are often more prone to taking risks on vacation than they would be at home (leaving valuables in their car, for example), often carry large sums of money, and are seen as vulnerable or easy targets. An additional factor in understanding tourist crime is the fact that, if a perpetrator is caught, it is less likely that a tourist (particularly from out of the country) would return at a later date to prosecute in criminal proceedings.

Sonmez, Apostolopoulos, and Tarlow (1999) saw cooperation between the tourism industry and police as critical when proactively addressing tourism safety. They reported that tourism policing, whereby police officers infuse traditional community-oriented policing with tourism techniques, is a relatively new concept in the United States. Tourism policing includes identifying tourist areas and geographical hot spots, analyzing and responding to tourism cycles and seasons, identifying needed services for tourist populations, and working closely with and identifying tourist destinations within the community. To accomplish this, police agencies throughout the United States and the world have begun developing and implementing specialized units whose "sole responsibility is the protection of tourists and have trained selected personnel to deal specifically with tourist matters" (Pizam *et al.* 1997: 23).

Tourism-oriented policing also shares some similarities with problem-oriented policing (POP). The POP model utilizes educated and well-trained police officers in a proactive manner, working with and drawing on the community to assist in solving problems. The concept of POP is often used interchangeably with the concept of COP (Thibault *et al.* 2001). Although both models share a common foundation in broken windows theory, there are some basic differences. First introduced in 1979 by Herman Goldstein, POP posits that police officers should be more aware of the contributory and fundamental crime problems in a community, rather than crime incidents in particular. Crime is a collection of related incidents that affect the community and create policing concerns, including order maintenance, reducing fear, and protecting people from crime. Whereas COP is viewed as collaborative and preventive, POP is seen as analytical and creative in solving long-term problems (Cordner and Biebel 2005).

Although American literature largely ignores the concept of tourism-oriented policing (TOP) compared with the literature in some other countries, TOP can be equated to a great deal of contemporary COP, but utilized in areas where a large segment of the "community" is visitors. However, significant pieces of the traditional community policing model, including getting to know people who live and work in the area, building confidence among the community residents, and creating community groups to assist in distributing information, cannot work with a large tourist population given its transformational nature. Consequently, in TOP, police work is not confined to working with tourists, but rather concerns itself with the people who work the tourism areas, including hotel owners, managers, taxi drivers, resort staff, baggage handlers, shuttle drivers, shop owners, and other private businesspeople. Although these people do not often live in the location that is being policed, they do spend a significant amount of time there, and are able to share information with the police. The tourism policing model is built on the community policing model of creating a partnership between the police and the community they serve (Glensor *et al.* 2000; Glensor and Peak 2004; Miller and Hess 2002; Purpura 2001; Sims *et al.* 2002; Wolf 2002, 2008), by serving a migratory population of tourists while utilizing the people who work in the area as a conduit. The TOP model is used extensively in both Las Vegas and Orlando within very different tourism environments.

Two distinctive tourism destinations

Orlando

Orlando is America's twenty-seventh-largest metropolitan area (United States Census Bureau 2008) and is also known as one of the world's top tourism destinations. Tourism brings in an estimated $30 billion to the local economy (Orlando/ Orange County Convention Visitor's Bureau 2010b). The Orlando Metropolitan Statistical Area (MSA) had over 2.1 million residents in 2008 (United States Census Bureau 2008). Walt Disney World, one of the major tourism attractions in Orlando, employs over 58,000 full-time and over 39,000 part-time employees ("Jobing" 2006; Shanklin and Barker 2001). The area promotes, and the economy relies on, family-centered activities, attractions, and resorts. The Orlando MSA has over 180,000 workers employed directly in leisure and hospitality (United States Bureau of Labor Statistics 2010). According to Uniform Crime Reporting (UCR) data in 2009, the Orlando MSA had 3,366 sworn law enforcement officers and 2,065 civilian law enforcement employees.

Orlando acts as host to over 48 million tourists a year (Shifflet and Associates 2010), and has developed a multiple-agency law enforcement Tourist Oriented Policing Sector (TOPS) specifically for the tourism area of southwest Orange County and southwest Orlando. The police officers and sheriff's deputies assigned to the TOPS unit work closely with other law enforcement agencies, retail managers and loss prevention officers, airline officials, victim advocates, and the Central Florida Hotel-Motel Security Association to prevent crime and prosecute criminals (Channell 1994; Chioji 2004). An example of tourism policing can be seen in the annual grant provided to the Orange County Sheriff's Office since 2005 from Walt Disney World, to provide a full-time law enforcement presence on Disney property with uniformed law enforcement officers and criminal investigators. Outside Disney property, the tourist corridor policing area in Orange County works closely with the Orlando Police Department tourist policing units. The corridor includes attractions, resorts, hotels, golf courses, malls, restaurants, and the Orange County Convention Center. The sheriff's office has formally recognized the role that tourism plays in the economy and vitality of the area by establishing a full-time presence of officers in the area. Deputies and officers that work the area respond to crime calls, make arrests, and police traffic infractions, but also work extensively to develop partnerships in the prevention of criminal activity.

Las Vegas

Las Vegas acts as host to over 36 million tourists a year (Center for Business and Economic Research 2010) and is America's thirty-first-largest metropolitan area (United States Census Bureau 2008) with a population of over 1.8 million people. It is known as one of the world's top tourism destinations, and tourism brings in an estimated $43 billion to the local economy (Center for Business and Economic Research 2010). The area relies on and promotes adult-themed industries. The Las Vegas Metropolitan Statistical Area has over 240,000 workers employed directly in leisure and hospitality (United States Bureau of Labor Statistics 2010). According to UCR data in 2009, the Las Vegas MSA had 2,835 sworn law enforcement officers and 1,675 civilian law enforcement employees.

Frey, Reichert, and Russell (1981) described a tourism economy in Las Vegas intent on fulfilling the needs of clientele. Their research portrayed a Mecca of prostitution (even though it is illegal in most of the area in and around the city), enabled by hotel bellmen, taxi drivers, and illegal organizations that supply prostitutes to hotel customers as a focal and contributing factor to the Las Vegas economy. This research found that law enforcement efforts successfully eliminated most visible forms of street prostitution in Las Vegas. However, this organized subeconomy was allowed to flourish because it was not brazenly flaunted and because of practices that legitimized the use of prostitutes within the Las Vegas resorts at the time of their research. Although prostitution continues to exist in Las Vegas, police and security officers work together to identify and criminally charge both prostitutes and "johns" (clients of prostitutes) within major resorts. Las Vegas police also employ TOP tactics, but in a very different social environment from their Orlando counterparts.

Table 9.1 shows the demographics of the populations in the Orlando and Las Vegas MSAs. The civilian and sworn law enforcement employee data are also included and shown as ratios to the population. The average weekly tourist population was added to the resident population for an average weekly population

Table 9.1 Orlando v. Las Vegas population, tourist population, and law enforcement ratios

	Orlando MSA	Las Vegas MSA
Population[a]	2,103,480	1,865,746
White/Caucasian	44.7%	70.8%
Black/African American	27.4%	10.6%
American Indian	0.3%	0.7%
Asian	2.9%	5.0%
Hispanic/Latino	22.2%	29.2%
Other	9.5%	9.3%
Law enforcement employees	*5,431*	*4,510*
Civilian (no law enforcement powers)	2,065	1,675
Sworn (law enforcement powers)	3,366	2,835
Ratio of sworn officers to population (/1000)	1.60	1.52
Average number of tourists per week	923,076	692,307
Ratio (/1000) sworn officers to population + tourists	1.11	1.10

Sources: Information compiled from Center for Business and Economic Research (2010), Visit Orlando (2011), United States Department of Justice (2009), United States Bureau of Labor Statistics (2010).

a   Totals may not add up to 100% as respondents could select more than one category.

in each MSA, and then divided into the number of sworn officers for a sworn officer per total population ratio. This is useful when comparing the data between these two agencies, as the ratios are similar. This shows that, although the two areas have different total populations and different average tourist populations per week, the resultant ratio of officers to population plus tourists is almost identical.

Policing methods

Whether in Orlando or Las Vegas, police officers in each of these MSAs have significant interaction with private security officers. All of the major theme parks in Orlando and the casinos in Las Vegas utilize security officers for a variety of functions outside the most typical visible security presence including combating underage drinking, transportation of large sums of money, employee audits, dignitary protection, and risk management. These police agencies often team up with private security personnel to provide training on Crime Prevention Through Environmental Design (CPTED) and first-responder crisis issues. Both Orlando and Las Vegas have a Tourism Oriented Police corridor, where police administrators work to not only serve the businesses, hotels, business owners, employees, and hoteliers, but also spend a significant amount of time being visible to tourists to create a sense of safety and security.

In Orlando, police officers are encouraged through public/private agreements to work for the theme parks as off-duty law enforcement, whereas Las Vegas officers are not authorized to work in the gaming industries in an off-duty capacity. However, every major theme park and hotel in Orlando, and every casino and hotel in Las Vegas, utilizes private security personnel to supplement public police efforts. Loss prevention and risk management positions are commonplace in both of these vicinities, as they are in other tourism destinations.

The largest of central Florida's theme parks created its own political subdivision to enhance county-provided services. Walt Disney World (WDW) created the Reedy Creek Improvement District, which was approved by the Florida Legislature in 1967. The Reedy Creek Improvement District is a political entity with a voting populace of a five-person Board of Supervisors who are elected by landowners in the district; Walt Disney owns all 27,000 acres within the improvement district's jurisdiction. Reedy Creek has its own fire department, its own utilities, and its own emergency communications center. However, even though WDW security once conducted traffic stops and other police functions, case law has developed that severely limits the powers of security personnel (Emerson 2009). WDW instead provides financial incentives to the Orange County Sheriff's Office to supply several uniformed and plain-clothed officers, along with supervisory and command personnel, with offices within the theme park. This partnership creates a unique relationship between public law enforcement personnel and private security, not only for the WDW property, but also in the surrounding areas. As mentioned earlier in this chapter, WDW and security personnel in other theme parks and hotels are very cognizant of how broadcast news can influence tourist decisions, and work diligently to keep potentially harmful events from becoming the focus of the media.

Civil containment

Leaders and businesses in both Orlando and Las Vegas want tourists to feel safe while visiting, to enjoy their stay, to feel comfortable recommending their location to friends, and to return for another visit. This can be accomplished through the legislation or prohibition of certain activities. For example, the acts of exotic dancing, gambling, and consumption of alcohol can all be expressly criminalized through statute or ordinance. Criminalization generally requires action at the state level in the United States and Australia, or by the semi-autonomous local government entities of the United Kingdom. Such criminalization generally carries the threat of loss of money or freedom and represents the putative consensus of the residents of the entire political area. Criminalization can be defined as serious offenses (i.e., felonies, indictable crimes) or as less serious offenses (i.e., misdemeanors and summary crimes). The more serious the offense, generally, the harsher the penalty following conviction.

At the level of state criminal law, at which such laws are generally defined in the United States, the structure of the most extreme of adult sexually oriented entertainment services is almost uniformly criminalized across the United States. Nevada is the only state among the United States to have legalized prostitution, though only in licensed premises (brothels). Prostitution is not legal within Clark County, where the Las Vegas metropolitan area is situated, but it is legal in other areas of the state. Nevada Revised Statutes Chapter 201 deals with the definitions of prostitution, prohibition of prostitution outside of counties and cities where it is decriminalized and regulated, penalties, and health-related requirements for legal establishments of prostitution. In Florida, prostitution is illegal, regardless of where it occurs. Florida Statutes Chapter 796 (Sections .04–.09) provides the definitions of prostitution, prohibits establishing premises for the act of prostitution and profiting from prostitution, and sets out the penalties associated with convictions for such behaviors. It also provides for the HIV/STD testing of persons arrested for prostitution (voluntary testing) and those convicted of such behaviors (mandatory testing).

State laws regarding "exotic dancing" or "stripping" enjoy a much less clear-cut definition in both states. This may be due to the protections of such artistic expression by the First Amendment (the right to enjoy free speech) of the US Constitution. However, criminalization is not the only tool available to communities to control undesired commerce, persons, or behaviors. In both states, the primary responsibility for regulation of non-prostitution adult entertainment is ceded to the local governments, counties, and/or cities. This is done through the creation of zones, or areas, where certain types of activity are sequestered. This second level of prohibition, generally enacted at the local level, involves land use authorization, or "zoning." In the US context, zoning represents more local control by counties or cities/towns to dictate land use. Similar local control can be found at the shire and city levels in Australia, as well. Zoning decisions and rules are often made by local boards. Those boards may be composed of either elected or appointed officials in the US context.

Over the past several decades, as zoning and land use planning increased in use across the United States, zoning has been used to exclude categories of business in the development of urban space, in particular (Ellickson 1996; Hozic 2002; Papayanis 2000; Sanchez 2004). Zoning has also been used to exclude particular groups of people deemed to be "undesirable" in certain public space (Amster 2004; Barak 1992). These "undesirable" populations include the homeless, mentally ill, substance users, and sex workers, among others. Examples of "undesirable" businesses include adult entertainment venues, alcohol-serving establishments, and tobacco shops. In the realms of policing pleasure, zoning plays a strong role in "zoning-out" or restricting both problem individuals and businesses. Zoning infractions are generally civil citations, though some may carry misdemeanor (summary) criminal charges. Ignoring the civil citations may also result in a criminal contempt citation. Thus, although zoning is a more "civil" tool to control businesses, persons, and behaviors, it can develop into a criminal matter.

For example, Orange County, Florida, the home county of Walt Disney World, Sea World, and Universal Studios, does have exotic dance bars, hotels that cater to same-sex couples, theaters, bars, and attractions. However, county ordinance severely limits the locations of those establishments away from the more family-friendly theme parks. Orange County also has regulations concerning open containers of alcohol, and gambling is illegal in the state of Florida except on land owned by American Indian tribes. Whereas Las Vegas does allow open containers of alcohol on the Las Vegas strip, the city does not have legalized prostitution (although it is commonly believed that it does), although select locations outside Las Vegas do have government-monitored, legal houses of prostitution.

Las Vegas utilizes the term "sexually oriented businesses," whereas Orange County employs the term "adult entertainment establishment" to encompass a range of adult-focused venues for zoning purposes. The Las Vegas zoning purposes are expressed in terms of preserving and enhancing the present qualities and advantages of the city; efficient utilization of natural resources; and protection of human, environmental, social, natural and economic resources. Orange County, by comparison, describes the zoning code related to adult entertainment as an attempt to "establish reasonable and uniform regulations that will protect the health, safety, morals, and general welfare of the people of the county" (Orange County Code 2010, section 3.4).

Definitions of sexually oriented businesses are descriptive and succinct in the Las Vegas zoning code (Las Vegas Zoning Code 1997, chapter 19.04). Orange County's zoning code not only defines the type of establishment and the activities that might take place within such establishments, but devotes considerable space to a series of allegations about those who work there. In particular, the Orange County Code attributes high levels of criminality and immorality to those who work in such establishments. The establishments themselves are described as contributing to the decline of civility, real estate value, and ultimately the desire of new commerce to locate in the county. The framers of the zoning code for Orange County conclude that it is necessary for the county to license and monitor the operators, employees, and patrons of these establishments in order to protect citizens, especially minors, "from the adverse effects of the activities that accompany such establishments" (Orange County Code 2010, section 3.4). Like other problematic domains (see above), it appears Orange County utilizes zoning codes to control activities and undesirable population segments. Las Vegas, on the other hand, appears to utilize zoning codes to control land use more pragmatically, without moral comment.

Dichotomous pleasure: activities of Convention and Visitor's Bureaus/Associations

Convention and Visitor's Bureaus/Associations (CVBs) are generally public/private partnerships operating as non-profit private organizations to promote tourism and events in a geographic area. Both Orange County/Orlando and the Las Vegas metropolitan areas have large, active CVBs. Wang (2008) argues that CVBs provide several essential services to the tourism and entertainment sectors of a community: information provider; community brand builder; facilitator and liaison of community tourism activities; catalyst of collaborative initiatives; advocacy for the tourism industry; organizer of destination marketing campaigns; funding agent for collective marketing activities; partner and team builder; and network management organization.

For our purposes here, the key interest is in the differences in the ways in which the CVBs promote and advocate for adult/sexually themed entertainment, assist in developing collaborative initiatives and destination marketing campaigns, and assist in the funding of such campaigns. A four-question assessment questionnaire sent to both CVBs in these counties was returned by one, and the other referred us to its website. We also utilized an analysis of recent tourism campaigns developed by the two CVBs to gauge the involvement with the adult/sexually themed entertainment world.

As mentioned earlier, many around the world are familiar with the "What happens in Vegas, stays in Vegas" campaign from the Las Vegas Convention and Visitors Authority (LVCVA 2010). These promotional spots have a distinctly adult theme to them, highlighting night-life and gambling activities. Although not directly or sexually explicit, a subtext of the availability of more sexually themed entertainment is apparent. A review of the list of conventions that are held in the Las Vegas area reveals a number of well-promoted sexually themed conventions and events that range from major adult entertainment industry association conventions to events that promote sexual partner exchanges among married and unmarried participants. Las Vegas is also the annual home to the Adult Video News Awards, celebrating the adult video industry ("X"-rated videos in the Australian classification scheme; see Potter 1996). These conventions and conferences are presented alongside organizations as diverse as the American Bar Association and university technology managers' meetings. In short, adult/sexually themed entertainment is treated as any other industrial sector by the LVCVA.

The Orange County Convention and Visitor's Bureau (OCCVB), by contrast, has no listings for adult/sexually themed entertainment venues or conferences. In response to the questionnaire, it answered "no" on all categories of consultation/involvement with, or promotion of, adult/sexually themed entertainment. The primary themes of the OCCVB advertising campaigns are family focused. The images presented are primarily of children and families enjoying the theme parks and natural features of the central Florida area. There is little subtext of "naughtiness" in any of the campaign media from the OCCVB.

In sharp contrast to the conservative presentation of the area, "Orlando Gay Days" (http://www.gaydays.com/) has been a major annual event in the Orlando area since 1991, and is not officially sanctioned by the OCCVB. Sometimes referred to as "Gay Day at Disney World," the event bills itself as "the world's most popular gay and lesbian celebration," bringing in as many as an estimated 150,000 persons to the area. There is a somewhat political element to the event, as well. In an area known for political conservatism, "Orlando Gay Days" stands out as one of the few activities in which behaviors some might consider socially deviant are openly featured. This stands in sharp contrast to the Las Vegas situation.

In Las Vegas, adult/sexually themed entertainment is treated as just another segment in the local economy by the public/private marketing venture known as the LVCVA. In the Orange County/Orlando area, the adult entertainment sector is absent from official information from the OCCVB. The differences found in official government zoning/land use plans are carried through into the public/

private partnerships that promote the "community brand" associated with the two areas. We turn next to an examination of how the organization of the sector itself might contribute to the ways in which it is viewed, and its activities and customers policed.

Private sector involvement in destination labeling

In Las Vegas, the adult-/sexually oriented business segments are competitive and well organized. The Sin City Chamber of Commerce mixes the adult entertainment sector of the business community with the "mainstream business" community (Sin City Chamber of Commerce 2010). The Sin City Chamber was "created to promote with equality, respect and fairness the businesses that provide the products and services that Sin City Las Vegas is noted for worldwide" (para. 4). It provides a series of networking and advertising opportunities to businesses. It does not, however, have a code of conduct or ethics for members, and expressly notes that it is not a regulatory organization.

The situation in the Orlando area is quite different. There are no adult entertainment merchants' associations or industry associations. Interviews with managers of adult-oriented businesses in the Orange County area revealed that they separate themselves along three dimensions: retail, entertainment, and adult services. Retail establishments generally sell lingerie, novelties, sexual aids, videos, and print materials. In one shop, the manager attributed about 60 percent of the store revenue to the three aisles containing "couples" items such as massage oils and "toys." About one-third of the store revenues were obtained through lingerie sales and only about 10 percent came from video and print media sales. In the Las Vegas code, these are known as "adult emporium" establishments, and require that 35 percent or more of the inventory fall under the adult video, print, or other product category.

The second Orange County category of adult-themed "entertainment" includes dancing, stripping, modeling, and other low- or no-physical-contact performances. These are known colloquially as "strip joints," "gentlemen's clubs," and so forth. Curiously, in the Las Vegas code, such establishments do not appear in the "sexually-oriented businesses" land use plan. As discussed earlier in this chapter, the Orange County zoning code takes great pains to explain the links between alcohol consumption, adult entertainment, and a variety of social ills.

The final category of "adult services" refers generally to activities requiring more direct physical contact, ranging from massage parlors to prostitution services. "Massage parlors" and "sexual encounter centers" (including "bath houses") are expressly listed and defined in the Las Vegas code of acceptable land uses. The Orange County zoning code expressly prohibits such establishments and services. Whereas it appears that Las Vegas seeks to regulate the operations and locations of adult services, the Orange County zoning code is employed to prevent their establishment.

In conclusion, the two communities are organized differently at all levels when it comes to the adult/sexually oriented entertainment sector. These differences are reflected in zoning, industry promotion, and sector organizing in the two communities. Orange County/Orlando zoning codes contain specific attributions of deviant and/or criminal behaviors to the adult entertainment sector and those who work in and utilize its services. In the remainder of the chapter we will test whether there are substantive differences in major crimes between these two cities. If the zoning codes are any guide, we would hypothesize that the Orange County/Orlando MSA will have lower rates of reported serious crimes than does the Clark County/Las Vegas MSA.

Variety of crime

Both the Orlando MSA and the Las Vegas MSA have unique opportunities for criminal behavior. Whereas crime that happens in other jurisdictions also happens in these areas, specific crimes may flourish in these environments. Orlando has unambiguous problems with counterfeit merchandise related to the theme parks, domestic violence, vacation/holiday voucher scams, counterfeit tickets to theme parks and attractions, slip-and-fall scam artists, and organized crime (including connections with terrorism, drugs, and gypsy travelers). Las Vegas has different specific problems, including casino robberies, casino cheating, counterfeit casino chips, sex clubs and prostitution, escort and massage services, and organized crime (including sex trade, drugs, and loan sharking). However, both environments have common opportunities for criminal behavior. These include distraction thefts, "smash and grab" thefts, "follow home" robberies, hotel burglaries and employee theft from hotels, auto theft (including rental car theft/fraud), counterfeiting, trespassing, shoplifting, drug use/sale, financial scams, and false reporting of crimes as examples. The general crime data for the Orlando and Las Vegas MSAs can be seen in Table 9.2.

This table depicts the crimes listed in the Uniform Crime Reporting Program as

Table 9.2 Orlando and Las Vegas 2009 MSA crime data comparison

	Orlando MSA rate	*Las Vegas MSA rate*
Violent crime	820.6	840.4
Property crime	4,468.40	3,667.70
Murder/manslaughter	7.9	7.3
Forcible rape/sexual assault	38.8	47.1
Robbery	239.4	307.6
Aggravated assault/battery	534.5	478.4
Burglary	1,212.50	1,015.70
Larceny/theft	2,853.60	1,905.40
Auto theft	402.2	746.6

Source: United States Department of Justice (2009) data.

Note: Rate per 100,000 inhabitants.

"Part I" offenses. As depicted in this table, "violent crime rate" refers to data listed in the Uniform Crime Reporting Program and includes murder and non-negligent manslaughter, forcible rape/sexual assault, robbery and aggravated assault/aggravated battery. Murder and non-negligent manslaughter is defined as the willful killing of one human being by another; forcible rape/sexual assault is defined as a sexual act directed against another person, forcibly and/or against that person's will; robbery is the taking of, or attempted taking of, anything of value from the care, custody, or control of a person by force, threat of force or violence, and/or putting the victim in fear of receiving serious personal injury; and aggravated assault/aggravated battery is the intentional causing of, or attempted causing of, serious bodily harm, or the threatening of serious bodily injury or death.

"Property crime rate," however, is used to identify several non-violent crimes, including burglary, larceny/theft, and auto theft. Burglary is the actual or attempted unlawful entry of a structure to commit a felony or a theft; larceny/theft is the unlawful taking, carrying, leading, or riding away of property from the possession or constructive possession of another; auto theft is the unlawful taking or attempted taking of a motor vehicle (Federal Bureau of Investigation 2001). Researchers of Uniform Crime Reports are cautioned when comparing the data of two cities, as we are doing here, as it may result in a simplified or incomplete view of the crime that has been reported. However, Table 9.2 and Figure 9.1 are utilized to show how two apparently dissimilar cities are actually very similar when it comes to crime.

Figure 9.1 also shows that, although Orlando's violent crime rate in 2009 is lower than that of Las Vegas, and Las Vegas's property crime rate in 2009 is lower than Orlando's, this has not been consistent through time. Reported crime may be a result of many different factors, and may change over time not because actual crime rates change, but because reporting methods change or citizen attitudes toward police change.

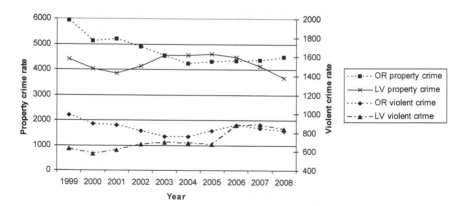

Figure 9.1 Ten-year comparison of Orlando and Las Vegas crime rates. Note: data obtained from the Uniform Crime Reports. Las Vegas data in 2002–3 were subjected to changes in reporting practices, annexations and/or incomplete data. Crime rate is shown as per 1,000 residents.

Because this chapter has focused to some extent on the arena of sexually explicit adult entertainment, it is also important to review the crime most often attributed to these environments: forcible rape (as defined in the UCR). Figure 9.2 presents a 10-year comparison of forcible rape complaints made to police in both the Las Vegas and Orlando metropolitan areas. Over that course of time the two cities have remained relatively similar in the rates of reporting. Las Vegas began with a slightly higher reported rate, merged with Orlando in 2005, and returned to a higher rate for the remainder of the period for which data are available. The difference in rates is, though, barely substantial. Contrary to common crime-control theory, it would appear that the differences in the control and availability of sexually explicit adult entertainment between the two cities are not reflected in the most serious of sex-specific criminal acts.

Many people would assume, because of the comparative environments, that the overall crime rate in Las Vegas would be higher than the crime rate in Orlando. This comparison of 10 years of data shows that the Orlando property crime rate has been higher in six of the last 10 years, and the Orlando violent crime rate has been higher than the Las Vegas violent crime rate in all but three years. These rates are depicted in Figure 9.1, and show that, while the property crime rate dropped in Las Vegas from 2006 to 2008, the Orlando property crime rate remained steady. The Las Vegas violent crime rate, although lower than the Orlando violent crime rate from 1999 to 2005, shot up in 2006 and remained higher.

When reviewing this data, it is also important to remember that the crime rates do not take into account the home residence of the victim. Certainly a considerable portion of the crimes depicted in both Table 9.1 and Figure 9.1 have a local resident as victim. We cannot therefore assume, for example, that, because the robbery rate in Las Vegas was higher than that of Orlando in 2009, more tourists

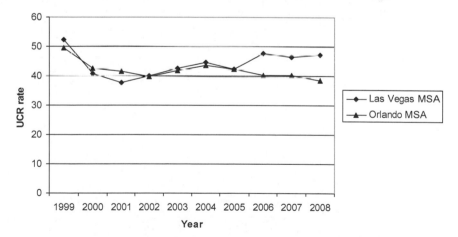

Figure 9.2 Ten-year comparison of Orlando and Las Vegas forcible rape rates. Note: data obtained from the Uniform Crime Reports. Las Vegas data in 2002–3 were subjected to changes in reporting practices, annexations and/or incomplete data. Crime rate is shown as per 1,000 residents.

were victim to this type of crime. What we can take from both Table 9.2 and Figure 9.1 is that similar crimes occur in both cities at similar rates, and this is contradictory to our original hypothesis.

Conclusion

Although Orlando and Las Vegas may seem to be polar opposites when reviewed from a criminal justice perspective, in reality it appears that they are not that diverse. Both areas utilize similar policing methodologies and comparable civil ordinances to manage business enterprises. Both have a visitors' bureau responsible for the marketing of an image, and both market to a particular type of tourist. However, although these destinations significantly differ in regards to their promotional image and the attractions offered, this does not appear to affect criminal activity.

This review is limited, however, through its use of Uniform Crime Reports. Although these reports are an important resource and are meticulously crafted, they are not the only reports regarding the occurrence of crime. Crime data from victim reports may yield different results, as may other methods of examining crime in a particular area. The authors note that in both Las Vegas and Orlando crime rates may be skewed by public officials who may not wish to tarnish public perception of their area, or by individuals who may not report crime to the police for a multitude of reasons.

What our review has shown us is that tourism marketing, local regulations, and state laws, created to protect members of society from decidedly immoral businesses, may actually not be providing the intended consequence of a safer community. This review has shown that two decidedly different cities, with similar tourism policing strategies, may have analogous crime problems, regardless of the clientele and type of leisure activities offered or promoted.

10 'There can be no orcs in New Zealand'

Do media representations of crime tarnish tourism?

John W. Buttle and James Rodgers

Introduction

Occasionally New Zealand's tourism industry promotes lucrative urban events such as the America's Cup Yacht Race of 2000 hosted by Auckland City (Barker, Page and Meyer 2002) and the Rugby World Cup, but the majority of international tourists view New Zealand in a more rural context. New Zealand is a place of pristine rural beauty with spectacular beaches and coastline vistas, green subtropical bush land, picturesque mountains and volcanoes, and grand fjords. Therefore, it comes as no surprise that the tourism industry utilizes the rural aspects of New Zealand to construct an image to sell vacations to the international tourism market. The countryside is also a favoured destination for the domestic holidaymakers and in December, during the height of the summer, cities such as Auckland vacate as inhabitants take their annual camping trip or visit the family holiday home (known in New Zealand as a bach) to relax (Buttle 2006).

Tourism provides considerable income for the New Zealand economy from both international and domestic holidaymakers. Statistics for 2009 indicate that international holidaymakers visiting New Zealand expended $9.3 billion. Likewise, domestic tourists spent $12.4 billion (Ministry of Tourism 2009). Given the revenue provided by tourism, any incidents that tarnish the image of New Zealand can be perceived as a threat to the economy.

Perhaps the biggest threat to the revenue provided by tourism comes from the perception that a particular destination is dangerous. There is evidence to suggest that crime and safety issues can adversely affect the behaviour of tourists (Bentley and Page 2001; Pizam and Mansfield 1996; Tarlow 2000). This is especially the case where media coverage of sensationalized accounts of crimes against tourists has highlighted the possibility of victimization to potential holidaymakers (Chesney-Lind and Lind 1986). Mawby (2000) suggests that incidents of violence, robbery, and terrorism can also raise concerns about the safety of holidaymakers, which in turn may lead to holiday cancellations and economic decline in areas dependent on tourism.

In this chapter we examine how sensationalized media representations may pose problems for the tourism industry in New Zealand. This will be achieved by utilizing the rural idyll (Halfacree 1996; Jones 1998), as the means of understanding how New Zealand's image as a desirable destination has been constructed to represent a peaceful holiday haven. Likewise Innes's (2004a) notion of signal crimes and disorders will be the means of explaining how the fear of crime may have a negative impact on tourism.

Selling the rural idyll

New Zealand is a place of scenic grandeur, so it is not surprising that the tourism industry utilizes the rural aspects of New Zealand to construct an image to sell vacations to prospective holidaymakers. Butler (1998) suggests that this image is often achieved through the utilization of rural settings by the entertainment media. This is especially the case with prospective international vacationers, whose introduction to this beautiful scenery most probably occurred while watching Peter Jackson's film adaption of Tolkien's *The Lord of the Rings* trilogy or other productions that have been filmed in New Zealand (Bell 2008; Buchmann *et al.* 2010; Hudson and Ritchie 2006). Although the analogy with *The Lord of the Rings* may seem stereotypical, the influence of popular culture on social policy and the tourism economy should not be underestimated (Bell 2006b; Rojek 1997). This is a group of films that showcased New Zealand to the world and it also provides an interesting metaphor with which to explain how tourism has been sold to the international and to a lesser extent domestic markets. Indeed, the filming locations for *The Lord of the Rings* have also become tourist attractions (Buchman *et al.* 2010).

The scenic vistas that promote the rural aspects of tourism in New Zealand go beyond the mere depiction of geographical attributes to encompass a sense of tranquillity often associated with rural locations (Swaffield and Fairweather 1998). This notion of rural tranquillity corresponds to what has been termed the rural idyll. The concept of the rural idyll is contested and its meaning is dependent on historical and cultural factors (Short 2006), but it often portrays the countryside as a peaceful tranquil place characterized by a romantic beauty and nostalgic traces of simpler times in a more rustic past (Mingay 1989). The countryside is seen as both innocent and clean (Bell 1997). Furthermore, this rural idyll is often perceived as being inhabited by respectable people who are good-hearted, hospitable, kind, virtuous, community-orientated and with higher moral integrity than their urban counterparts (Howitt 1971). This corresponds with the relaxed and friendly nature of the Hobbits from the Shire, as the following extracts taken from *The Hobbit* indicate:

> Hobbits are little people . . . They love peace and quiet and good tilled earth. They dislike machines, but are handy with tools. They are nimble but don't like to hurry . . . They are inclined to be fat. They wear bright colours . . . They like to laugh and eat and drink. They like parties and they like to give and receive presents. They inhabit a land they call The Shire . . . a wide respectable country inhabited by decent folk, with good roads, an inn or two and now and then . . . a farmer ambling by on business.
>
> (Tolkien 1982: 1, 31)

Although this extract from *The Hobbit* exemplifies the rural idyll, the peaceful nature of the countryside, like this example, is fictitious, or at the very least exaggerated.

Perhaps the most pertinent version of the rural idyll is described by Bell (2006b) as the tourist idyll. From this perspective the production of a tourist rural idyll must be globally recognizable by international consumers (Duruz 1999), especially those from the countries, such as Australia, Britain, the United States, China and Japan, that provide New Zealand's greatest tourism markets (Ministry of Tourism 2009). Furthermore, tourists' concepts of the rural idyll may not be an exact duplicate of how life in the countryside is understood by New Zealanders. Rather it is the peaceful enjoyment and friendly welcome along with safe aspects of the rural idyll that are emphasized when marketing New Zealand's opportunities to the world, because this is how rural life is viewed by most, if not all, cultures. Therefore, it is important to New Zealand's tourism industry that this national image of peace and tranquillity remain intact.

Beware the anti-idyll

The rural idyll refutes the dangers and moral decay that is characterized by city life. Therefore, crime and disorder must be perceived as next to non-existent in order to maintain the idyll. For the image of beautifully peaceful New Zealand to be maintained, the notion of safety must be ensured for prospective holiday-makers. As the countryside must be seen to remain free from crime, disorder and deviance (Cloke and Little 1997; Halfacree 1996; Jones 1998), so too must a nation that promotes itself to visitors as a safe destination. Whereas images of Tolkien's Shire populated by respectable Hobbits can be seen as promotable, other less respectable aspects of the 'Lord of the Rings' story characterized by the dark and dangerous land of Mordor are not so desirable. In short, where New Zealand's tourism industry is concerned there can be no mention of orcs in the Shire.

There is another view of the countryside that is the antithesis of the rural idyll. What Bell (1997) terms the anti-idyll is also depicted in popular culture, for instance the New Zealand-made film *The Locals*. Bell states that slasher movies, such as *The Hills Have Eyes* and action movies such as *Deliverance* characterize rural people as depraved criminals or deviant. All three of the aforementioned films are based on the premise of urban dwellers who take a trip to the countryside only to find themselves being hunted by the deranged and often deformed local inhabitants. Here, the picturesque countryside becomes a desperate isolated fear-producing location that should be avoided. In the anti-idyll, it is the backpackers that must be wary of the horrors waiting to be perpetrated against them by chainsaw-wielding mass murderers. Given that the New Zealand tourism industry has traditionally catered to international backpackers, this image of the fear-evoking anti-idyll may be damaging to the tourism industry. Again Tolkien offers a perfect analogy of the anti-idyll in his description of Mirkwood:

> Mirkwood is dark, dangerous and difficult . . . Water is not easy to find there,
> nor food . . . in there the wild things are dark, queer and savage . . . Straight
> through the forest is your way now. Don't stray off the track!
>
> (Tolkien 1982: 132–7)

This warning evokes imagery of the anti-idyll and portrays an image of the aptly
named forest of Mirkwood that is not conducive to tourism because it does not
cater to the wellbeing of holidaymakers, even the most hardy backpackers would
not want to travel this way.

News values crime reporting

The media plays an integral role in informing the public of crime stories through
domestic and international media outlets (Barak 1994; Cohen and Young 1973;
Cottle 2003; Ericson 1995; Garofalo 1981; Manson 2003; Potter and Kappeler
1998; Pritchard and Hughes 1997; Reiner 2007). However, there is a large disparity between the types of crimes that are reported and those that are most prevalent.
For example, dishonesty offences such as theft or burglary are far more common
than violent crimes, with dishonesty making up 56.7 per cent of all reported
crime in 2005, and violent crimes accounting for only 11.9 per cent (Statistics
New Zealand 2006). Yet, when viewing mainstream media, and in particular
news broadcasts, violent crimes account for the majority of reported crime news
(Ericson 1995; Reiner 2007). Indeed, the cliché phrase of 'if it bleeds it leads'
holds very true within the majority of media organizations. To a large extent,
coverage of crime is sensationalized with a view to selling news to a public that
the media believe want to be deeply mortified. Owing to society's ever-increasing
reliance on the media for information regarding crime, the disparity between reality and what is presented on the news can have unintended consequences. Most
notable is the perceived level of violent crime within society and an elevated
fear of victimization (Barak 1994; Ericson 1995; Jefferson and Holloway 2000;
McRobbie and Thornton 1995).

Victims often report greater levels of fear than those members of the public
who are relatively untouched by crime, which indicates that information regarding crime is mediated by personal experience (Brunt *et al.* 2000). So, even though
the chances of becoming a victim of crime are statistically minor (Reiner 2007;
Statistics New Zealand 2006) the perceived level of violent crime is higher than
the risk of becoming a victim (Ericson 1995; Reiner 2007; Jefferson and Holloway
2000). Therefore, a public that has little experience of serious crime is instead
informed by sensationalist media accounts. This can have major consequences
for a destination that is attempting to market itself to tourists using the image of a
rural idyll, because when people are deciding where to take a vacation they do not
want to consider being victimized (Brunt *et al.* 2000), even if the possibilities are
remote. However, news values based on the notion of 'if it bleeds it leads' assume
that the public are interested in sensationalized stories about violence and crime. It
may be that some sensationalized violent incidents are not fear-inducing, or at least

not as frightening as other incidents. Furthermore, there may be occasions when sensationalized crime stories have less influence than holiday brochures depicting scenic paradises, at least from the perspective of potential holidaymakers.

Signal crimes and disorder

The notion of signal crimes and disorders provides a theoretical framework from which to understand the process by which one criminal incident can go virtually unnoticed by the public and another can instil considerable anxiety (Innes 2004a). In essence, signal crimes are incidents that cause a person to use that crime as a signal to influence their understanding of a neighbourhood and to adjust their behaviour accordingly (Innes 2004b; Innes and Fielding 2002). Some crimes in particular, which have exaggerated 'signal values', are highly influential in forming the beliefs concerning a particular area or incident (Innes 2004b; Innes and Fielding 2002). According to Innes (2003) signal values can vary, but strong signals invariably relate to what are considered as serious crimes such as homicide or sexual assaults. Strong signal crimes often involve a 'good victim' such as a middle-class female, an attractive woman or a child who is portrayed by the media to embody a sense of innocence and purity (Manning 1996). Some of these crime stories may have a greater impact than others depending, on the period of time over which the story is covered and how widely the media spread the news (Innes 1999). Innes also noted that it is not just singular sensationalized events such as homicide that can instil a sense of public anxiety about being victimized but that a series of smaller events also create a signal of danger. This supports Pizam's (1999) assertion that the effects of crime against tourists can have long-lasting repercussions. He explains that the perception of constant violent crimes against tourists can cause a significant decrease in the likelihood of tourists visiting that particular location. Pizam also notes that international media coverage of violent incidents can prolong the negative impact on the tourism industry in countries perceived as problematic. Therefore, these signal crimes may provide insight into the perceptions and presuppositions held by tourists in relation to crime within the rural idyll that is New Zealand.

Innes (2004b) indicated that when a strong signal is generated by a crime, or a series of incidents, people's understanding of the world may shift towards concerns about safety. From Innes's perspective, this expression of the fear of crime is characterized by changes in behaviour focused on avoiding perceived dangers. For example, those who do suffer from this fear of victimization will take preventative measures in order to protect themselves, such as avoiding areas and situations that they perceive to be dangerous (Innes and Fielding 2002). Therefore, holiday destinations perceived as dangerous may prompt potential visitors to take extra precautions, or stay away entirely.

It is also relevant to note that signals can be interpreted in different ways by differing demographics (Jefferson and Holloway 2000). Research shows that female's fear of crime is associated with sexual assaults, whereas a male's fear is largely associated with physical assaults. Little, Panelli and Kraack (2005) suggest that, within a rural setting, the fear of crime is based on the introduction of the unknown – or to be more specific the unfamiliar that is often associated with the presence of outsiders encroaching on the rural way of life. For international tourists, the unknown may also influence their level of concern as they are now located in an unfamiliar country and are often exposed to different cultural values that challenge how they view their way of life. Given this, the interpretation of danger signals can be mediated by the sense of cultural familiarity that the vacationer feels is present at the holiday destination. So cultural familiarity plays an important role in how tourists perceive areas of potential disorder or crime.

Media depictions of crime against international tourists

Given that people are prone to concern about issues they perceive to have a personal effect on them, the victimization of tourists in New Zealand may be considered pertinent to prospective international holidaymakers. A central issue to media representations of crime stories is the way in which bystander quotes are used to show the devastation of a crime and to create an image of a peaceful community suffering because of this horrendous crime. The following quotes are an example of how printed media co-opt the views and concerns that local residents feel about incidents of crime and disorder:

> 'It was the worst possible thing that could have happened to them when they went out of their way to help these two men,' said Kaitai Detective Sergeant Trevor Beatson. 'They had come to New Zealand fully believing it was a safe place to holiday and now their holiday and impressions of our country have been shattered.'
>
> (Kohler 2009)

> It is a sickening attack from the point of view that their own safety and well-being was put at risk, but also because this area is regarded by tourists to be a beautiful place to come . . . The girls were just parked up on the beach in the van, here for a nice vacation. It's horrible what has happened, we don't want things like this to happen to visitors.
>
> (Lewis and Gilespie 2008)

> We consider ourselves to be one big family up the Coast, and everybody thinks it is just horrible that it could happen here.
>
> (NZPA 2008)

By emphasizing the shock and dismay that the residents feel about a crime, it further enhances the story's news value and coverage it will receive (Ericson 1995; Reiner 2007). The discourse of concern by local residents demonstrates their respectable family values, while repudiating any challenge to the rural idyll by implying that theirs is a good community where crime is not tolerated. To this extent, local residents' fear of crime may be closely linked to concerns about public respectability and the impact that being perceived as dangerous by tourists may have on the local economy.

Media construction of a strong signal

From a signal crimes perspective, the media and interest groups have picked up two sexual assaults against Dutch tourists travelling in New Zealand in 2006 and 2009 to highlight that New Zealand must alter its stance in dealing with people who commit crimes against tourists (Kohler 2009; NZPA 2008; *NZ Herald* 2008; Savage 2007; The Press 2009a) by imposing harsher sentences on offenders. The first attack occurred in Northland, New Zealand, on Friday 9 November 2006, where a couple were held at gunpoint by a masked attacker within their own campervan (Woulfe *et al.* 2006). They were then tied up and driven around the local town whilst the offenders forced them to empty their bank accounts at ATMs. During this time the woman was raped. The offenders abandoned the campervan in a rural cemetery and fled with several items of property (Woulfe *et al.* 2006). On Thursday 22 February 2007, two men were convicted of the attack, with sentencing deferred to the Auckland High Court in order for a sentence of preventative detention to be considered (NZPA 2007). The second attack occurred on 15 January 2009 in Southland, New Zealand, where a local man broke into the victim's car at 6:40 a.m., raped her and stole approximately NZ\$700 (The Press 2009a). Police later apprehended the offender, after his mother recognized her filleting knife and tea towel, which had been used in the attack, and alerted police. The offender was sentenced to serve 10 years in prison on 9 April 2009 (The Press 2009b).

These two attacks have become the focal point for discussion regarding the potential impact of crimes against tourists and New Zealand's image as a safe place to visit. The coverage of these incidents is typical of the media treatment of crimes occurring in a rural setting. The bystander quotes from these news articles attempt to show just how devastating the attacks have been not only for the victims, but also for the surrounding community (Wallace 2008):

> Tuatapere Community Board deputy chairman Les Johnston said residents would be horrified when they learned what had happened. 'We certainly would never expect anything like that to happen here. This sort of thing is not good for us; it is not good for any community. We are trying to be a nice happy little community . . . This is just horrible.'
>
> (Porteous 2009)

As Wallace (2008) notes, the most popular phrase is: 'things like that don't happen here'. This type of comment is usually associated with crimes that occur in rural communities, where the perceived chances of violent crimes occurring are relatively low compared with those of the city. This is especially true of crimes against tourists that occur within rural New Zealand, who are usually staying in isolated areas or in small rural towns to enjoy New Zealand's scenic beauty (see

Chapter 8 in this book). Again the bystander comments are a denial that these incidents are in any way a breach of the rural idyll by emphasizing that serious crime is a rare occurrence and that the residents of the area are fine respectable people. These bystander comments are in effect making a plea to prospective tourists to 'please continue visiting our peaceful paradise'.

The reporting of these two sexual assaults has created a signal that was significantly strong enough for action to be taken at the level of the nation state and by individuals planning to holiday in New Zealand. A serious consequence of these sexual attacks was that the Dutch government issued a travel warning about the supposed dangers of camping in New Zealand (DutchNews 2009; Gay 2009a,b; The Press 2009b) and as a result of this some tourist operators began to report a decline in inquiries and bookings (The Press 2009a; Gay 2009a; APN 2009).

It can be argued that international media may have detected a trend of serious crime, tarnishing the peaceful rural image of New Zealand. It is certainly the case that the Dutch authorities have considered these two sexual assaults as signal events that depict a dangerous trend for their citizens and have acted to warn against holidaying in New Zealand. However, it can also be argued that this has had only a limited impact on tourism in New Zealand. People are generally self-interested (Epley and Caruso 2004; Moore and Loewenstein 2004) and are often more influenced by news that pertains to them, so it is likely that the bulk of, if not all, the reporting of these two tragic incidents was focused only on the two countries, because a danger signal was received through media outlets that cover the Netherlands and New Zealand. Prospective tourists in other European countries are probably less aware of these incidents and still associate New Zealand with the rural idyll. From a signal crimes perspective this is demonstrated by the fact that the authorities in other European countries have not acted to warn their citizens against travelling to New Zealand because the victimization of these Dutch tourists failed to generate a strong signal in other countries. Furthermore, the financial costs of these two crimes to the tourism industry are likely to be limited because the Dutch are not among the most prominent of New Zealand's international tourism markets, such as Australia, Britain, United States, China and Japan (Ministry of Tourism 2009). Indeed, adverse press such as this is more likely to have an effect on the more lucrative domestic market.

Media construction of a weak signal

The murder of the British tourist Karen Aim has also become part of the discourse in regards to the effects that crimes against tourists can have on New Zealand's image. Karen Aim was attacked and murdered in Taupo, by 15-year-old Jahche Broughton, in 2008 (BBC 2009; Eriksen 2009; NZPA 2009; Sky News 2008). Broughton attacked her with a baseball bat while she was walking home from a night out with friends. Broughton later pleaded guilty to the murder and was sentenced to 15 years' imprisonment, with 12.5 years without the chance of parole (NZPA 2009). The media reaction to her death should have ensured that the crime would be seen as a signal crime to potential tourists who were looking to travel in New Zealand. By referring to the murder as 'ghastly' and 'vicious', the articles tempt the reader to visualize the experience of what it was like during the murder (BBC 2009; Eriksen 2009; NZPA 2009; Sky News 2008). By utilizing these adjectives and the connotations that they carry, the articles can be seen as exaggerating the potential fear of victimization felt amongst those who read the stories. To further highlight the devastation caused by the crime, the article contains comments from the victim's family, such as:

> It's felt as though we're watching a bad film on the television and could we not change channels? But we're stuck on this channel for the rest of our lives … We just wish that we could change over, instead of this absolute nightmare that we're going through.
>
> (Sky News 2008)

This indicates to the readers what the family of the victim is going through on account of their loss, and, although it is understandable that a family would be grieving during such a time, it also serves to show potential tourists exactly what would happen if they too were murdered whilst in New Zealand on holiday. If a strong signal were generated by discourse such as this there could be a profound effect on New Zealand's image as a safe destination for British tourists by eroding or refuting the rural idyll. Furthermore, British visitors make up a significant portion of New Zealand's international tourism market, so any concerns about the safety could result in a reduction of British vacationers and a considerable reduction in tourism profits. As Pizam (1999) suggested, crimes such as these can have substantial negative consequences for the country that can last for many years to come. However, for this to occur the incident would need to produce a clear sign that New Zealand was dangerous to vacationers.

What is notable about the Karen Aim murder is that it did not appear to produce a signal strong enough for the British authorities to post an official warning about visiting New Zealand. From a signal crimes perspective, this lack of action would indicate that New Zealand's image as a peaceful and tranquil paradise remains intact for the majority of prospective British tourists. As is noted by Mawby in Chapter 8 of this book, if anything it is neighbouring Australia that takes the lead as a dangerous place for British tourists to visit, at least in the eyes of the media (Venditto and Mouzos 2006). This is because greater media attention has been focused on a number of particularly gruesome murders of tourists who were vacationing in Australia.

Media depictions of crime against domestic tourists

Tourism in New Zealand is not limited to international visitors. Domestic tourism accounts for a larger portion of holidaymakers within New Zealand, and the issues that affect international tourists can also be seen to alter the perceptions and behaviour of domestic tourists as well. Arguably, residents of New Zealand may have a better understanding of the risks associated with certain areas or activities.

Nevertheless, exaggerated media portrayals of crime ensure that New Zealand's domestic tourists and residents are affected by the fear of crime. As seen by the Rotorua District Perceptions of Safety Survey 2009, residents themselves are concerned about the impact that crimes have on their community and are aware of signals that indicate danger in their local area (APR Consultants 2009). It is a popular New Zealand tradition to go to the bach or camping ground over the Christmas and New Year's holidays, with many families vacating the city in search of their own slice of paradise near the beach or lake. However, New Year's revellers are also located within these areas, and regions such as the Coromandel Peninsula become hot spots for youth to congregate and celebrate the new year (Koubaridis 2007). The consequences of the mixture of youth, alcohol and revelry often produce inebriation and violence. The reputation for disorder in these areas has grown over the years. They are now reported as 'towns that explode' over New Year's Eve with drunken celebrations and the crimes that follow such as being drunk and disorderly, driving under the influence, theft, burglary, assaults and sexual crimes.

> Nelson proved to be the nation's black spot when it came to the nation's New Year celebrations last night. While revellers nationwide largely behaved themselves, Nelson police were struggling to cope with a number of serious offences, including three reported rapes and an alleged stabbing . . . Senior Sergeant Stu Koefoed said '59 people were arrested. Among the more serious charges were an attempted murder, an indecent assault, three counts of male assaults female and two of assault' . . . Officers also had their work cut out for them on the Coromandel Peninsula, where they were kept busy throughout the night with disorder and liquor ban offences, and a number of assaults and fights. About 155 people were arrested at Whangamata and 38 at Whitianga.
>
> (NZPA 2010)

Residents and tourists alike are confronted with an area that is perceived as having a large increase in crime over the holiday period. The fear of victimization due to this may result in travellers staying at home or going elsewhere. In addition, the usual reports of drunken arrests and violence that occur over New Year are often portrayed on the news, which further associates crime and inebriated revellers with that particular location.

In the case of incidents of serious crime that do not involve the victimization of international tourists, the media report less about how these crimes are an exception to the rule and focus more on the implied innocence of the victim and how the crimes breach the traditional family values that supposedly characterize New Zealand. For example:

> Drunken thugs prevented a young mother and her baby leaving a Wanaka camping ground during a New Year's Eve riot . . . Jorden Wyatt . . . said 'the woman was trying to drive away in her car but a group of young men with shaved heads would not let her go' . . . The riot started at the Albert

Town camping site after the men had rolled over a car they had painted with obscene words and set it alight. Mr Wyatt said . . . 'it was his first time at the Department of Conservation-run camping ground and he would not be going back.'

(New Zealand Herald 2006)

Here the discourse is situated in the production of outrage to produce social censure and unlike reports that involve victims from other countries there are no statements that repudiate challenges to the rural idyll. This may be because the media assume that domestic holidaymakers have less need to buy into the rural idyll when shopping for holidays than their international counterparts.

The problem of volume crime

Although the press often sensationalizes homicide, it is still a fairly rare occurrence in New Zealand (Newbold 2000). Senior Sergeant Nicky Sweetman of the New Zealand Police succinctly describes the core issue: 'Attacks on tourists are not on the increase but they do get a lot of media attention' (stuff.co.nz, 2009). Indeed, the risk of becoming a victim of homicide while on holiday is extremely low (Venditto and Mouzos 2006); instead vehicle crimes against tourists are far more numerous. According to Kazmierow and colleagues (2009), travelling by vehicle is the most accessible and convenient way for a tourist to view the countryside, yet New Zealand, like many other Western countries, has a significant number of vehicle crimes (Statistics New Zealand 2006). What increases the risk is that tourists themselves are susceptible to theft from a motor vehicle, because they believe themselves to be safe thanks to the relaxed atmosphere associated with being on vacation, and it is this that makes holidaymakers complacent where the consideration of crime prevention is concerned (Brunt *et al.* 2000; Pelfrey 1998; Pizam 1999). Losing passports, travel documents and accommodation bookings can be a huge inconvenience for a traveller and so a number of travel organizations have issued warnings about leaving valuables in a car or leaving a car in certain locations (Kazmierow *et al.* 2009). Tourists are naturally vulnerable to crime involving a motor vehicle because of the actions of travelling (Kazmierow *et al.* 2009). By frequenting areas that are conducive to crime, such as isolated car parks or areas with a high turnover of vehicles, and presenting themselves as lucrative targets by failing to take precautions against crime the chances of victimization are greatly increased (Kazmierow *et al.* 2009). Moreover, a higher volume of vehicle crime incidents may cost New Zealand's tourism industry more than the impact of sensationalized media coverage of serious crime. Tourists often spread the news to their friends and family about their time in New Zealand and, as noted by the old dictum, a bad review lasts much longer and spreads further than a positive one.

The Rotorua District Perceptions of Safety Survey indicated that approximately 20 per cent of the respondents felt that factors such as the high crime rate or the possibility of violent crime made Rotorua an unsafe town to live in (APR

Consultants 2009). However, a survey conducted in Britain by Brunt, Mawby and Hambly (2000) indicated that only 9 per cent of holidaymakers felt crime played a considerable role in their choice of destination. Although Brunt and colleagues did not conduct their research in New Zealand, it is possible that their findings highlight an interesting comparison that could be made with the role that crime plays between residents of a location and visiting tourists. As noted by Harper (2001), a common trend is that tourists are more likely to become the victims of larceny, theft or robbery than residents of that particular location (see Mawby in Chapter 8). The features that draw tourists to New Zealand, its scenic beauty and the vision of a pristine rural idyll, also prompt them to visit isolated locations that may put these holidaymakers at greater risk of being victimized (Kazmierow *et al.* 2009; Harper 2001). Potential visitors are not particularly concerned about crime at their destination despite the possibility that their actions will enhance the risk of becoming victims of crime.

Discussion

Research that highlights the relationship between crime and tourism will never be popular with state-run funding institutions and the rest of the tourism industry because of the need to preserve the image of New Zealand as a country that embodies the rural idyll. This work goes some way to fill the paucity of academic literature on this topic but as this is a fairly large hole to fill it can be assumed that much of what has been written here may falter under the weight of future research. Nevertheless, a number of important issues have been raised about the relationship between crime and tourism in New Zealand.

New Zealand owes much of its international reputation as a tranquil rural paradise to Peter Jackson's interpretation of Tolkien's *Lord of the Rings*, which along with other cinematic productions has showcased the beauty of this country to the world. The promotion of New Zealand as a country that embodies the positive characteristics of the rural idyll is strong in the minds of international tourists. However, like other civil societies, New Zealand is a country with no shortage of social problems, which in reality is far from a crime-free paradise. There are also occasions when challenges to the notion of the rural idyll arise from sensationalized media coverage of serious crimes such as homicide, violence and sexual assaults. In this, New Zealand is similar to the majority of Western-style democracies.

Innes's notion of signal crimes and disorders provides a useful means of examining to what degree media accounts of crime elicited fear in prospective holidaymakers, the most serious being when reported crimes generated a signal strong enough to produce avoidance behaviour of some sort. In one instance this avoidance behaviour manifested as a travel warning by the Dutch state to its citizens. The effect that this travel notice had on New Zealand's tourism trade was minimal because Dutch tourism is only a marginal market that accounts for a small percentage of visiting tourists. Whereas some Dutch holidaymakers will have been put off booking a holiday, it is New Zealanders whose fears were more likely to be exacerbated. When an international tourist becomes a victim of serious crime, some residents of the area where the crime occurred express a degree of trepidation regarding the local economy, and they put forward denials such as 'this never happens in our peaceful town'. These denials of danger seek to secure the holidaymaker-friendly image of the rural idyll. Unlike international tourists, domestic tourists are constantly exposed to sensationalized serious crime coverage by New Zealand's media, as well as reports about the victimization of international holidaymakers. So, for the domestic market, it is probable that the image of New Zealand as a rural paradise has never been as strong as it is in the international market. The real threat to visitors to New Zealand remains the risk of becoming a victim of less serious criminal activity such as theft, although many holidaymakers appear to be less concerned about these more mundane volume crimes.

Returning to the earlier analogy with *The Lord of the Rings*, the comparison between New Zealand and the fictional Shire is to some extent correct. Both are places of scenic rural splendour populated by respectable, friendly and well-meaning people, but like most places there are some orcs and goblins to contend with. Therefore, the wizard Gandalf's advice to the Hobbit Frodo about not wearing his ring because it will attract the attention of the evil Ringwraiths is also pertinent to those on vacation in New Zealand. While holidaying, the risks from serious violent crime are minimal but there is wisdom in giving some thought to the protection of the 'precious things'.

11 Visitor perceptions of crime-safety and attitudes towards risk

The case of Table Mountain National Park, Cape Town

Richard George

Introduction

South Africa is admired for its natural beauty, vibrant culture and relative novelty as an international tourist destination. Since 1994, tourism has increasingly been recognized as a key economic growth sector by the South African government and commercial businesses. The government has channelled substantial resources towards tourism development and marketing over the past few years and the country's tourism industry is now one of the fastest-growing contributors to its economy. In 2009, South Africa hosted 9.9 million international visitors, an increase of 3.5 per cent over 2008 (South African Tourism 2010).

Over the last decade, South Africa's major cities – Johannesburg, Durban and Cape Town – alongside other international destinations such as Rio de Janeiro, Mexico City and Kingston, Jamaica, have gained a reputation for being crime-ridden tourist destinations. South Africa reportedly has one of the highest violent crime rates (incidents of murder, rape, car hijackings and assaults) in the world (Altbeker 2005). Since re-admittance to the international community in 1994 (after an era of profound economic and social exclusion under apartheid), the country has received negative media attention as a tourist destination following several high-profile cases involving crime against tourists.

Cape Town, also referred to as the 'Mother City', situated at the southwestern tip of Africa, is considered a popular tourist destination for international, regional and domestic tourists. It boasts numerous world-class tourist attractions such as Robben Island, Table Mountain, Cape Point, the Victoria and Albert Waterfront and idyllic wine farms. Table Mountain National Park (TMNP), which covers over 29,000 hectares, is an urban park on the fringe of the Cape Town metropolis. This situation – being bounded by city limits – has made it difficult to manage and has raised safety and security concerns for TMNP's management.

Table Mountain National Park, South Africa's second most visited tourist attraction, is one of 22 national parks countrywide managed by South African National Parks (SANParks). The Park received approximately 4.3 million visits (including repeat visitors) in 2007 (South African National Parks 2008). However, TMNP has experienced an escalation of criminal activity in recent years, tarnishing its image as a world-class visitor attraction. During 2007, there were 30 reported crime incidents in TMNP (South African National Parks 2008). The majority of these incidents were muggings and theft of visitors' personal belongings from parked vehicles. Most visitors to the park are day visitors – hiking, picnicking or taking a trip on the cable car – which is reflected in the nature of these crime incidents. According to research carried out by South African Police Services (SAPS), 70 per cent of crime victims in TMNP are South Africans (South African National Parks 2008). These and numerous other 'mountain muggings' have been highly publicized in the local and international media and have been condemned by national and local tourism authorities. Furthermore, these crime incidents, along with the associated negative publicity, may have affected tourists' decisions to return to the attraction or to Cape Town in the future. This study focuses on tourist perceptions of crime-safety while visiting TMNP. This makes it a unique study in that most previous research studies have focused on tourist crime at various urban tourist destinations.

Before the study results are presented and discussed, the literature on tourism and crime, tourist perceptions of crime-safety and perceived tourist risk is reviewed.

The association between tourism and crime

Over the last 35 years, there has been a growing body of literature that has investigated the relationship between tourism and crime. The tourism–crime literature can be divided into seven main themes: (i) tourism impacting crime levels; (ii) tourist locations with high crime rates; (iii) tourist crime victimization; (iv) locals and tourists' perceptions of crime; (v) tourists as offenders of crime; (vi) terrorism and tourism; and (vii) tourism crime preventative measures.

Tourism and crime researchers have sought to establish whether the tourism in different locations generates criminal activity. An increase in tourist activities may well result in an escalation of various types of crimes. For example, McPheters and Stronge (1974) reported higher crime rates in the Miami, Florida, tourist season. Similarly, Jud (1975: 328) found that property-related crimes were more associated with tourism in Mexico. A recent study by Walker and Page (2007) looked at patterns of crime in central Scotland and compared locals and visitors in terms of the types of criminal incidents and at what time of day these incidents occurred. The researchers found that tourists are more vulnerable to crimes of dishonesty and motor car theft, and that they are most at risk in the afternoon and early evening. Other tourist areas where increasing crime rates are seen as an externality of tourism development include Hawaii, USA (Chesney-Lind *et al.* 1983; Fujii and Mak 1979; Fukunaga 1975), Tonga (Urbanowicz 1977), Cairns, Gold Coast, Australia (Kelly 1993; Prideaux and Dunn 1995), North Carolina, USA (Nicholls 1976), and the USA in general (Pizam 1982). Most of these studies, which were confined to a single city or state, found that tourism does contribute to increased crime rates. However, several researchers found it difficult to measure accurately the direct link between increases in crime levels with the development of tourism. Several studies examined this association in specific countries, including Mexico (Lin and Loeb 1977; Loeb and Lin 1981) and the USA (Pizam 1982). Conversely, these studies did not find a significant relationship between tourism and crime. A number of issues were raised by several of the tourism–crime researchers, including limitations in available tourist crime victim data, how crime can be measured, and the extent to which tourism can be quantified (Chesney-Lind *et al*. 1983; Fujii and Mak 1980; Jud 1975). The literature unanimously reports that in areas where large numbers of tourists are present during peak season criminals have attempted to benefit illegally from their presence.

There is sufficient evidence amongst the tourism–crime literature to suggest that acts of crime committed against tourists will have a negative impact on tourist arrivals (Alleyne and Boxill 2003; Bloom 1996; Cavlek 2002; Dimanche and Lepetic 1999; Elliot and Ryan 1993; Fujii and Mak 1980; Kelly 1993; Levantis and Gani 2000; Pelfrey 1998; Pizam and Mansfeld 1996: 1; Prideaux and Dunn 1995; Tarlow 2000). The general consensus amongst these researchers is that any threat to the safety of a tourist (i.e. criminal activities against tourists) along with associated media publicity (i.e. news reporting, government travel warnings) is likely to negatively affect a specific location, be it a destination, region, country or neighbouring countries. The murder of a British couple on their honeymoon and the rape of another British tourist in Antigua in 2008 severely tarnished the image of the Caribbean island and caused a downturn in visitor arrivals (https://webmail.glos.ac.uk/exchweb/bin/redir.asp?URL=http://eturbonews.com). In recent years, the upsurge in murders, rapes, gang violence and armed robberies has tarnished the flattering perception of the Caribbean as a 'paradise' for tourists. A study by Alleyne and Boxill (2003) also found that crime had a negative impact on tourist arrivals to Jamaica. They found that respondents who felt most unsafe were those who did not stay in the all-inclusive resorts, possibly making them more vulnerable to crime. Most travellers will seek safer and secure destinations and avoid those that have high crime rates. As Richter and Waugh (1986: 230) note, 'when concerns for wellbeing are perceived to be excessive, tourists will cancel, postpone, or choose alternative destinations that involve less risk'.

Research has also focused on tourist crime victimization at certain destinations including Hawaii, USA (Chesney-Lind and Lind 1986), Washington, DC, USA (Demos 1992), Guam (Pinhey and Iverson 1994), Miami, Florida, USA (Crotts 1996; Schiebler, Crotts and Hollinger 1996), Malaga, Spain (Stangeland 1998), Sydney, New South Wales, Australia (Allen 1999), Barbados, Caribbean (de Alburquerque and McElroy 1999), New Orleans, Louisiana, USA (Dimanche and Lepetic 1999), and Budapest, Hungary (Michalkó 2003). Certain tourist locations and tourists, therefore, have been found to be vulnerable to crime.

Numerous theories drawn from the field of human ecology have been used to help explain why certain locations in tourist destinations appear to expose tourists to increased incidences of crime victimization (Crotts 1996). Two widely cited theories are the Routine Activities Theory (Cohen and Felson 1979) and the Hot Spots Theory (Sherman *et al*. 1989). The Routine Activities Theory views criminal acts in the course of their everyday, routine activities such as work and leisure; criminals need to satisfy themselves by taking something of value from victims (Cohen and Felson 1979). The theory postulates that, in order for a predatory crime to occur, three basic elements are required: a suitable victim or target, a motivated offender and a relative absence of police and private security forces (or 'guardianship'). Any one of these components missing is enough to prevent the criminal act from occurring (Crotts 1996: 4). The Hot Spots Theory examines locations which provide convergent opportunities in which predatory crime can occur (Sherman *et al.* 1989). Areas ranging from tourist resorts to transportation hubs may be considered by criminals as desirable locations for conducting crime, whether against tourist or locals.

Perceptions of crime-safety and its effects on tourist revisitation

A research topic of particular relevance to this study is the impact of victimization and perceptions of fear of crime on a tourist's decision to revisit a destination. Barker, Page and Meyer (2003) propose that tourists' fear of crime and threat to personal safety are just as important as the issue of tourist victimization in terms of assessing their impact on tourist behaviour. A perception of high crime rates is likely to negatively affect a destination's image, deter visitors, reduce the desire to revisit, and spread negative word-of-mouth recommendations.

Sönmez and Graefe (1998) found that previous international travel experience influenced individuals' perceptions of safety/risk, and in turn affected their future travel behaviour. Sönmez and Graefe concluded that a traveller's perceptions are of more detriment to travel decision making than actual safety and risk at a particular destination. The researchers, however, examined this relationship in the context of perceived terrorism risk.

Mawby, Brunt and Hambly (2000) conducted an investigation on a sample of UK holidaymakers – victims and non-victims – in relation to revisiting destinations. The researchers found that 56 per cent of tourist victims and 55 per cent of non-victims indicated that they would definitely return to the destination affected. Thus, in Mawby and colleagues' (2000) study, victimization does not appear to have a major influence on a tourist's decision to return to a destination.

George (2003) investigated tourists' perceptions of crime-safety whilst visiting Cape Town, South Africa. George found that little more than half (54 per cent) of visitors claimed that they would probably return to Cape Town even though they had encountered a criminal incident or felt that their life was in danger during their stay. The study showed that there was a negative association between having been a victim of crime or feeling unsafe and the likelihood of return. In addition, the study found that purpose of the respondents' visit was a significant factor in their perception of crime-safety. Respondents who were travelling on holiday and visiting friends and relatives were less likely to return than were business tourists.

Holcomb and Pizam's (2006) study of US travellers found that personal theft or knowing someone who has been a victim of theft while on a trip did not affect the likelihood of visiting a destination where the theft occurred. Notably, the manner in which the crime report was handled by authorities was found to be the only factor to have a statistical effect on the likelihood to travel to the affected destination. Holcomb and Pizam's study revealed that over 41 per cent of the respondents gave a negative evaluation to the manner in which authorities handled the crime report. Holcomb and Pizam's results support those of Mawby and colleagues (2000) and George (2003), who found that tourists who experience personal theft or know someone who has had such an experience would still return to the destination.

Perceived tourist risk

Consumer decisions are frequently made under a certain level of risk (Blackwell *et al.* 2006: 123). Risky decisions are defined as 'choices among alternatives that can be described by probability distributions over possible outcomes' (Weber and Bottom 1989: 114). In addition, at least one of the possible outcomes must be undesirable (or at least less desirable than the others) for risk to exist. Perceived risk refers to the individual's perceptions of the uncertainty and negative consequences of buying a product or service (Dowling and Staelin 1994), performing a certain activity or choosing a certain lifestyle (Reisinger and Mavondo 2005). This element of risk becomes more evident during the decision making by prospective tourists. It is logical to assume that they will compare destination alternatives according to perceived benefits and costs. These costs may be monetary (getting to the destination, accommodation, travel insurance and so on), physical distance, time costs and risk associated with the journey such as accident, sickness or crime. Tourists, like other consumers, would be interested in minimizing any risk, thus helping them to maximize the quality of their travel experience (Fodness and Murray 1998).

To certain groups of individuals, 'safety' or 'feeling safe' is an important factor that affects destination selection. Dowling and Staelin (1994) acknowledged that the consumer involvement with the purchase decision influences the individual's perception of risk. Tourism activity is considered a high-involvement purchase decision. There are numerous risks and uncertainties associated with travel. For example, the 'outcome of a decision' such as the risk of choosing the wrong destination and the 'consequences of a decision' including consuming valuable time and money, health and danger risks, and dissatisfaction as a result of the quality of services at the destination not living up to expectations. According to Moutinho (1987), the degree of risk may vary with the costs involved in a decision and the degree of uncertainty that the decision will lead to satisfaction. Cook and McCleary (1983) identified time, budget and physical distance as constraints prospective tourists take into account when evaluating destinations. Similarly, van Raaij and Francken (1984) suggested that travel decisions are likely to be made based on weighing constraints against economic situations. Van Raaij and Francken (1984) noted that tourists might choose less expensive options or decide to abort travel plans during economic hardship. Crompton (1977) postulated that tourists make a destination decision after time and money constraints have been measured against destination image. These findings indicate that tourists, when choosing where to holiday, weigh up the perceived costs and benefits associated with destination alternatives.

Five major risk factors in terms of tourism safety have been identified in previous research studies: terrorism (Aziz 1995), war and political instability (Gartner and Shen 1992), health concerns/spread of disease (Carter 1998), natural disasters (Faulkner and Vikulov 2001) and crime (Pizam and Mansfeld 1996). It would therefore be reasonable to assume that tourists are just as likely to make destination decisions based on perceived risk from various threats such as high crime rates at a destination. For instance, if a holiday destination is perceived as too high a crime risk, consumers then may make alternative decisions.

Perceptions of risk may vary depending on the types of risk perceived. In a study of travel and risk, Roehl and Fesenmaier (1992) identified seven types of risk associated with travel decisions. These were equipment, financial, physical, psychological, satisfaction, social and time risks. The researchers found that social risk did not appear to be related to the perceptions of risk associated with leisure travel. Roehl and Fesenmaier further classified respondents into three types of risk-taking tourists: risk neutral, functional risk, and place risk. Most relevant to this study is place risk, which refers to tourists who develop a risk perception based on the risk factors related to the destination and its political, social and/ or security situation. Roehl and Fesenmaier (1992) found that those respondents perceiving the most risk were least likely to have relied on information sources. This finding contrasts with consumer behaviour literature according to which information search is typically used as a risk reduction strategy (for example, Dowling and Staelin 1994; Roselius 1971), and is inconsistent with several tourism researchers who noted that sources of information act as risk minimizers or 'decision reinforcers' (Um and Crompton 1990; Witt and Moutinho 1989).

Nevertheless, several researchers noted a positive relationship between past travel experience and future travel intentions (Chen and Gursoy 2001; Goodrich 1978; Mazursky 1989; Perdue 1985; Sönmez and Graefe 1998). In particular, Chen and Gursoy (2001) found conclusively that past trip experience induce tourists to perceive less risk and feel safer when travelling to new destinations. Mazursky (1989) suggested that future travel is influenced not only by the extent but by the nature of previous travel experience as well. Mazursky suggested that personal travel experience may be more of an influence than information acquired from external sources.

Besides types of risk and individual past travel experience, tourists' perceptions of risk may vary according to factors such as an individual's age, gender, nationality, personality type, travel arrangements, culture, motivation and tourist role (Lepp and Gibson 2003; Reisinger and Mavondo 2005, 2006). Gibson and Yiannakis (2002), in their study of tourist role preference over a life period, found that preference for risk-related tourism tended to decrease with age. In terms of gender and its influence on perceptions of risk in tourism, the literature is inconsistent. Gibson and Jordan (1998) reported that women are more susceptible to risk than men. Likewise, other researchers noted that preference for risk in tourism differs according to gender (Carr 2001; Kinnaird and Hall 1996; Kozak, Crotts and Law 2007). However, Sönmez and Graefe (1998) did not find gender to influence an individual's perceptions of terrorism risk. Similarly, Lepp and Gibson (2003) in their study of US students' perceptions of risk associated with international tourism did not find gender to affect perceptions of crime risk. Research has found that an individual's perceptions of risk associated with international tourism also vary according to nationality. As Richardson and Crompton (1988) noted, travellers of different nationalities may perceive the same risk differently. For instance, Barker and colleagues (2003) found that international tourists attending the 2000 America's Cup in Auckland, New Zealand, placed a higher importance in demands for safety than domestic tourists. Seddighi, Nuttall and Theocharous (2001) also reported that travel agents' perceptions of risk are influenced by nationality. Fuchs and Reichel (2004) in their study of tourists to Israel found that quality and level of perceived risk as well as risk reduction strategies vary according to cultural background and nationality. Reisinger and Mavondo (2006) revealed significant differences in travel risk and safety perceptions among tourists from different cultures. For instance, the researchers found that US and Australian tourists perceived more risk and felt less safe than British, Greek and Canadian tourists. Tourism safety research by George (2003) and Barker and colleagues (2003) revealed that differences in length of stay at the destination affect the exposure to risk and need to be considered in any interpretation of relative levels of crime risk faced by tourists. Lepp and Gibson (2003) found that perception of risk associated with international tourism varies depending on the tourist role and tourists' preferences for familiarity or novelty. Their study, however, did not find that tourists seeking familiarity perceived higher levels of crime-related risk than those seeking novelty.

In summary, the literature on tourist risk perceptions suggests that, to understand the perception of crime-safety and risk associated with tourism, individual factors such as past travel experience, personality, age, gender, culture and nationality should be taken into account.

Purpose of the study

This study has three main objectives. The first objective aims to test various causal links between tourist perceptions of crime-safety and their intentions to revisit and recommend TMNP. The second objective is to determine whether visitor attitudes towards risk moderate these direct relationships. The third objective is to identify individual factors which may significantly influence visitor perceptions of crime-safety.

Methodology

Sample

The sample consisted of a total of 303 respondents interviewed during their visit to TMNP. The survey was undertaken from mid-June to mid-July 2008, during Cape Town's winter season. Visitors to TMNP were interviewed at six strategically chosen points: Signal Hill, Kirstenbosch Gardens, Lion's Head, Newlands Forrest, Cecelia Forrest and Table Mountain Cableway. Figure 11.1 shows these

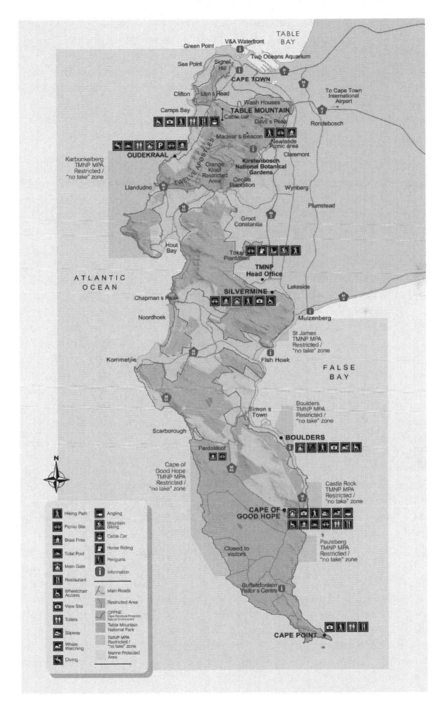

Figure 11.1 Table Mountain National Park (TMNP) within the Cape Peninsula, Western Cape.

six sites. These locations were chosen as it was felt that the majority of visitors visiting TMNP would congregate at one or more of these points and would therefore provide a reasonable representation of the target survey population. Respondents were specifically interviewed as they were exiting the various TMNP sites in order to ensure that they had some experience upon which to form perceptions of safety and security in the park.

Research instrument

The research instrument used a self-administered, two-page structured questionnaire. The first set of questions in the survey employed ordinal scales. Respondents were asked about the nature of their visit to TMNP: how many times they had visited TMNP, whom they were visiting with, reasons for visiting the Park and how aware they were of incidences of crime in TMNP.

Subsequently, respondents were asked whether or not they were aware of any incidences of crime or had previously encountered crime in TMNP. If they answered 'yes' to indicate awareness of criminal incidence, they were asked to specify where they had obtained information about the incident (TV, magazines, newspapers; friends and/or family; other tourists; tourist guides; travel advisory website; or other). If they answered 'yes' to indicate having personally experienced crime in TMNP, respondents were asked to specify the type of crime that they had experienced.

Respondents were then asked, using a five-point Likert scale, how safe they thought Cape Town and TMNP to be, how risky they thought their visit to TMNP was, how willing they were to recommend TMNP and whether or not they would return to TMNP. In addition, this part of the questionnaire classified respondents' risk profiles.

The final part of the questionnaire included user questions relating to respondent's purpose of visit (i.e. holiday/leisure, visiting friends and relatives or business trip) and demographic questions (i.e. gender, age and nationality). With the exception of one open-ended question that asked about the type of crime experienced, all other questions were closed. The survey questions were tested in a pilot study carried out with respondents who had visited TMNP.

For this study an attempt was made to test causal relationships between crime-safety perceptions and revisitation and likelihood to recommend TMNP, as well as the moderating influence of attitudes towards risk on these direct relations. Prior to conducting linear regression analyses, reliability and validity were assessed on the two main constructs (visitor perceptions of TMNP and visitor attitudes towards crime-safety). Summated scales were created by summing the scores on individual items and dividing by the number of items in the scale.

Finally, tests of one-way ANOVA were carried out to test whether various individual factors such as age, gender, purpose of visit, and frequency of visit influenced respondents' crime-safety perceptions.

Findings and discussion

Demographic characteristics

Of a total sample of 303 respondents, 52 per cent (157) were male and 48 per cent (146) were female. The majority of respondents (69 per cent) were under the age of 44. Most visitors (43 per cent) were South Africans, 23 per cent were from the UK, 8 per cent from the USA, 5 per cent from Germany and 4 per cent from the Netherlands. A high ratio of local to overseas visitors was expected given that the research survey was carried out during the months of June and July, in the middle of the Cape's winter season. The composite of international visitors is consistent with SA Tourism's – the country's national tourism organization – main target overseas markets (UK, Germany, the USA and the Netherlands) (South African Tourism 2008).

Frequency of visits

Nearly half of the study respondents (46 per cent) were first-time visitors to TMNP, whereas 22 per cent of respondents had previously visited the Park between two and five times. Interestingly, over a quarter of respondents (25.7 per cent) had visited TMNP on 10 or more occasions. It can be assumed that many of these respondents were local 'Capetonians' and thus possessed a fair amount of experience in visiting the Park.

Size of travelling party

A majority of respondents (95 per cent) were visiting TMNP with other people; only 5 per cent were visiting alone. Of those who were visiting TMNP with others, 40 per cent of respondents were accompanied by family members and 45 per cent by friends, while 18 per cent were part of a tour group. As far as reason for visiting TMNP was concerned, 33 per cent of respondents were visiting to hike, 11 per cent to picnic, 30 per cent to use the cable-car and 39 per cent for sightseeing.

Experiences of crime incidents

With regards to incidents of crime, over half of respondents (55 per cent) had heard about crime in TMNP. Of these respondents, over one-third of respondents (36 per cent) had heard about crime incidents in TMNP from the media (TV/ newspapers), 27 per cent from friends and relatives, and 7 per cent from other visitors.

Of the total sample, 10 were found to have personally experienced crime (either mugging or theft of belongings) on a previous visit to the Park. All but one of the respondents who had previously experienced crime in TMNP were South Africans. This finding is consistent with South African Police Services' (SAPS) statistics which indicate that 70 per cent of crime victims in TMNP are local visitors (South African National Parks 2008). In general, most of these victims had visited TMNP on numerous occasions (five victims had visited TMNP more than 10 times), thus increasing their likelihood of falling victim to crime (see Table 11.1).

Awareness of crime

Table 11.2 shows the cross-tabulation of nationality of respondents and whether they had heard about crime in TMNP. Results suggest that South African visitors were far more likely to have heard about crime in TMNP than overseas visitors. Indeed, 81 per cent of South African visitors had heard about the problem of crime in TMNP. This finding is not entirely surprising given that a number of crime incidents in TMNP have been reported in the local media over the last several years.

Visitor perceptions of crime-safety in TMNP

Cronbach alpha and composite reliability of two main constructs, visitor perceptions of TMNP is unsafe and visitor attitudes towards risk, were at acceptable levels (α and $\rho_c \geq .69$). Individual items measuring each construct had item-to-total correlations well above .40, suggestive of internal consistency. Completely standardized solutions of the items loaded $\geq .50$ on their factors, and thus suggestive of convergent validity (see Table 11.3). However, the AVE (averages) of the two constructs were below the reasonable threshold of .50; therefore, items designed for visitors perceptions of TMNP is unsafe and visitors attitudes towards risk are relatively weak indicators of the two factors and cannot capture the necessary variance. Additionally, Table 11.4 demonstrates that both measurement models had excellent model fit.

Table 11.1 Profiles of TMNP crime victims

Incidents	Nature of crime	Nationality	Gender	Age	No. of previous visits
1	Mugging	RSA	Male	24	6–10
2	Theft (from parked car)	RSA	Male	41	10+
3	Mugging	RSA	Female	18	2–5
4	Mugging	RSA	Male	23	10+
5	Mugging	RSA	Female	22	10+
6	Mugging	RSA	Female	30	10+
7	Mugging	Other African	Male	32	1
8	Theft (from parked car)	RSA	Female	23	1
9	Mugging	RSA	Female	34	1
10	Mugging	RSA	Female	58	10+

Table 11.2 Cross-tabulation of 'heard of crime' for each nationality group

Heard of crime	SA	UK	Germany	Netherlands	Other Europe	N. America	S. America	Australia	Asia	Other Africa	Total
Yes	106	22	6	4	10	8	2	3	3	2	166
No	24	48	10	9	13	23	4	1	3	2	137
Total	130	70	16	13	23	31	6	4	6	4	303

Table 11.3 Summary of reliability and validity scores

Constructs and indicators[a]	α^b	$\rho_i{}^c$	$\rho_c{}^d$	$\rho_v{}^e$	λ^f	t-value
Visitor perceptions of TMNP	.76		.69	.31		
TMNP is unsafe*		.42			.53	8.76
I might fall victim to crime		.50			.55	9.00
TMNP is just an unsafe as other attractions*		.46			.60	10.05
People have told me that TMNP is dangerous		.56			.64	10.95
I felt worried about my personal safety		.58			.66	11.32
I will tell other people to be careful of crime in TMNP		.54			.59	9.92
Visitor attitudes towards risk	.70		.70	.38		
I like to take risks*		.49			.62	9.79
I live life on the edge		.52			.67	10.51
I like to take chances*		.40			.47	7.24
I like to gamble on things		.51			.67	10.46

Notes
a   Measures were collated in the form of a five-point Likert scale.
b   Cronbach alphas are reported.
c   Average inter-item correlations are reported.
d   Composite reliabilities are reported.
e   Average Variances Extracted are reported.
f   Factor loadings from completely standardized solution are reported.
*   This indicator is reversed before it is included in the calculations.

Table 11.4 Confirmatory factor analysis: summary of Model Fit Indices

	χ^2	d.f.	p-value	GFI	RMSEA	NNFI	CFI	ECVI
Visitor perceptions of TMNP (unsafe)								
Hypothesized 6-factor 1st-order model	25.35	9	.003	.97	.078	.96	.98	.16
Visitor attitudes towards risk								
Hypothesized 4-factor 1st-order model	2.47	2	.29	1.00	.026	.99	1.00	.061

Univariate statistics also demonstrate on average that visitors do not feel that Cape Town is an unsafe city (refer to Table 11.5). Overall, the majority of respondents agreed that TMNP was a safe destination, over 70 per cent of respondents agreeing to this statement and only 13.5 per cent disagreeing (question 9 in survey). Likewise, most visitors agreed that they would recommend and return to TMNP.

Table 11.5 Univariate statistics for summated scales and single-item measures

Scales and measures	N	Mean*	Standard deviation
Cape Town is an unsafe city	303	2.44	.994
Visitor perceptions that TMNP is unsafe	303	2.58	.725
Visitor attitudes towards risk	303	2.90	.780
I plan to revisit TMNP in the future	303	4.34	.662
I will recommend TMNP	303	4.47	.591
I will not return to TMNP for fear of my safety	303	4.41	.549
I will not recommend TMNP because it is not safe	303	4.44	.605

* Based on 1 – 5 scale where 1=strongly disagree and 5=strongly agree.

Respondents who visited TMNP frequently were more likely to warn other people to be careful of crime in the Park (see Table 11.6). In addition, as the number of respondents' visits to TMNP increased, their perceptions of an unsafe environment (both the city of Cape Town and TMNP) increased. Furthermore, the more frequently respondents visited the Park, the more they felt they were likely to be a victim of crime. This finding may well be attributed to visitors being made aware of crime in TMNP and exposure to various crime-safety initiatives such as signage and Visitor Safety Officers (VSOs) on patrol in the Park.

Respondents' perceptions of crime-safety can also be explained by respondents' age, nationality, and purpose of visit. The test for ANOVA found that age influences visitors' perceptions of TMNP being dangerous ($F = 2.08$). Thus, as respondents' age increased (up to 55 years) they were more likely to have felt worried about their personal safety. This is consistent with Gibson and Yiannakis (2002), who reported that preference for risk in tourism decreases with age.

Respondents from North America, South Africa and the UK feared for their personal safety in TMNP more than those visitors from Germany and the Netherlands. This supports Reisinger and Mavondo's (2006) finding that international tourists' perceptions of safety vary among tourists from different cultures. South Africans (domestic tourists) were also more likely to inform other people about crime in TMNP. Most South African respondents (82 per cent) had heard about crime in TMNP and were therefore likely to warn others about the safety concerns.

With reference to tourist's purpose of visit and its effect on perception of travel risk, respondents visiting Cape Town for visiting friends and relatives (VFR) reasons were more likely to feel unsafe in both Cape Town and in TMNP than those visitors on business and those on holiday. In addition, the study found that VFR tourists were more likely to feel that they would be a victim of crime in TMNP than those tourists on business or those on holiday. This is consistent with George's (2003) finding that purpose of visit is an important factor in visitors' perceptions of crime-safety. These findings might be explained by the fact that friends and relatives were more aware of crime issues in TMNP and in turn likely

Table 11.6 One-way ANOVA results of variations of TMNP visitor perceptions of crime-safety

Factors	CT unsafe	TMNP unsafe*	Fall victim	Unsafe attraction*	TMNP danger	Fear safety	Tell others crime	Not rtn TMNP*	Not rec TMNP*	Not rtn TMNP fear safety	Not rec TMNP fear safety
No. of visits	$F = 4.52^c$	$F = 7.23^c$	$F = 8.94^c$	$F = 4.75^c$	$F = 6.04^c$	$F = 5.33^c$	$F = 10.49^c$	$F = 16.71^c$	$F = 4.22^b$	$F = 9.00^c$	$F = 1.71$
1	2.41	2.13	2.88	2.28	2.43	2.06	2.51	4.04	4.30	4.30	4.27
2–5	2.45	2.20	3.29	2.59	2.61	2.00	2.79	4.52	4.67	4.45	4.36
6–10	2.16	2.16	3.32	2.32	3.11	2.00	3.21	4.68	4.58	4.37	4.37
>10	2.55	2.65	3.33	2.72	3.08	2.31	3.49	4.67	4.59	4.68	4.40
Heard of crime	$F = 2.57^a$	$F = 6.55^c$	$F = 7.30^c$	$F = 4.48^b$	$F = 4.70^c$	$F = 1.18$	$F = 12.05^c$	$F = 12.63^c$	$F = 3.04^a$	$F = 8.11^c$	$F = 2.97^a$
Yes	2.52	2.46	3.32	2.61	2.92	2.16	3.25	4.55	4.54	4.52	4.38
No	2.34	2.07	2.86	2.28	2.38	2.05	2.41	4.09	4.39	4.33	4.27
Gender	$F = 1.94$	$F = 0.78$	$F = 0.37$	$F = 1.03$	$F = 1.57$	$F = 0.56$	$F = 1.95^a$	$F = 1.06$	$F = 1.48$	$F = 1.78$	$F = 1.07$
Male	2.46	2.29	3.08	2.51	2.82	2.19	3.04	4.35	4.52	4.46	4.37
Female	2.41	2.27	3.15	2.41	2.52	2.02	2.68	4.34	4.42	4.40	4.29
Nationality	$F = 1.08$	$F = 1.75$	$F = 0.98$	$F = 0.47$	$F = 0.54$	$F = 2.41^a$	$F = 1.90$	9.86^b	11.18^c	4.39^b	3.75^b
SA	2.43	2.40	3.24	2.65	2.87	2.15	3.05	4.65	4.58	4.49	4.39
UK	2.25	2.10	2.99	2.20	2.33	2.13	2.87	4.16	4.42	4.45	4.38
Germany	2.19	2.38	2.94	2.56	2.69	1.69	2.75	4.12	4.63	4.62	4.31

Netherlands	2.38	2.15	2.92	2.69	2.46	1.92	2.85	3.85	3.92	4.31	4.00
USA	2.50	2.23	3.04	2.35	2.92	2.15	2.62	4.12	4.54	4.42	4.46
	$F = 1.19$	$F = 1.80$	$F = 1.02$	$F = 0.95$	$F = 2.08^a$	$F = 0.31$	$F = 0.80$	$F = 0.73$	$F = 1.37$	$F = 3.12^a$	$F = 0.85$
Age											
<24	2.58	2.22	3.19	2.54	2.79	2.05	2.91	4.35	4.47	4.47	4.32
25–34	2.40	2.27	2.99	2.43	2.67	2.01	2.45	4.41	4.51	4.43	4.27
35–44	2.31	2.41	3.22	2.47	2.84	2.26	3.29	4.29	4.45	4.47	4.53
45–54	2.33	2.12	3.14	2.61	2.73	2.90	2.90	4.27	4.45	4.39	4.18
≥55	2.35	2.41	2.82	2.24	1.97	1.88	2.85	4.26	4.44	4.32	4.47
	$F = 5.62^c$	$F = 3.36^b$	$F = 3.16^a$	$F = 1.87$	$F = 2.13^a$	$F = 1.66$	$F = 3.63^b$	$F = 9.04^c$	$F = 3.76^a$	$F = 4.13^b$	$F = 1.16$
Purpose of visit											
Holiday	2.32	2.10	2.94	2.27	2.43	1.96	2.58	4.12	4.35	4.38	4.37
VFR	2.74	2.42	3.26	2.76	2.85	2.42	3.08	4.44	4.52	4.24	4.24
Business	2.36	2.27	3.16	2.39	2.89	2.18	3.00	4.48	4.61	4.50	4.27

*Reverse coded item

[a] $p < .10$, [b] $p < .01$, [c] $p < .001$

to have warned their visitors. In addition, as stated earlier, almost a third of visitors (27 per cent) had heard about incidents of crime in TMNP from friends and relatives. Business and holiday tourists may be less likely to have been informed (from the media, tourism businesses) about crime-safety issues in TMNP, and therefore may well be less fearful of crime in TMNP than VFR travellers.

Gender did not appear to be a significant demographic factor affecting visitors' perceptions of crime-safety in TMNP. This finding is consistent with other tourism research that did not find gender to influence an individual's perception of risk. Notably, Sönmez and Graefe (1998) did not find gender to influence an individual's perception of terrorism risk. Similarly, Lepp and Gibson (2003) reported that gender did not influence a tourist's perception of crime-related risk, as did George (2003), who did not find gender to be a factor affecting visitors' perceptions of safety in Cape Town.

Linear regression analyses revealed that, although visitors perceived TMNP as unsafe, they are still likely to recommend TMNP to others ($\beta = .20$, t-value = 3.62) (see Table 11.7). In addition, the results show that, although visitors in general perceived TMNP to be unsafe, they are still likely to return to TMNP ($\beta = .22$, t-value = 3.69). Furthermore, 'risk' does appear to affect the relationship between visitor perceptions of unsafety and their likelihood to recommend ($\beta = .03$, t-value = .12) and return to TMNP ($\beta = .29$, t-value = 1.06). These results are supported by the findings of Mawby and colleagues (2000), who in a survey of British tourists found that 56 per cent of victims and 55 per cent of non-victims would definitely return to the destination where the crime occurred. Similarly, George (2003) found that 54 per cent of visitors to Cape Town claimed that they would very likely return even though they had encountered an incident or felt that that their life was in danger during their stay in the city.

Conclusion and recommendations

There is a wealth of literature on the association between perceived risk and tourist decision making and behaviour. However, previous research has not addressed crime-safety perceptions and risk attitudes in a particular subsector (e.g. visitor attractions) of the tourism industry. More specifically, it has not examined the influence of tourists' perceptions towards crime-safety and intentions to revisit and recommend a particular tourist attraction. This research study is also unique in that it focuses on a rural area (a national park) situated in close proximity to a metropolitan city. It tested these causal links within a tourist attraction and determined whether risk attitudes influence them. Finally, the study assessed which individual factors influence crime-safety of visitors and attitudes towards risk.

According to this study's results, regardless of whether tourists perceived TMNP to be an unsafe environment, they were still willing to revisit and recommend the attraction. Since most respondents were domestic visitors, this finding could be attributed to public attitudes of patriotism and a sense of national pride in their city's iconic tourist attraction. This finding could also be indicative of a host

Table 11.7 Summary of regression effects: linear and moderated regression models

Independent variable (reference level stated first)	Dependent variable: likelihood of recommending TMNP to others for fear of safety					
	β^a	*t-value*	β	*t-value*	β^b	*t-value*
Visitor perceptions of TMNP is unsafe	.20	3.62**	.17	.80 (NS)		
Moderator: Visitor attitudes towards risk					.03	.12 (NS)
F-statistic	13.07*		4.55**			
Degrees of freedom	301,1		299,3			
R^2	.01		.04			

	Dependent variable: likelihood of returning TMNP for fear of safety					
	β^a	*t-value*	β	*t-value*	*Interaction effect*	*t-value*
Visitor perceptions of TMNP is unsafe	.22	3.90***	.01	.06 (NS)		
Moderator: Visitor attitudes towards risk					.29	1.06 (NS)
F-statistic	15.17***		6.96***			
Degrees of freedom	301,2		299,3			
R^2	.00		.01			

Notes
a Standardized regression coefficient is reported.
b Unstandardized regression coefficients are reported.
*$p < .10$, **$p < .01$, ***$p < .001$, NS=non-significant.

population that is well adjusted to living in a society with a high crime rate. These results are consistent with those studies carried out by Mawby and colleagues (2000) and George (2003), which found that tourists were still likely to return to the affected destinations.

In addition, respondents' attitudes towards risk do not appear to influence the link between crime-safety and their intentions to revisit or recommend TMNP. This non-significant finding may be explained by the fact that most respondents were South Africans, who are perhaps more willing to tolerate higher risk than other nationalities. This is supported by Hofstede's (2005: 168–9) widely cited work on national culture, which found that individuals from low uncertainty avoidance (UA) cultures (risk-tolerant) – such as South Africa – are generally more comfortable with situations involving risk than high UA cultures (risk-avoiding).

This study results indicate that a number of individual factors influence perceptions of travel crime-safety and risk. It found that age, nationality, frequency of visits and purpose of visit influenced tourist perceptions of crime-safety in TMNP. In particular, domestic tourists and international tourists have different perceptions of crime-safety. Local visitors generally have lower perceptions of crime-safety and possess greater awareness of incidents of crime in TMNP than overseas visitors. Potential TMNP visitors could therefore be segmented according to purpose of visit and nationality, and then targeted to ensure that safety communications and messages are tailored towards these different users. Such targeted safety messages may then encourage a change of visitor behaviour and improve perceptions.

Although it is difficult to prevent criminal activity in TMNP entirely, the management should continue to prepare itself for the occurrence of such incidents through crisis planning and collaboration between stakeholders, citizens and visitors. A unified effort and involvement of all stakeholders are required to combat crime against local and international visitors. In particular, cooperation with the private sector tourism industry responsible for informing visitors concerning safety and security is paramount. Safety and security resources such as additional park rangers and policing may be required to protect visitors and provide a safe experience for visitors to TMNP.

In terms of future tourism–crime research, the study could be repeated during the peak season in TMNP to ascertain if a seasonal component changes crime-safety perceptions across different nationalities. Further work is called for to determine the level of awareness of current safety initiatives in TMNP and whether or not these initiatives are effective in altering visitors' perceptions of safety and security. Another study could be carried out to assess the impact of physical risk perception – the risk of being physically injured in an accident – on visitor decision making and behaviour at TMNP.

The study could also be replicated at other visitor attractions in destinations perceived to have high crime rates in order to gain insight into the effects of perceived risk crime on visitation and visitor behaviour. Differences in crime-safety perceptions in other sectors of the tourism industry (e.g. accommodation, transportation) could also be examined to build a more comprehensive picture of the differences among these sectors as perceived by tourists of different nationalities. Finally, further research might consider analysing the differences in crime-safety and risk perceptions and intentions to travel, on respondents from different education levels and occupations and at various life-cycle stages.

12 Crime and safety within caravan populations

An Australian survey[1]

Elaine Barclay and R. I. Mawby

Introduction

Caravanning and camping are popular leisure pastimes in most Western countries, particularly Australia. In fact caravan and camping has been the fastest growing domestic tourism sector in Australia over the past 10 years. This is in stark contrast to the overall slump in domestic tourism particularly since the economic downturn of 2008 (CCIA 2010). Caravanning and camping provide the freedom to tour at one's own leisure, access to prime locations and camaraderie with like-minded people. Most importantly these activities are affordable. In Australia, families form 60 per cent of the market, with many leasing a caravan site on a semi-permanent basis for weekend and annual holidays. Seniors, those over the age of 55, account for 21 per cent of the market. This group comprises cashed-up retirees or pensioners commonly known as *Grey Nomads* and their numbers are increasing. Some circle Australia several times and their recreational vehicle becomes their permanent home. A further 7 per cent of the market is international tourists mostly from the UK, Germany and other European countries (CCIA 2010).

Little is known about safety and security within these populations. Yet campers and caravanners are likely to be vulnerable to crime because being in a 'leisure state' they are often nonchalant about their personal safety and security (Prideaux and Dunn 1995). Crime and safety within caravan parks is an issue that has not been previously researched in Australia. Official crime data provide no specific data on crime within caravan parks. Nor is it a subject that the caravan park industry has been keen to discuss. As with crime and tourism in general, in a classic refutation of the adage that 'all publicity is good publicity' there is a reluctance to assess whether or not a problem exists.

However, as other chapters in this volume testify, it is clear that both tourists and tourism are closely associated with crime. In Australia (Prideaux 1996; Prideaux and Dunn 1995; Ross 1992; Walmsley *et al.* 1983) as well as elsewhere, there is very little research to identify variations between different groups of holidaymakers or the different types of accommodation they choose. In this context, for example, there is no evidence about whether tourists who stay on park sites are more worried about or at risk of crime and disorder than those staying in hotels (Mawby *et al.* 2010). Nor do we know if there are variations between caravan parks in different areas. Given the proven relationship between lifestyle and victimization (Cohen and Cantor 1981; Maxfield 1987; Rountree and Land 1996), it is thus pertinent to ask if those who opt for a caravan holiday thereby increase their vulnerability to victimization.

Just as there are various definitions of a 'tourist', so caravan parks vary considerably, both in their typical occupants and in the nature of the dwellings within them. Although park sites are commonly associated with tourists, a number of other groups also reside there on a temporary or permanent basis. Some choose to live permanently in a park because they enjoy the lifestyle, the community, access to communal facilities, and the affordability and flexibility compared with other forms of housing. Some may own park accommodation as second homes,[2] or may be timeshare owners, or older residents who have downsized to live in park homes. There are temporary residents such as itinerant or seasonal workers and those who have no other housing alternatives such as homeless people located by welfare agencies to park sites on a semi-permanent basis. At the same time, accommodation on park sites may include tents, towed caravans, static caravans, cabins and more permanent structures. Therefore, there can be an eclectic group of Australians as well as overseas visitors in one closely confined space. There can be the very young and the very old; the very wealthy and those most marginalized in life.

What is unequivocal, however, is the importance of caravan parks to the Australian economy. As at September 2009, Australia-wide there were 1,646 caravan parks with a total capacity of 228,481 tourist sites for caravans, tents, park homes and the like. There were 34,950 long-term residents and another 39,594 permanently reserved sites (ABS 2010). In 2009, the sector employed 10,458 people and generated an annual income of AU$1,090,953,000 (ABS 2010). This market accounts for around 10 per cent of total visitor nights spent by international and domestic visitors. The importance of tourism to the national economy demands a duty of care. More importantly, the safety of tourists is paramount at a time when tourists generally are disenfranchised from the otherwise more inclusive community safety dialogue (Mawby 2008).

This chapter, consequently, addresses four questions:

•   What do tourists and residents of caravan parks feel about crime and safety?
•   Are they at relatively high risk of victimization?
•   Are there variations between different types of park or park resident?
•   How can the findings best be explained?

First, though, we shall briefly set out the research strategies we deployed.

The research

The research was conducted in two Australian states, New South Wales (NSW) and Western Australia (WA). In each state, a mixture of coastal and rural locations was included, with 36 parks in all being surveyed. Of these, four were tourist-only parks and one a residential-only park, whereas the majority hosted a blend of varying proportions of permanent and temporary residents and tourists. Nine parks were members of park chains. Ten were located close to a town's central business district but most were located on the outskirts of towns, often adjacent to a natural feature such as bushland, a river or a beach. Parks ranged in size from 20 to 400 sites (mean 108). All provided powered and non-powered sites for caravans and motor homes, onsite vans, cabins or chalets and tents. Overnight fees ranged from $10 for a campsite to $147 for a cabin. Some parks had only basic facilities whereas others constituted tourist resorts complete with swimming pools, spas, pool and games rooms and tennis courts. Primary data were collected from four key sets of players: park users ($n = 62$), park managers ($n = 36$), police ($n = 6$) and other interested parties ($n = 17$).[3] Park users comprised 40 tourists and 22 permanent residents.

Park owners were originally contacted by telephone and asked if they would consider being a part of the study. Information on the research was then forwarded by email or fax. Arrangements were subsequently made with the managers to set a time and date for the interviews to be conducted. The first author visited the community and stayed on site in one park for one or two nights to observe park life. Some cold-call visits to parks were made and all were well received. Face-to-face interviews were conducted with park managers, followed by tourists and permanent residents staying on the parks. Although the original aim was to interview a random sample, it became evident very early in the study that a large proportion of those contacted were aged 60 and over. Therefore it proved necessary to seek a purposive sample in order to gather the perspectives of a wide range of the population in age, family structure, accommodation type and type of traveller.

Caravan parks as safe and secure environments

Previous studies have suggested that, despite above-average levels of victimization, tourists express low levels of concern about crime (Mawby 2000). To test this out among tourists using caravan parks, we asked a range of questions, in some cases comparing the views of tourists and permanent residents.

In line with earlier research (Mawby, Brunt and Hambly 2000), only 16 per cent of tourists/residents questioned reported that crime and safety was a very important consideration in where they chose to go, and 38 per cent never thought about it. Only 36 per cent of tourists and even fewer residents (14 per cent) said there were places in Australia where they would not stay because they would feel unsafe. Caravan parks in some outback towns that had high crime rates were identified by some tourists as places where they would not stay, but there was an acceptance that this was the way things were if one wanted to see outback Australia, and one would be safer in a park than camping on the side of the road. Some viewed parks with high proportions of permanent residents, particularly in cities, as undesirable. Others reported that they used their common sense. If a park appeared to be poorly maintained or was in an unsavoury area, they would elect to move on. Some tourists did make a practice of asking park managers about any safety and security issues when making a booking. Even if they were advised that petty theft was an issue, this would not dissuade them from staying on the park; they would just be a little more aware. Moreover, while a greater proportion of tourists considered security when choosing a park, it was not the deciding factor (see Figure 12.1). A park's location and the quality of the facilities were far more important than were safety and security.

Tourists and park residents were also asked how safe they felt in varying situations: walking around the park during the day and after dark; staying in the van/cabin alone at night; and walking outside the park during the day and after dark. The results are summarized in Table 12.1. This shows clearly that residents, and especially tourists, felt very safe on the park, but less safe off the park. Although these figures are not strictly comparable with general victim survey findings, they strongly suggest that tourists on caravan sites are less fearful, especially at night. Participants were also asked how concerned they were about the safety of their children or other family members, and again registered low levels of worry.

Perceived problems on park sites

To seek a further understanding of the extent and nature of crime and antisocial behaviour on parks, tourists, permanent residents and managers were asked to rate a list of 10 antisocial behaviours according to the degree each was a problem. Table 12.2 summarizes their opinions. Some managers may, unsurprisingly, be a little defensive about such questions, albeit we found most to be extremely candid in their responses. For example, managers generally identified more disorder and antisocial behaviour than either residents or tourists. It is also notable that each group prioritized slightly different issues: tourists, noise and dangerous driving; residents, drug and verbal abuse; and managers, noise and drunkenness. With few exceptions, though, the evidence suggests that tourists express less concern than permanent residents or park managers, and low levels of concern about antisocial behaviour compared with standard victim survey results.

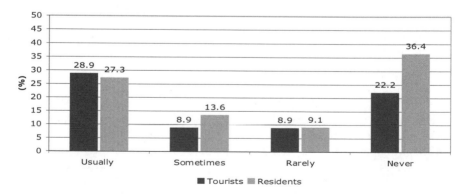

Figure 12.1 Degree to which safety and security was considered when choosing a caravan park.

Table 12.1 Participants' fear of crime

Fear of crime	% very safe		% safe		% unsafe		% very unsafe	
	Residents	Tourists	Residents	Tourists	Residents	Tourists	Residents	Tourists
Walking around park: during the day	90.9	97.5	4.5	2.5	–	–	–	–
Walking around park: after dark	81.8	92.5	9.1	7.5	–	–	–	–
Staying home alone at night	81.8	95.0	9.1	5.0	–	–	–	–
Walking outside park: during the day	77.3	55.0	–	22.5	4.5	–	9.1	2.5
Walking outside park: after dark	27.3	40.0	27.3	15.0	13.6	17.5	31.8	2.5

Table 12.2 Percentage of each group perceiving the following as a (major or minor) problem

	Tourists	Residents	Managers
Domestic violence	6.6	11.6	1.1
Fighting	6.6	9.1	13.9
Drug abuse	0	27.1	16.7
Drunkenness	11.1	11.6	33.4
Verbal abuse/bad language	8.9	18.2	19.5
Loud parties/noise	26.6	11.6	33.4
Dangerous/noisy driving	20.0	13.6	19.5
Groups of teenagers hanging around	11.1	9.1	25.0
Rubbish dumping	2.2	9.1	11.1
Graffiti	4.4	9.1	13.9

Table 12.3 Percentage of each group perceiving the following as a (major or minor) problem

	Tourists	Residents
Petty theft	20.0	27.3
Burglary	6.7	22.7
Vehicle thefts/attempts	2.2	0
Thefts from vehicles/attempts	4.4	4.5
Vandalism (dwelling)	0	9.1
Other vandalism	6.7	4.5
Robbery/attempts	2.2	0

Tourists and permanent residents were then asked to rate a list of seven property crimes according to the degree each was seen to be a problem on caravan parks (Table 12.3). Only minor thefts were considered a problem by a significant minority of each group and, with the exception of burglary, which was perceived to be a problem by 22.7 per cent of residents, the figures are again remarkably low.

Levels of victimization

Earlier studies on tourists' perceptions and experiences of crime have also suggested low levels of concern. However, they have also pointed to a paradox, in that tourists tend to experience high levels of victimization (Mawby 2000). The very nature of caravan parks renders them vulnerable to property crime. Tourists, particularly overseas tourists, will carry considerable sums of money, credit cards, cameras, mobile phones and other valuables that are of interest to thieves (Crotts 1996). Many retirees will travel with their own four-wheel-drive vehicle, caravan or mobile home as well as a trailer and boat, all valued between $150,000 and $600,000. With the transient nature of park residents and the easy access to caravans, tents and cabins, caravan parks may be attractive targets for offenders.

With regard to the present study, we addressed the question of experience of crime by asking park managers about the problems they had experienced on their parks, and permanent residents and tourists about their experiences on park sites that had occurred within the previous two years. Figure 12.2 displays the proportions and types of offences that managers reported having occurred on parks within the sample. At first sight these figures appear high. However, they refer to whole complexes rather than individual units, and would require dividing by the average number of units per site (108) to get actual rates. Bearing this in mind, it seems that the major problems experienced by tourists and residents (as opposed to site owners) involved petty theft, burglary and theft from vehicles.

Our interviews with tourists create a problem in that tourists spent a relatively short time on any particular site, so victimization experiences during one particular stay will almost certainly appear low. We therefore asked them about their lifetime experiences of crime on a caravan park, and their experiences over the preceding two years. Permanent residents were asked about their experiences living within caravan parks.

When asked if they had ever been a victim of crime, several of the permanent residents noted that they had very little to steal. Nevertheless, seven (32 per cent) reported one incident of victimization. Three of the permanent residents had been victims of a break-and-enter. However, these spanned a number of years. For example, one resident who had been living on a park for 15 years had been a victim of a break-and-enter in the third year of living in the park. Her neighbours,

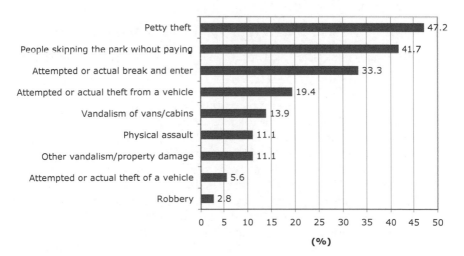

Figure 12.2 Reported crimes on caravan parks by managers.

who had been living on the park for 20 years, had also experienced one break-in five years ago.

Of the 40 tourists interviewed, only nine (23 per cent) reported experiencing some type of crime on a caravan park in their lifetime. All reported they had been victimized only once. Three said that they had experienced a crime in the past two years. These figures are well below those for tourists in general (R. I. Mawby 2010). Most of the offences reported were petty theft. The types of items reported stolen included clothing from clotheslines or washing machines, alcohol and food from cooler boxes, bicycles, surfboards, wetsuits, fishing rods and other sporting equipment, mobile phones, laptop computers, wallets and handbags, generators, tools, barbeques and gas bottles. For instance, one British couple, who were back-packing around Australia, had food stolen from a camp kitchen refrigerator. The offence was not reported to police because of its trivial nature but the loss still amounted to $100.

These findings have demonstrated that crime and antisocial behaviour were not a major problem for caravan parks in this study. Even where tourists were targeted, there was no indication that they saw this as a significant problem. For example, asked if they would revisit a park where they were victimized, one tourist said:

> Well, we did actually. We still went back . . . Because it was a nice park, closer to town centre, all the sort of things you look for when you're travelling. You always try and look for proximity to the town centre. That's why we always come here. Of all the caravan parks that there are here – there are quite a few, and there are a lot fancier and flashier ones – this one, because you can walk into town, it's ideal. I mean, the showers and toilets are my main thing. And they are very clean, they're nice. If they weren't, then I wouldn't stay here, because that's the first thing I look at.

Variations between different types of park and resident

Research demonstrates clearly that crime is rarely a random event. Why particular property or victims are targeted is thus a key question for researchers. In the case of park site crime in Australia, two questions arise. First, why are those using parks apparently at lower than average risk of victimization? Second, why are some parks and residents at greater risk than others?

One explanatory approach is routine activity theory (Cohen and Felson 1979). This attempts to explain the incidence and distribution of crime in terms of three sets of actors: potential offenders, potential victims, and law-enforcement agencies and other 'capable guardians'. It may also be used to explain the relationship between tourism and crime, and it is interesting that some tourism researchers have adopted this approach (see, for example, Crotts 1996).

Opportunity theorists, in contrast, have emphasized the extent to which offenders take advantage of the behaviour of citizens to commit crime. For example, Lynch and Cantor (1992) identified four dimensions covering the interaction of victims' behaviour and 'policing' and the impact on offenders' target choices, namely:

- *target exposure* – the visibility and accessibility of the target;
- *guardianship* – the extent to which victims and their property are protected;
- *target attractiveness* – value of property that might be stolen;
- *proximity* – distance of target from potential offenders.

A slightly different emphasis is adopted by rational choice theorists such as Cromwell, Olson and Avary (1991), who address the processes by which an offender chooses a criminal career, selects targets, and carries out criminal acts. They subsequently identify three types of cues used by burglars in assessing risk:

- *surveillability* – the extent to which premises are overseen by passers-by and neighbours;
- *occupancy* – as suggested by the presence of a car, noise, lights etc.;
- *accessibility* – including the presence or absence of window locks, an alarm, open windows etc.

Combining these approaches, it seems that the ways in which offenders identify their targets can be addressed using at least three criteria:

- *Guardianship* – the extent to which the target is protected and able to be protected: for example, whether it is visible to others with the motivation to provide protection. Guardianship can be distinguished according to whether it is physical (e.g. alarm) or social, that is where the source is the public police, private security, neighbours or the potential victim.
- *Accessibility* – the extent to which easy access is afforded. Again, accessibility may be physical (e.g. barriers restricting access) or social (e.g. offender lives some distance from potential target).
- *Rewards*, which is a more specific term than 'target attractiveness' – the extent to which the target possesses, or is perceived to possess, property that is of value.

How, then, can we explain both the low rates of crime and disorder on park sites, and variations between sites and tourists, according to these three criteria?

Guardianship

At first sight, park site guardianship would appear poor, suggesting high levels of risk. Few park sites or park homes were fitted with burglar alarms or security cameras, many had no formal policing arrangements, and the routine activities of tourists minimize the likelihood of self-guardianship. Furthermore, economic disparity exists within park populations ranging from wealthy tourists with large expensive caravans and four-wheel-drives to the most economically and socially disadvantaged homeless people in society. These factors might be thought to inhibit 'collective efficacy' (Sampson *et al.* 1997) within a community to effectively maintain control over crimes.

Nevertheless, many park sites evidenced high levels of guardianship, and these parks especially tended to experience fewer crime and disorder problems. In particular:

- *Good visibility increased the potential for guardianship.* Good lighting did seem to reduce crime, as lit sites and caravans were better able to be 'policed' by residents and staff. In contrast, where users had chosen to position their caravans in shaded areas under high trees, their risk increased.
- *Formal policing reduced crime.* Sites that were regularly patrolled by the local police and where the police responded quickly to calls from site managers experienced less crime and disorder. These were invariably rural sites, where the police were more able to provide a presence. In contrast, in urban areas police considered patrolling of park sites peripheral to their work and a low priority. Tourists and residents experienced less crime and less fear of crime on parks that employed private, in-house (but not episodic external) security, or where the manager assumed a security function. Often one of the management team (more often than not, the woman) acted as the 'security guard' presenting a warm, friendly exterior but quite formidable when necessary. When some managers were asked what security features they had on the park, they responded: 'My wife!' One added: 'She hears, sees, smells everything. Nothing gets past her.' Another manager believed troublemakers would often respond more readily to a rebuke from a woman than from a man.
- *Informal guardianship was crucial.* Given the transient nature of tourists, it might seem unlikely that they would fulfil a policing function. However, it seemed that the nature of caravan parks, in Australia at least, created a subculture and feelings of shared responsibility among regular 'caravaners'. One manager observed: 'Tourists talk to one another, particularly people in the caravans. They can tell you from one end of Australia, to the other side – where to stay, where not to stay, how to do it, and all the rest of it.' This proved to be even more so in the case of permanent residents, even where these residents were primarily social housing cases, who provided a significant level of informal policing within sites that covered the units of both permanent residents and tourists. As one manager noted: 'the permanents – they're your eyes and ears. If anything is going on, they will let you know.'

Collective efficacy is particularly important because, among tourists at least, self-guardianship is limited. Permanent residents may adopt routine behaviours similar to those of occupants of conventional homes. In contrast, tourists behave in very different ways on holiday than they do at home (Crotts 1996; Mawby, Brunt and Hambly 1999; Stangeland 1998). Of particular relevance here, they tend to spend more time engaged in leisure activities away from the park, for example in the evenings. This limits self-guardianship, where accommodation is left empty for significant lengths of time in the daytime and evenings, as well as impacting on tourists' ability to act as capable guardians of their neighbours' property. Their routine activities also increase accessibility (see below).

Accessibility

In the case of park homes, accessibility applies on a number of levels: the extent to which the site is readily accessible to offenders, in terms of whether they are themselves staying on site and, if not, where they live or travel from and how easy it is to access the site once there. In general, and perhaps unlike in the UK (Mawby *et al.* 2008), there was little evidence that park users themselves created crime and disorder problems, and some park managers detailed how they excluded or managed potentially troublesome groups such as schoolies (school leavers).[4] Additionally, many park sites evidenced low levels of accessibility, and these parks tended to experience less crime and disorder problems. Overall, accessibility varied according to:

* *Where the park site was located*: this played an important part in determining social accessibility. Just as researchers have shown how crime and disorder are concentrated in the city, predominantly where or near to where offenders live or travel through in the course of their routine activities, so parks in town centres, near high-crime areas and within walking distance of where offenders lived experienced higher rates of offending and were perceived as less safe, as were those bordering routes to and from leisure centres. In contrast, parks that were more likely to be away from the coast and in small rural communities experienced less crime and disorder and were considered to be safe.
* *The location of the park home within the site*: this was also important in affecting social accessibility. Thus park homes located on the perimeter of sites were most vulnerable.
* *Real or symbolic boundaries*: structural features were important at the park level where boundary fences and security barriers restricted physical access. The lack of physical barriers, notably fencing, facilitated access, while security gates added an additional barrier. However, symbolic boundaries were almost as important. At one extreme, parks that flowed into adjacent townships, without any obvious separate identity, experienced greater problems. Similarly, parks that merged into bushland, particularly rural areas that were themselves easily accessible, experienced greater risk. However, several of the parks used environmental features such as rivers, national parks, beaches or railway lines as natural boundaries. This also applied at the level of the individual unit. At the extreme were annexes that provided little protection. Thefts of goods left under or outside units were also common. The confined space in park homes meant that goods that would be kept within a conventional home (bicycles, eskies etc.) may be left outside, becoming readily accessible to the offender.

As a police officer noted: 'Tourists tend to pull things out of a van and leave them lying about. There is a need for simple security measures to stop opportunistic crime – better ways to secure equipment such as, bikes on bike racks.'

And a park manager noted:

One of the major things that we battle with is the people who lock up their house for fifty weeks of the year, like it's a fortress, and they come here and think that they can leave their surfboards, wetsuits out. And if there's one thing the local kids love, is getting into caravan parks and relieving people of their surfboards and wetsuits.

- *Park residents as offenders:* Although 'outsider' access may be restricted, some offences on sites are committed by park users. Park sites are, to a certain extent, melting pots where the barriers of distance that usually separate affluent middle-class potential victims from property offenders among the impoverished lower classes are dismantled. However, whereas our initial impression was that offences might be the work of other residents, especially some groups of permanent residents, the overwhelming view of park managers was that the main problem group was not residents but schoolies. This was the group most commonly excluded and, when admitted, most carefully policed.

Rewards

We found no evidence that offenders targeted more affluent sites in prestigious areas, nor that they targeted more affluent or better-kept vans or cabins. It seems that accessibility counterbalances the attraction of rewards. On the other hand, there was some indication that potential rewards were influential, with tourists more vulnerable than permanent residents. This may be explained in two ways. First, many permanents, notably social housing cases, had fewer valuables worth stealing. Second, and reinforcing the relevance of repeat victimization, a high turnover of tourists meant a speedy replenishment of goods that would attract an offender back. In this sense, offenders had no need to wait for insurance claims to be settled (Anderson *et al.* 1995; Polvi *et al.* 1991; Robinson 1998) before returning for new consumables (Shaw and Pease 2000). However, unlike in the study in Cornwall (Mawby *et al.* 2008), there was less indication that holidaymakers took significant amounts of valuables with them, hence reducing their attraction to thieves.

Some tentative conclusions

Although no previous research had considered crime on caravan parks, and indeed little attention has been paid to variations in risk between different subgroups of tourists, our preliminary assumption had been that rates would be relatively high.

Our findings do not support this, and indeed contrast with ongoing research in Cornwall (Mawby *et al.* 2008, 2010). The fact that some parks did experience relatively high levels of crime and disorder provides us with some clues to why this was not the norm. Three factors seemed particularly important. First, in terms of guardianship it appeared that collective efficacy, both in terms of a caravan park tourist subculture (particularly among the Grey Nomads) and through the involvement of permanent residents, was particularly strong, influencing both the amount of crime and disorder and perceptions of safety. Second, there was less suggestion of crime and disorder problems created by other campsite residents than the British research implies, with permanent residents more likely to be seen as an asset than a liability and schoolies either excluded or well policed. Third, we would suggest that many caravan parks, in restricting accessibility, provided some of the features of gated communities (Low 2004; Vesselinov *et al.* 2007), with physical and/or symbolic barriers restricting access. There is some emerging evidence that such communities may reduce both crime and, especially, anxiety (Waszkiewicz 2007); this chimes in with our findings.

Our conclusions suggest that caravan parks in Australia provide some of the characteristics of all-inclusive resorts where tourists relax within a secure protected community (Alleyne and Boxill 2003). This in itself raises the need for further research to compare the experiences of different groups of tourists with different holiday experiences, and to assess the extent to which such differences impact on the relationship between leisure and crime and disorder. It is now well accepted that tourists are at high risk of victimization. It is thus timely to move on to more refined comparisons that contribute to both the tourism literature and wider victimological theories.

Notes

1 The research that forms the subject of this chapter was funded by the West Australian Office of Crime Prevention.
2 Although Stangeland (1998) demonstrated that second home owners in Spain experienced lower burglary rates than tourists, in the one study of burglary to address second-home owners on 'park sites', the authors found break-ins to *dachas*, or weekend homes in Hungary, to be particularly high (Mawby and Gorgenyi 1997).
3 Predominantly private security staff and relevant local council employees.
4 In Australia, the end of the school year regularly sees thousands of school leavers ('schoolies') descend on coastal resorts to celebrate. This has on a number of occasions resulted in significant, and well-publicized, crime and disorder problems. See Homel *et al.* (1997) and Fickling (2003).

13 Tourist victimization

An exploratory survey from Ghana

Kwaku Boakye

Perhaps, apart from natural disasters, human-induced insecurity remains the single most potent threat to a viable tourism trade. This manifests itself in the form of crimes against tourists. These impact on individuals (in terms of bodily harm or loss of property or trauma) and destinations, which tend to suffer (sometimes) irreparable damage to their image with undesirable outcomes on their patronage (Breda and Costa 2006; Prideaux 1996; Tarlow 2006). Consequently, the fact that image is an important ingredient in tourism development has been very well documented, and destinations would go to any length to present themselves as a safe and enjoyable paradise.

The African continent remains, perhaps, the region hardest hit by an image crisis. Though no destination in the world can be free from perceptions of insecurity or the incidence of crime (Crotts 1996), such images are more prominent in Africa (Ankomah and Crompton 1990; Brown 2000; Teye 1998). The image of the continent as being war-prone, insecure, famine and disease-ridden and a hotbed of all types of crime tends to overshadow the otherwise vast untapped potential for tourism development. Although there can be no denying the fact that some of the perceptions have been fuelled by actual events (e.g. civil wars, famine and political unrest), it is also true that the greater part of these negative images are normally predicated upon anecdotal information and unsubstantiated generalizations. Many a visitor to the continent has been known or heard to have expressed surprise about how positively different they have found their destination from the images fed them in their home countries (Boakye 2008).

The quandary of many African countries is clear. On the one hand, they wish to attract the much-needed tourist dollars by developing their attractions/infrastructure and various marketing campaigns, while on the other hand they have to consistently battle with a reputation of being volatile and anything but ideal for tourist patronage.

Generally, available literature on the subject has tended to be based largely on the context of mature tourist destinations in Europe, North America and Oceania. Save a few studies which capture tourists' perceptions of their security (e.g. Boakye 2008; George 2003) there is limited information available on the general security situation in an African tourist destination. This study seeks to contribute to reducing that knowledge gap by providing results from a preliminary study carried out in Ghana.

Conducting a study about tourism security within an African setting has three justifications, the first of them being the increasing flow of inbound tourist traffic to the continent. According to the United Nations World Tourism Organisation (UNWTO 2010), Africa is the only region that witnessed positive arrival growth (5 per cent) in 2009. In fact, Africa is one of the regions whose growth is projected by the UNWTO to continue to exceed the world average. Second, research affords the opportunity to understand the phenomenon of tourist-induced crime within the framework of the continent's unique characteristics (e.g. largely undeveloped and informal tourism sector). Finally, it gives first-hand information to policymakers to protect tourists better.

The context

Ghana is a West African country of about 23 million people with a per capita income of US$600 and a recurring balance of payment deficit. Though cocoa and gold have traditionally been the key exports, the revenues accruing have often fluctuated. Currently, minerals and remittances from Ghanaian citizens abroad constitute the second and third highest foreign exchange earners respectively, with tourism being the fourth major foreign exchange earner. Tourist arrivals and receipts have increased at an average of 10 per cent over the past decade. According to the Ghana Tourist Board (Ghana Tourist Board 2009), tourism is of increasing importance to the Ghanaian economy; since 2005 tourist arrivals have grown by over 60 per cent. Equally, receipts have increased significantly. Between 2005 and 2006 there was an 18 per cent increase and between 2008 and 2007 it was almost 20 per cent. Perhaps no indicator better mirrors the growth of the sector than the construction of hotels. In 2008 alone, 163 new hotels were constructed, adding 3,622 rooms to the then existing room space.

Recognizing the potential benefits from the tourist trade, the government has since the late 1990s been actively involved in the sector through:

- the creation of a ministry solely for tourism;
- implementation of a 15-year national tourism development plan to end in 2010 with an aim to attract more than 1 million inbound tourists;
- various marketing campaigns to attract more inbound tourists;
- development (with the aid of the United States Agency for International Development) of major tourist attractions in the Central Region.

With the country's recent discovery of oil in commercial quantities, the growth of tourism is likely to be accelerated, attracting more high-end 'business tourists' and creating more recreation-based infrastructure.

Background to the research

The research addressed four principal questions:

* What are the most common crimes suffered by tourists in Ghana and what spatial patterns underlie their distribution?
* Does vulnerability to victimization differ by tourist type?
* How do tourists in Ghana perceive their security?
* How attuned are the Ghanaians to addressing the problem?

With these questions in mind, an exploratory study was undertaken to assess the dynamics of tourist victimization in Ghana in terms of its incidence, forms and patterns; analyse tourists' perceptions of security in Ghana; and appraise the ability of police as capable guardians.

Three towns, Accra, Cape Coast and Kumasi (Figure 13.1), were chosen on the strength of their patronage by tourists. Hot Spots Theory suggests that tourists are most likely to be victimized in places where they cluster most (Sherman *et al.* 1989). These three towns, collectively described as Ghana's 'tourism triangle', are the cities most visited by tourists in Ghana and, collectively, receive a disproportionate number of the country's tourist arrivals (Abane *et al.* 1999).

All the cities are well endowed with different attraction offerings. It must be noted, however, that tourist presence in Accra is accentuated by the presence of the only international airport. Cape Coast, on the other hand, is better endowed in terms of popular attractions, but does not have adequate supporting facilities to cater for tourists on an extended basis. The city was included because it normally attracts a fairly large number of student-tourists (pre-university volunteers, student nurses and university groups) who visit the country through various study-abroad programmes. These programmes are structured to promote local integration; thus the students stay with host families and are more familiar with local customs than the conventional tourists. Finally, Kumasi is considered in many unofficial circles as the 'cultural capital' of the country and is mainly patronized because of the possibility of viewing some authentic historical and cultural edifices. Both Accra and Kumasi are likely to have more conventional tourists than Cape Coast.

The focus was on international tourists for at least three main reasons. First, they dominate the tourist arrival figures. Second, it was hypothesized that they would be most at risk because of their way of dressing, and because they are unfamiliar with the local terrain, not to mention that they look different mainly in terms of skin colour and language (Allen 1999; Holcomb and Pizam 2006). All these traits are likely to render them more vulnerable than the domestic tourists, albeit domestic tourists are not immune to crime. Third, domestic tourism in Ghana is arguably characterized by excursionism (Akyeampong 1996), which is markedly different from tourism.

In all, a total of 420 questionnaires were administered over the period, with 336 (80 per cent) valid responses: 114 from Cape Coast, 75 from Kumasi and the remaining 147 from Accra. Tourists were reached using the accidental sampling

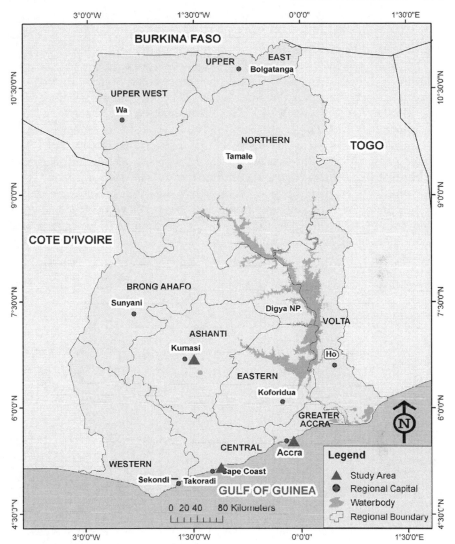

Figure 13.1 Map of Ghana showing areas.

method at major tourist attractions. Tourists visiting the attractions in their own tour buses in groups of six or more were designated as 'institutionalized' whereas those moving alone were categorized as being 'non-institutionalized' or independent. The inherent shortcomings of this method make generalization difficult. Deliberate efforts were made to control against the predominance of group tourists by issuing arbitrary quotas. In effect, no more than three persons from a group each day were chosen. Likewise, non-institutionalized tourists were relatively easier to identify and approach. Unlike the institutionalized tourists, most of the non-institutionalized were found away from attraction sites and in public places of the main towns. Owing to the strong potential for the same tourist to be approached more than once at different locations, the strategy devised was to space the data collection periods two months apart from each other.

Overall, respondents were broadly representative of the profile given by the Ministry of Tourism. Almost half were from Europe, and over a third from the USA. It is worth noting that the majority of the respondents from Europe were from Germany and, especially, the United Kingdom. On the whole, the sample was predominantly youthful (dominated by volunteers and those on study-abroad programmes) with those aged below 30 accounting for more than half of the sample (Table 13.1). A little over two-thirds (71 per cent) were visiting Ghana for the first time and culture was the major attraction (over 68 per cent).

The modal travel party size was two to five. Middle-aged females were generally more likely to travel in larger groups and use hotels whereas young males tended to travel in smaller groups and normally chose the much cheaper home-stay option. Most home-stay programmes are structured to provide accommodation

Table 13.1 Socio-demographic profile of tourist respondents

Variable	Frequency	Percentage
Age		
<30	171	50.9
31–49	90	26.8
50+	75	22.3
Total	336	100
Sex		
Male	165	49.1
Female	171	50.9
Total	336	100
Highest educational level		
Secondary	13	3.9
Polytechnic, training college etc.	38	11.3
Degree and above	285	84.8
Total	336	100
Country of origin		
Europe	155	46.1
USA	128	38.1
Africa	4	1.2
Asia	49	14.6
Total	336	100

and two meals daily. Their emphasis is on cultural integration and the host families are selected mainly on having a building which has decent accommodation.

Additionally, a police sample of 22 officers, was purposefully chosen across the three study areas, consisting of the three crime officers of the towns, five divisional commanders, six station officers and eight officers from the Criminal Investigation Department. In-depth interviews were conducted with these officers.

Finally, a total of 73 stories from actual victims, tour guides, tour operation/ground-handling companies and the police were collated at the same time as the questionnaire was being administered. The information gathered included type of crime, place names, circumstances under which it took place and what action was taken. These served as the basis for plotting the maps found in the later sections of this chapter.

Tourist victimization

Overall picture

The figures in Table 13.2 are drawn from a checklist in which respondents were asked whether or not they had experienced five different types of crime since arriving in Ghana. As Mawby, Barclay and Jones (2010) point out, tourists anywhere in the world are a high-risk group (see also Boakye 2009, 2010). In line with previous studies, tourists were found to be particularly vulnerable to crime and harassment. Approximately one-third of the respondents (108) had suffered from at least one crime. Property theft (which was defined to include theft of money) was found to be the most frequently occurring crime, experienced by 14.9 per cent of respondents and accounting for 46.5 per cent of the crimes against victims. Wallets, personal effects and electronics were the items most often mentioned. Following at a distance was verbal assault (34), which accounted for close to a third of all incidents, and was mentioned by one-tenth of tourists.

The findings noted above are in consonance with the known literature (Chesney-Lind and Lind 1986; Harper 2006; Holcomb and Pizam 2006; R. I. Mawby 2010) which identifies property crimes (especially theft) as the most frequently committed crimes against tourists.

Table 13.2 Frequency of tourist-related crimes

Type of crime	Frequency	% of victims (n = 108)	% of overall (n = 336)
Property theft	50	46.5	14.9
Assault – verbal	34	31.4	10.1
Assault – physical	13	12	3.9
Phone snatching	7	6.4	2.4
Fraud	4	3.7	1.2
Total	108	100.0	32.5

Patterns of incidence

In the context of this study, the crime pattern indicators (based on earlier studies by Crotts 1996; George 2003; Harper 2006; and McPheters and Stronge 1974) used were time of day; location and site of crime; and whether the victim was alone or not. To this end, layered cross-tabulations were carried out between these pattern indicators (*time of day*, *site*, *town* and *accompaniment*) and the various crimes suffered by the tourists. In some cases, the respondents did not fill the details out completely. For example, some respondents would only indicate that they had been verbally abused without providing the other details on the patterns. For this reason some of the totals may not be necessarily congruous with already stated totals in Table 13.2.

As regards the towns of victimization, Cape Coast appears to be the most insecure destination because the majority of the crimes happened there – theft, verbal assault and physical assault – albeit neither phone theft nor fraud was recorded in Cape Coast. All the fraud cases reported were from in Accra – probably because it is the most economically developed of the three. Overall, Kumasi had the lowest victimization rate, scoring the lowest on all types of crimes. Perhaps Prideaux's (1996) proposition about the positive relationship between tourist numbers and incidence of crime could be applicable here. Cape Coast is touted as the most visited town in Ghana (Abane *et al.* 1999) and has been part of the area constantly referred to as the 'tourism heartbeat of Ghana'. Similarly, work by Teye and colleagues (2002) points to some degree of resentment among the residents of Cape Coast towards tourism development and tourists. The reality is that Cape Coast could be described as the earliest tourist destination in contemporary Ghana. Indeed it was the birthplace of the Natural Resource Conservation and Historic Preservation Project, the country's first ever deliberate tourism development effort.

Over the years, it has become evidently clear that the town has not received benefits commensurate with the increased tourist inflows. Such sentiments have been expressed by many opinion leaders at various fora and have been the subject of many a conference, the most recent being one organized by the Central Regional Development Commission in 2007. It could well be the case that after almost 17 years of exposure to tourists the locals are feeling disenchanted and therefore choose to victimize them both as a statement and for economic gain.

Notable differences are also observed when considering the *site of victimization*. Attractions were found to 'host' most crimes. With the exception of theft, all the crimes took place at attraction sites. Physical assault stands out in this regard; all the incidents occurred at attraction sites. It is also worth highlighting that the hotel was the site which witnessed the least crime, though it hosted the majority of property thefts (56 per cent). Not surprisingly, the market place was the leader in terms of phone snatching and verbal assault with 61.7 per cent and 57.2 per cent respectively. The open-air nature of Ghana's markets and their general disorganization coupled with huge traffic (both human and vehicular) provide the perfect setting for victimizing the uninitiated tourist. For phone snatchers such conditions would be most ideal.

Dynamics of victimization

A spatial analysis of the victimization sites showed some patterns which confirm the propositions by Jarrel and Howsen (1990) as well as Meithe and Meier (1990), to the effect that the use of space contributes to tourist victimization. The findings from this study as represented in the maps (Figures 13.2, 13.3 and 13.4) confirm the assertion that victimization is more prone to take place in entertainment-oriented areas. The basis for plotting the maps was the place names/areas mentioned in the 73 victimization stories received from both the tourists themselves and the service providers. An analysis of the maps shows a very clear pattern of the concentration of victimization around the key tourist attractions and entertainment spots in the study towns. The cases of the three towns are discussed in turn.

In Cape Coast for example, all the places mentioned fall within the shaded area and this stretches from the Victoria Park area through the Central Business District (CBD) towards Tantri. It will be noted that with Cape Coast, though there are many hot spots, victimization was concentrated around the main attraction, the Cape Coast Castle.

The shaded area in Figure 13.2 suggests that the criminogenic zone stretches from Bakaano through the Tantri area. It is noteworthy that this area runs parallel to the beach and is dotted with a number of drinking spots and two night clubs. It is an area where white tourists are spotted especially during the night. In this area mugging and theft were the crimes mentioned most.

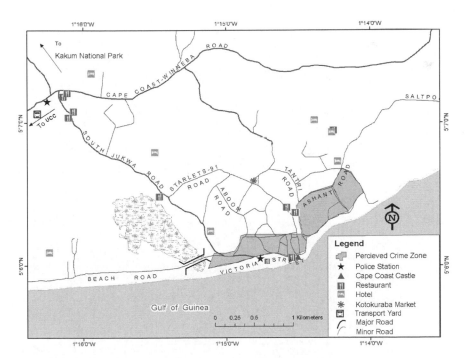

Figure 13.2 Map of Cape Coast showing some crime incidence spots.

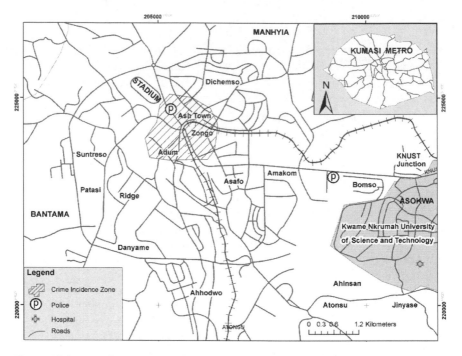

Figure 13.3 Map of Kumasi showing crime incidence spots.

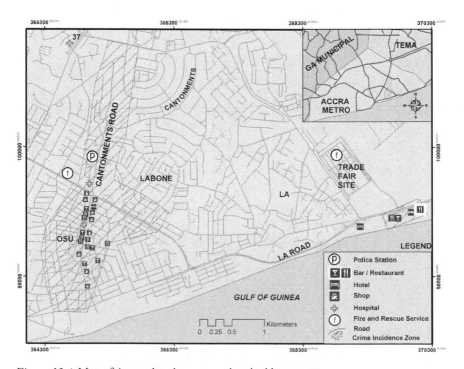

Figure 13.4 Map of Accra showing some crime incidence spots.

Similar patterns were noted in Kumasi and Accra (Figures 13.3 and 13.4 respectively). As can be seen from the maps, there are relatively few entertainment places within the hot spots area, but most victimization takes place there.

The shaded areas in Figure 13.3 cover Adum and Manhyia. It is also worth mentioning that within this zone are the famed Kumasi Cultural Centre, the former City Hotel and the Manhyia Palace Museum. These are three of the most patronized attractions in the Kumasi Metropolis and the area is dotted with countless entertainment and food and beverage spots.

With Accra it can be observed from Figure 13.4 that the areas highlighted fall between Osu Oxford Street and the Cantonments area. It is not surprising that these areas were mentioned in the victimization stories because, as in Cape Coast, they have a heavy concentration of entertainment and shopping spots. In addition, the La Pleasure Beach area was mentioned in a number of victimization cases and it can be adduced that the presence of the beach contributes largely to this situation.

The trend emerging from these maps is that tourist victimization takes place not just near entertainment spots but also around those spots and criminogenic places which are located close or within the vicinity of major tourist attractions. As observed from Figures 13.3 and 13.4, all the places mentioned were not only concentrated around spaces which are normally used for entertainment, food and beverage, shopping and nightlife but also close to major tourist attractions. Mention can be made of the Cape Coast Castle (for Cape Coast), Cultural Centre and Manhyia Palace (in Kumasi) and Oxford Street and Labadi pleasure beach in Accra. Thus an extension of the Hot Spots Theory may be suggested to include the assertion that it is hot spots located near tourism attractions which are more likely to witness tourist victimization.

Socio-demographic dynamics

As indicated in Table 13.3, the quintessential tourist victim was the European male aged more than 30, non-university educated and in informal occupations. This finding conforms with and departs from existing literature. Interestingly, Michalkó (2003) made similar findings identifying European tourists as the most frequent victims of crime in Hungary. Tourists with largely the same characteristics have been identified by Alleyene and Boxill (2003) as being particularly susceptible to crime whilst in Jamaica.

It is also clear that the youngest age group had the lowest proportion of theft victims compared with the other age groups. Interestingly, a smaller proportion of males fell victim to property theft than females. *Level of education* also appeared to have some influence as tourists without tertiary education were more likely to fall prey to theft than their university counterparts. Perhaps, two striking features about theft concerned the variables *occupation* and *country of origin*. With occupation, a notable trend was the relatively low victimization rate of students compared with those in the formal and informal sectors. Likewise, considering country of origin, tourists from Africa did not experience any theft whereas the most victimized were those from Europe.

Table 13.3 Percentage distribution of crimes by socio-demographic characteristics

	Crime				
	Theft	Verbal assault	Physical assault	Phone theft	Fraud
Age					
< 30 (n = 170)	12.9	14.1	0.6	4.1	1.2
31–49 (n = 90)	17.8	6.7	13.3	0	1.1
50+ (n = 75)	17.3	5.3	0	0	1.3
Sex					
Male (n = 165)	15.8	9.1	7.3	2.4	1.2
Female (n = 171)	14.6	11.1	0.6	1.7	1.2
Educational status					
Non-university (n = 51)	12.2	11.3	6.2	4.8	1.6
University (n = 285)	14.5	6.8	1.3	2.9	0.9
Occupation*					
Formal (n = 94)	8.1	5.3	8.5	0	2.1
Informal (n = 84)	11.6	15.6	4.8	1.2	1.2
Student (n = 147)	20.2	2.4*	0.7	4.1	0.7
Continent					
Europe (n = 155)	19.4	8.4	5.2	4.5	1.3
America (n = 128)	13.3	9.4	0.6	0	1.6
Africa (n = 4)	0	25	0	0	0
Asia (n = 49)	8.2	16.3	8.2	0	0

As compared with those in other occupations, the low level of victimization among students needs mention. Similar findings were made by Allen (1999) and Barker, Page and Meyer (2002). It sounds paradoxical that young people identified in the literature as being highly susceptible to crime also have a lower vulnerability. The reason may be partly attributed to their length of stay. Since they spend longer periods than the average tourist, they appear to be more 'streetwise' and know the terrain better, and thereby avoid victimization. Another reason could be the level of preparation they undertake before embarking on the trip. It is possible that they learn a lot about the destination that they can even navigate without much help. In this regard, two popular sources are the Bradt's Travel Guide and the Lonely Planet website (http://www.lonelyplanet.com). Furthermore, there is the possibility that they are perceived by the local people as not wealthy, given their (normally) shabby dress and patronage of relatively cheap services or facilities (accommodation, transport etc.). In many ways, the student tourists show characteristics of Cohen's (1972) *drifter* or *youth tourist* (Cohen 1987a) or the *backpacker* (Barker *et al*. 2002).

As regards the crime of verbal abuse, the *sex* and *age* patterns observed were similar to what had been noticed earlier with regard to theft. The other age groups recorded a higher rate of verbal abuse than the young (aged < 30). Males were also found to have a higher victimization rate of verbal abuse than females, those without university education suffered more than those in the university. Again the students and those from the USA were found to have suffered the least verbal abuse.

The age and sex distributions observed earlier were also observed in the crime of physical assault. It is worth noting that a greater proportion of males (85 per cent) suffered from physical assault than their female colleagues (33.3 per cent). In terms of phone snatching, all seven victims were young Europeans. Otherwise, the earlier socio-demographic trend continued unabated, with males and non-university students dominating.

Travel behaviour dynamics

Aside from socio-demographic characteristics, victim profiles can be built using the tourists' travel behaviour. These were conceptualized as variables which define travel habits of tourists. In this context, travel indicators are *accommodation preference*, *travel arrangement* and *travel party size*. In this section, the results of cross-tabulations of the various crimes against these travel behaviour indicators are analysed. Here it was noticed that the victims were disproportionately non-institutional tourists.

More marked differences are observed across the different types of crimes and the various travel behaviour indicators. Considering theft, for example, it showed clearly that, in terms of accommodation type, those in home-stay programmes were the least vulnerable.

Likewise, those who travelled independently had a higher proportion falling prey to theft than those who relied on travel intermediaries. Still on theft, it was, perhaps, the variable *travel party size* that really brought out the differences. As can be seen from Table 13.4, the proportion of victims of theft increased progressively as the travel party size increased. Vulnerability to theft was highest amongst the groups of six to nine people.

As regards verbal abuse/assault, the hotel was found to record the lowest incidence among accommodation types. Similarly, in terms of travel arrangements, those who made their own ('self') were more victimized than their counterparts who relied on a travel intermediary. As in the case of theft, verbal abuse appeared to decrease with the growth in travel party size.

A statistically significant pattern was observed between accommodation type and vulnerability to theft, including burglary. The dominance of the hotel as a site of crime is corroborated in Table 13.5. This is consistent with Mawby's (2006) assertion that the rate of crime in such places is normally higher than in households. Generally, the formal, commercialized accommodations had the highest

Table 13.4 Percentage distribution of crimes across travel behaviour

	Crime				
	Theft	*Verbal assault*	*Physical assault*	*Phone theft*	*Fraud*
*Accommodation type**					
Hotel (*n* = 159)	13.2	3.8	2.5	0	1.3
Guest house (*n* = 70)	25.7	2.0	11.4	2.9	0
Family and friends (*n* = 106)	11.3	13.2	0.9	4.7	1.9
Travel arrangement					
Self (*n* = 244)	14.3	10.7	4.9	1.2	1.2
Intermediary (*n* = 92)	17.4	8.7	1.1	4.3	1.1
Travel party size*					
Alone (*n* = 100)	12.0	4.0	4	1	1.0
2–5 (*n* = 163)	14.7	11.7	4.9	3.7	1.2
6–9 (*n* = 18)	27.8	38.9	5.6	0	5.6
10+ (*n* = 55)	18.2	7.3	0	0	0

Note
* $p = 0.05$.

proportions of victims. It was noted, for example (Table 13.4), that patrons of the 'guest house' (a cheaper form of formal accommodation) had the highest proportion of theft victims, followed by those who used hotels, whereas the informal accommodation recorded the least victimization. There is a strong likelihood that this pattern has to do with the type of patrons and the degree to which the hotels invest in security. Normally it would be expected that lower-income tourists (be they backpackers or youth tourists) would patronize less formal accommodations. These people are known to seldom leave valuables in their rooms. Concerning the high proportions recorded by the hotels and guest houses, there is a possibility that the middle- to higher-income tourists who patronize them may bring easily transportable valuable items which they are likely to leave (Mawby *et al.* 2010). Thus the argument is that they have a false sense of security, with owners unable or unwilling to invest.

With the three remaining crimes (physical assault, phone snatching and fraud) the trend followed that seen earlier in this section with a few significant exceptions. The incidence of physical assault was higher among those who made independent travel arrangements, stayed in cheaper form of accommodation (guest houses and home-stay programmes) and moved in larger groups. The pattern is no different when considering the crime of phone snatching. Indeed, there were no cases recorded among those who patronized hotels or travelled in larger groups. Fraud was found to be more likely among those who used home-stay programmes, made independent travel arrangements and moved either alone or in small groups numbering no more than five persons. The reason may not be very difficult to

Table 13.5 Percentage distribution of crimes by pattern indicators

Indicator	Crime				
	Theft (n = 50)	*Verbal assault (n = 34)*	*Physical assault (n = 13)*	*Phone theft (n = 7)*	*Fraud (n = 4)*
Time of day					
Daylight	60	76.4	92.3	71.4	75
Night	40	23.6	7.7	28.6	25
Site					
Hotel	56	8.8	0	0	25
Attraction	28	29.4	100	42.8	50
Market	16	61.7	0	57.2	25
Town of occurrence					
Cape Coast	36	54.5	63.6	0	0
Kumasi	32	15.15	36.4	28.6	0
Accra	32	30.3	0	71.4	100
Accompaniment					
Alone	41	81.25	92.3	14.3	75
With others	59	18.75	7.7	85.7	25

fathom. By its nature, fraud requires a lot of space and time to commit. There must be enough time for an acquaintance to be struck up and confidence to be built. Thus, as has been observed, these conditions inure better to those who move alone or in smaller groups. It is therefore not surprising that those in the largest group had no fraud cases.

Looking at the variables in Table 13.4, it can be seen that the categories of the travel behaviour indicator associated with the non-institutionalized tourist recorded higher levels of victimization than the others. Using the variable *accommodation preference* as an example, the 'home-stay' category recorded the highest level of (non-theft) victimization compared with those using hotels and guest houses. Similarly, when considering the variable *travel arrangement* it is seen that those who relied on intermediaries and moved around in groups recorded less victimization than those who made their own travel arrangements ('self').

The notable exception to this trend emerges when observing the distribution under the variable travel party size. Contrary to the expected logical pattern, the incidence of victimization rather tends to increase with increasing travel party size. The reason for this strange happening may be that these non-institutionalized tourists (especially those who visit the country alone) normally tend to befriend local self-appointed tour guides who usually 'chaperone' or 'pilot' them around till departure. Tourists who rely on such 'pilot boys' are less likely to be victimized because of the knowledge, protection and goodwill offered.

Tourists' perceptions on security

Despite the high rate of victimization among respondents, Ghana was generally considered a safe country by the majority (305, or 89 per cent). This is further evidenced by the finding that desire to revisit the county was still strong even among those who had fallen victim to one crime or another while in the country (see Table 13.6). The majority of tourists (87 per cent) said they felt safe for varied reasons such as 'I am careful', 'crime happens all over the world, Ghana is no exception', and 'I am an experienced traveller'.

As Table 13.6 also indicates, willingness to recommend and revisit the country was high across all the five crimes. Considering property theft for example, 94.4 per cent and 90.2 per cent of the victims in each case were willing to revisit the country and recommend it to other people. These findings support the view by a school of thought (e.g. Holcomb and Pizam 2006; Mawby 2000) which suggests that being a victim of crime does not negatively affect repeat patronage. Special mention needs to be made of verbal abuse scoring the highest negatives, especially in terms of revisiting (32.4 per cent). Responses provided in the follow-up open-ended questions indicated that the respondents perceive verbal abuse as a clear sign of hostility from the hosts. By their reasoning, all the other crimes could happen fortuitously anywhere to anybody but verbal abuse is a clear 'statement of hatred' and a 'warning not to return' to the destination.

Though not technically classified as crimes per se, harassment and begging were also reported by almost all (92 per cent) respondents as constituting a threat to their security. Most tourists complained about the 'stressful' situations they normally encountered at some attractions, where they were either pestered to buy some wares or asked for all kinds of favours ranging from money to marriage proposals.

Of all the genres, historical attractions were considered the most secure (162, or 50.2 per cent). The reasons adduced for their choices were revealing. A majority of this number (97, or 59 per cent) claimed the historical attractions were secure because they had clearly defined guidelines for patronage (e.g. a clear

Table 13.6 Type of crime by willingness to recommend and revisit

Crime	Recommend		Revisit	
	Yes	No	Yes	No
Property theft ($n = 51$)	50 (94.4)	1 (5)	46 (90.2)	5 (9.8)
Phone snatching ($n = 7$)	7 (100)	0 (0)	6 (85.7)	1 (14.3)
Physical assault ($n = 13$)	13 (100)	0 (0)	13 (100)	0 (0)
Fraud ($n = 4$)	3 (75)	1 (25)	4 (100)	0 (0)
Verbal abuse ($n = 34$)	27 (79.4)	7 (20.6)	22 (64.7)	11 (32.4)

procedure, pricing and professional service delivery). Others also mentioned the availability of supporting tourism-related facilities at the attraction site as indicative of the security levels there. These include tour-guiding services, restaurants and accommodation.

Another major theme from the tourists' responses focused on the concept of shelter. To them, security constituted the ability of the attraction sites to 'protect' them from the marauding of 'all manner of sales people'. As one tourist wrote: 'once we were inside the wall of the [Cape Coast] castle and away from the hustlers, we felt very safe'.

Conversely, the attractions which were thought by tourists to be insecure were designated so for various reasons such as 'the unavailability of proper and efficient guiding services', 'too many people coming close to tourists', 'people forcing tourists to buy their wares', 'unavailability of tourist related services' and 'too many people grabbing your arm'.

These distressful remarks constituted some of the reasons for describing certain attractions as insecure. Other respondents (44, or 30 per cent) proffered psychological reasons for perceiving an attraction to be insecure. For example, the story of the Atlantic slave trade, with its gory details of torture and gross human rights abuses, made some feel depressed and, by extension, insecure. A few others blamed the tour operators and tour guides for making the attractions insecure in that they are constantly reminded of the need to be careful, thereby making them paranoid and insecure. Furthermore, a few tourists (24, or 10.1 per cent) assigned structural reasons for feeling insecure. The most 'guilty' attraction in this category was the canopy walkway of the Kakum National Park whose bridges were 'too high and shaky'. Also cited was the Mole National Park, whose motel was 'too close to the animals', and some beaches which were described as 'too obscure, dark and open to criminals'.

A little over half (189, or 56.4 per cent) felt safest in their accommodation whereas others nominated the attraction site (60, or 21 per cent) and fewer still the bus. Almost a fifth of the volunteer students (54, or 18 per cent) indicated that they felt safest in the villages where they stayed during the period. The reason for this could be the high level of informal contact with the locals and the fact that most of the villages are new to tourists and therefore are very welcoming to such tourists in the short term, and also because tourism is in its incipient stage. It is likely that in the short run they are accorded the best of hospitality and there is even the likelihood of a strong communal sense of protection for the visitors. Nonetheless, the finding that the accommodation was thought to be the safest place is not very surprising given the fact that most of these hotels invest in security for both the guests and the facility.

The views of police

Being the constitutionally mandated institution responsible for internal security, the Ghana police service represented an integral focus of this study. The essence was to find out their knowledge of tourism, attitudes towards securing tourists and the practices they employ in providing a safe environment for tourists. Capable guardianship is the third element in Felson and Cohen's (1979) Routine Activities Framework that contributes to the commission of a crime against tourists. As adopted for this study, it was conceptualized to focus on police capabilities in securing the tourist.

Generally most of the officers could correctly define who a tourist was but were obviously limited in their ability to distinguish between some international and domestic tourists. There was also a common perception that tourists are not specifically targeted for victimization. Consequently, to them, tourists become victims of crime primarily through their own acts of commission or omission ranging from carelessness to the search for the authentic (which, almost always, includes the desire for illicit activities). As one officer put it: 'They naively think nobody will harm them whilst they are on holiday'. Another said, 'they do not know the terrain very well but are adventurous and go to places even we the locals see as dangerous'. Others also said, 'the tourists are too relaxed while on vacation' and 'openly display their valuables'. Some police respondents described the tourists as being 'careless both in their handling of their own possessions and the type of relationships they enter into'. Little blame was placed on the criminals. As one rhetorically asked: 'if the tourist is careless and leaves his camera and someone picks it up, can you define that as a crime?' These findings confirm observations made by de Albuquerque and McElroy (1999) and Cohen (1987a) to the effect that police forces normally blame tourists for being victims of crime.

Another aspect of the study sought to determine respondents' views on capability of their guardianship using the three Ps framework (presence, prevention and processing). Each of the elements is discussed in turn.

Presence

Presence was defined in terms of visibility at tourism-related zones. In this regard, the prevailing view was that their presence has not been visible in the tourist zones of the study area. According to them, though, patrols are undertaken for the general populace, and the tourist spots which are included are covered because of their location along the routes, not because of any conscious attempts at tourism security. In a few cases, some units had received occasional invitations from the management of some key tourist attractions to provide security during certain public holidays. According to them they are paid by the inviting agency and their activities during such days include protection of people and property, crowd control and the maintenance of order.

Prevention: training, strategies involved in providing security for tourists

Prevention refers to the ability of law enforcement agencies to protect the tourist from being victimized. One rare tourist-specific measure was captured from Kumasi, where the police had attended a few seminars on tourism security organized by the regional office of the Ghana Tourist Board.

Another aspect of prevention relates to police capacities in terms of having the requisite resources (men, money and materials) to reduce victimization. Despite acknowledging the availability of weapons and vehicles for fighting crime, the respondents were almost unanimous in the perception that more could be done to fight tourist-specific crime. As with any other public servant, the policeman's conditions of work cannot be described as the best; however, for a majority of the respondents it was the lack of equipment such as patrol vans that constituted the most viable threat. This lack of resources is perhaps not limited to Ghana, as Pizam, Tarlow and Bloom (1997) also made similar findings on other police forces in more developed countries and mature destinations.

Still on prevention, the general perception pointed to inadequate training for tourism-oriented policing. Consequently, there was a unanimous claim by the police officers that they have not received any training on tourism-specific policing. It could safely be assumed then, that the officers and men of the service have limited insight into tourist-specific policing.

Nevertheless, the respondents were almost unanimous in their view about the importance of providing the tourists with security. As one officer astutely put it:

> It is very important because our image as a destination depends on it and ultimately, it will affect our attractiveness as a destination. Tourists share a lot of information with their friends when they return, thus it is important that we protect them so others will also patronize.

They were however, divided on the most appropriate method. Whereas some supported the idea of establishing a tourist-specific policing unit, another group viewed such an establishment to be discriminatory against locals and felt that general security should be improved instead. Though there was a general consensus on the need to protect tourists, there were divergent views on the nature of the protection. Some suggested a patrol system whereas a few thought a more comprehensive solution such as the creation of a special unit would be more appropriate.

Processing

Processing was defined in terms of the ability of the law enforcement agencies to expeditiously and efficiently pursue complaints either to their logical legal conclusions or to the satisfaction of the complainant or both. Literature (e.g. de Albuquerque and McElroy 1999; Alleyne and Boxill 2003; Pizam *et al.* 1997) suggests that in most cases the police have a reputation for being indifferent towards the welfare of the tourist, especially concerning reported crimes.

The respondents, however, insisted that they provide prompt attention to tourists who file complaints or request police forms. Though they pointed to a low level of reporting of tourist victimization, they were quick to add that the few cases that came to them were handled with the highest level of efficiency. A few reasons were adduced for the perceived low level of reporting. First is their claim that the tourists normally do not have the time to pursue cases of victimization to their logical conclusions: apprehension of the suspects and subjection to the due process of the law. In their opinion, most tourists report cases only when they need a police report form to enable them to make insurance claims for items lost. Another reason the police identified for the low reporting was the inability of the victims to positively identify perpetrators. Closely related is their suggestion that tourists (especially those who fall victim to criminal activities such as fraud and other con-games) were ashamed to report such victimization because of their fear of being implicated in such schemes. For example, one respondent told the story of a tourist seeking to buy gold illegally. After being duped, he reported the case to the police but declined to pursue it when he realized he could be apprehended for falling foul of the law. Thus, in their view, tourists also fail to report crimes because of the fear of being exposed as engaging in either illicit or immoral activities.

To sum, the respondents perceive tourists as being foreign and mainly in the country for leisure and entertainment. They also hold the tourists primarily responsible for being victimized. Finally it emerged that, in terms of the three Ps of capable guardianship, they have a less visible *presence*, and do not undertake enough tourist-specific *prevention* but insist that they *process* the complaints that come to them to the best of their ability. Perhaps the suggestion by one officer aptly reflects the desired strategy to secure tourists:

> We need to detail personnel permanently at attraction sites. It should be part of our postings. In such an instance, the attraction sites and the government can jointly bear the cost with the greater part borne by the attraction sites.

Discussion

This chapter has discussed the results of an exploratory study on the tourist security situation in Ghana. Though a third of the respondents had suffered from at least one form of victimization (or crime), Ghana is still generally considered to be safe. Nevertheless, the figures have suggested very significant and interesting variations especially in terms of the travel behaviour of victims. Space was also found to have some affinity with the incidence of victimization and it was mainly the case that, in all three study towns, victimization was clustered around entertainment spots that were close to major attractions and had key entertainment facilities. It has also emerged that, although blaming the tourists for their own victimization, the police generally appear ready and willing to commit themselves to providing a safe environment for the tourist. A few ramifications from these findings are discussed in conclusion.

The positive acclaim of the country as being safe for tourists does not necessarily constitute an exemption from future challenges of security. As has been proven lucidly in the literature, tourists and tourism are increasingly becoming targets for all forms of insecurity, with far-reaching consequences. Competing from a continent which is largely perceived to be unsafe, Ghana needs to take a more proactive stance towards providing security for the tourists. The passive approach of the police towards providing security for tourists is neither out of place nor unique to Ghana. The literature proposes a somewhat forward link between the level of a destination's development and police perceptions/attitude towards ensuring visitor safety. Citing examples from three relatively mature tourism-dependent towns (Cape Town, New Orleans and Miami), Pizam and colleagues (1997) found the respective police authorities to have a proactive stance towards perceiving tourist crime and to have institutionalized efforts to fight it. On the other hand, in relatively young destinations such as Ghana, where tourism is yet to emerge as the dominant economic activity, the attitude of law enforcement agencies appears to be passive. Though the safety of tourists is recognized as important by law enforcement agencies, there appears to be doubt about the degree to which instances of insecurity reduce the appeal of destinations. This explains the common view of police authorities, as observed in this study, that tourists were not necessarily under threat, and that, even when it occurs, it is to be blamed on the carelessness of the tourists rather than their being targets.

The seemingly passive approach adopted by the police must give way to more institutionalized tourist-specific policing strategies. For example, the finding from this study that most victimization takes place at the attraction sites can offer some justification for setting up a tourist police unit in each of the three major towns. Such a unit's core responsibilities could be the three Ps (maintaining a *presence* at attraction sites; *preventing* victimization through patrols and education; and swift *processing*, including documentation). Also important will be the need to institutionalize public/private partnerships in the provision of security. As observed from the findings, official invitations for security from managers of tourism facilities (especially attractions) appear to be few and far between and are mainly restricted to public holidays and festive occasions such as Christmas and Easter.

The phenomena of harassment, aggressive selling and begging at attraction sites should continue to be a major concern for the country's tourism authorities. Education and sensitization remain two important tools which can be used to curb these ills. Specific messages can be tailor-made for host communities about their roles and responsibilities in the tourism enterprise. The often-held fallacy that host communities should only benefit from tourism without any contribution towards it can be dispelled with such education. In addition there can be permanent security at these attraction sites to ward off people who victimize the tourists in these ways.

Finally, a conscious effort must be made to identify and provide protection for the non-institutionalized tourist. Normally, the travel behaviour of these tourists inadvertently places them outside the protection range of the formal security organizations (Boakye 2010; R. I. Mawby 2010). For example, a tourist living with a host family with a flexible itinerary and who travels freely across the country to unfamiliar attractions is not very likely to benefit from protection offered from police patrols in the tourist zone/cluster. There is, therefore, a need for such tourists to be identified, monitored and protected.

14 The tourist victim
Paradise lost or paradise regained?

Carol Jones

The tourist is one of the world's natural victims.

(Turner and Ash 1975: 238)

Introduction

Chapters 8–13 in this book identify and discuss issues of tourism and crime in a number of different countries across the world. Comparisons can be made with regard to the risk of crime in each jurisdiction and, to a greater or lesser degree, their responses to tourist victimization. This is particularly relevant as it has been shown that, in the case of international travel and crime victimization, the needs of tourist victims differ from those of resident victims and from country to country. For domestic victims, the literature emphasizes the emotional/psychological impact on the victim of the crime (see, for example, Ingram 2000; Lurigio 1987; Spalek 2006). In the case of victims who are away from home, the type of support most commonly sought is more practical: the need to replace lost credit cards, travel documents and cash.

The purpose of this chapter is to consider some of the problems in identifying levels of victimization generally and compare and contrast the problems in reporting and recording levels of victimization among domestic and tourist victims of crime. Drawing upon research in the United Kingdom, the Republic of Ireland and Florida in the United States of America, the impact of crime on tourist victims is considered and the different services available to tourist victims of crime in these countries are reviewed. From these descriptions and from the recommendations of the European Union a number of parameters are identified to determine a model of tourist victimization. The model is then applied to these services to characterize and distinguish each one from the other, and evaluate them from a tourist perspective.

Identifying levels of victimization

The difficulties of identifying levels of victimization in any jurisdiction are well recorded (see, for example, Nelson, Bromley and Thomas 2001; Ratcliffe and

McCullagh 1998). In the domestic scene they revolve around reporting and recording and additionally, in the case of transnational victims, comparison and categorization (van Dijk *et al*. 2007).

Any comparison of levels of victimization in different countries is problematic because methods of collection vary, as do the categories of crime type. Furthermore, a significant proportion of crime goes unreported (Kruttschnitt and Carbone-Lopez 2009). In England and Wales, police statistics identify all crimes recorded, while the British Crime Survey (BCS) provides evidence of a more limited range. However, neither source directly identifies the circumstances under which the crimes are committed. Smith (2006), in his review of crime statistics, noted that, whereas police data referred only to crimes that were reported to or known by the police and these tended to be the more serious crimes, the BCS relates to only certain types of crime, excluding some of the most serious offences.

Statistics of recorded crime considerably underestimate the level of crime in the community because, for many reasons, victims fail to report offences to police. A victim's decision to report crimes is affected by a number of interrelated complex factors, including the personal characteristics of the victim, the victim's perceptions about the seriousness of a crime incident, previous victimization experiences, the social influence of family and friends or bystanders to the crime, the likelihood of compensation for personal harm or property damage/loss (Coleman and Moynihan 1996; Ruback, Greenberg and Westcott 1984; Skogan 1984), the victim–offender relationship, particularly in the case of partner abuse (Felson *et al*. 2002), a sense of personal liability (Jones 2008) or a lack of confidence in the law enforcement agencies (Goudriaan *et al*. 2005). In the case of victimization while on holiday, a number of additional reasons prevail, including unfamiliarity with the location of a police station, language barriers, cultural differences or just the fact of having to spend valuable leisure time reporting the event. Law enforcement officers have indicated that many 'victims' do not want to return to the Florida area to participate in the prosecution process, which may occur four to six months after the incident. One reason often stated is the cost associated with returning despite the fact that the state attorney's office will pay expenses and financial support may also be available from the victim's advocate unit.

The limited research that has been undertaken on tourist crime victimization shows that visitors are more likely than residents to experience victimization (Mawby *et al*. 1999) but are less likely to report the incident to the police. Research indicates that this may be, in part, because tourist victimization can be due to unfortunate circumstances, but also due to the visitors own behaviour while on holiday (Mawby *et al*. 2010). For example, in interviews with tourist police officers in Florida, USA,[1] some tourists were described as 'volunteer victims' by one officer:

> It is amazing to note the number of tourists that will literally pull into a parking space at one of the theme parks . . . and be so excited to have reached Disney, they will leave their car in one or more of the following conditions – or any combination thereof: doors unsecured, doors left standing open, windows in

a down position, keys in the ignition, engine running, valuables left in plain sight to include passports, luggage, money, purses and electronics.

This sentiment was repeated by officers in the southwest of England in a study conducted there (Jones 2008):

> I can't believe some of the things that they get up to . . . and often they bring it on themselves. I have kids of their age and if I thought that they went on holiday to spend the whole time drunk I'd be jumping. Why do they think that they're invincible in Cornwall? When they cross over the Tamar Bridge, they leave their common sense behind.

Jones (2008) found tourist victims of crime had believed that crime did not occur in idyllic holiday locations and this belief had contributed to their victimization. These perceptions were greatly altered in hindsight. 'Cornwall is not the crime-free area it is assumed to be', 'It's increased my awareness of crime' and 'I didn't think it would happen to me!'[2] were comments commonly recorded from tourist victims of crime in the southwest of England in 2001 (Jones 2008).

This lack of awareness and subsequent victimization may suggest that crime is a significant problem in Cornwall but statistics indicate that this is one of the safest areas of the United Kingdom.[3] However, levels of acquisitive crime increase significantly in the main holiday months of May, July and August, which suggests that the influx of tourists contributes to this increase (Jones 2008). One explanation for this may be the lifestyles of tourists. Table 14.1 clearly indicates that people on holiday spend more time away from their accommodation, thus increasing the risk of burglary, and time spent in bars and clubs increased the risk of robbery and theft as they circulate in unfamiliar surroundings and lose inhibitions through increased socializing and increased alcohol consumption.

Although some crimes do go unreported it is also clear that some offences are reported which have not taken place. Insurance fraud, whereby a tourist submits a claim knowing it to be false, is a costly and increasingly common problem. In order to make a claim a victim must furnish an insurance company with a crime number issued by the police or another law enforcement agency (Morley *et al.* 2006). In the case of tourist victims of crime in Orange County, this problem was identified by the Orange County Sheriff's Office (OCSO), whose officers police the tourist areas of Disney and International Drive in Central Florida:

> suspicions have been raised over a very small percentage of reports that indicate the crime never actually happened and the victim (many times an international tourist) is filing a false report for insurance purposes.[4]

Although there has been to date little known research on this topic outside the insurance industry, we may suppose that this happens elsewhere. According to research undertaken on behalf of an insurance company in 2008, between 2003

Table 14.1 Comparison of resident and visitor victims of crime in Cornwall in 2000

	Percentage of visitor victims (n = 216)	Percentage of resident victims (n = 81)
Gender: male	56.5	46.9
Professional status	53.3	21.0
Retired	8.8	3.2
Income of less than £5,000	5.3	4.2
£5,001–£10,000	4.3	11.3
£10,001–£20,000	21.4	31.0
£20,001–£30,000	20.9	29.6
£30,001+	48.1	23.9
Age 16–24	24.3	5.3
25–54	53.8	65.8
55–64	12.6	19.7
65+	9.3	9.2
5+ hours away from home during the day	74.2	75.0
3 times or more out in the evening at home	15.7	5.3
Spare time at pubs/clubs	53.7	28.4
Eating out at restaurants in the evening	61.6	44.4
Socializing with family/friends	63.9	33.3
Very/fairly safe walking out after dark at home	72.2	70.5
3 or more times out in the evening in Cornwall	62.6	5.3
Those aged 16–24 who went out 3 times or more in the evening in Cornwall	86.3	25.0

Source: Jones (2008).

and 2008 5.8 million Britons were victims of crime while overseas, 2.8 million Britons reported theft of personal belongings and a further 2.3 million had bank cards or money stolen, and 640,000 were victims of physical or sexual assault.[5]

The effects of crime

Research into the fear and risk of becoming a victim has been widely studied (see, for example, Ditton and Chadee 2005; Jackson 2006; Mirrlees-Black and Aye Maung 1994; Romer *et al.* 2006) although most of the studies have concentrated on victims in their home environment. In 1984 Kidd and Chayet found that victims of crime were emotionally affected by their ordeal and displayed a variety of symptoms including nervousness, anxiety and anger. The impact on the victims' perception of their own security was also profound, with 60 per cent of the sample of victims feeling significantly less safe following the crime (Kidd and Chayet 1984). This evidence was gathered from victims who had experienced a level of violence; however, there is evidence that this effect can also occur in cases where violence is not part of the victim's experience (Jones 2008). The Scottish Crime Survey (Ingram 2000) found there was little difference identified among victims of vandalism, personal offences and household thefts. In general, the effects of crime do not relate to the type of crime, nor is there a template that dictates that victims of a certain type of crime will react in a specific manner (Lurigio 1987). Reactions may in part be dependent upon age, gender and socio-economic status as well as seriousness of the crime itself.

Mawby, Brunt and Hambly (1999) deduced from their research that people appeared to be more susceptible to crime while on holiday than at home, and this has been supported by others (see Harper 2006; Jones 2008). Research by Jones (2008) in the southwest of England found that visitors to the area who had been victims of crime often declared that they 'didn't think that crime happened in such areas' and they felt 'let down', 'surprised' or 'shocked.'

Similarly, Ryan's (1993b) study conducted in Spain in 1989 found that violence can contribute to the victim's distress. He identified a number of variables that were significant in addressing levels of violence, and more recent evidence shows that these have changed little in the intervening years. His study suggested that tourists were more vulnerable to violence if their cultural norms included peer group cohesiveness, intolerance of those outside their group, and values which justify behaviours of excessive drinking and indulgence in violence and casual sex where possible (Ryan 1993b: 159–60).

Victim support services

There is a need to define more clearly the nature of victimization and its effects to determine the nature of support services needed for individuals who are victimized away from home. This becomes even more necessary as the importance of tourism for the world economy increases. Bauman's (1998b: 77) statement that 'Nowadays we are all on the move' is becoming more and more true as globalization and consumerism have allowed ever-growing numbers to travel to ever more distant places to explore and experience the differences of place, or merely imbibe the 'tourist-made' attractions of the package holiday. It is the increased importance of tourism to just such economies that has led to a limited but important number of studies into tourists who have been victims of crime.

Being a victim of crime in an unfamiliar environment is an unwelcome outcome which can cause the victim to question preconceived assumptions about the cultural process, the legal system and practical commonsensical skills that assist the victim to cope with the incident.

Ryan (1993b) notes that the very process of 'being on holiday' may contribute to the likelihood of a tourist's being victimized. A holiday is 'time out of time', freedom from the normal constraints of home and work, supplemented by a belief that being on holiday is about 'having a good time'. It often involves 'risky behaviour' unrestrained by the unfamiliar because often tourists are in places that promote 'the British Pub', the 'Club Flamingo' or the 'Queen Vic', which for the British tourist invoke names that are reminiscent of home. Hence, while tourists are, on the one hand, away from the familiar, they frequently seek an environment that provides them with an air of familiarity. As a consequence, if they are then made a victim of crime, we may speculate that they will further expect and seek a similar level of service from a similarly familiar criminal justice system.

There is some recent empirical evidence to support this view. According to research undertaken for a UK-based travel insurance company in 2008, between 2003 and 2008 there were 871,569 reports of crime involving tourists in Spain,[6] the country that attracted the largest proportion of British visitors, drawn by low-cost flights, cheap accommodation and inexpensive bars and clubs. A significant minority of these victims felt that they were isolated and, in spite of financial losses, did not report the offence.

The insurance company research also found that up to 12 per cent of British tourists were victims of crime between 2003 and 2008 while on holiday. This is lower than the 18 per cent rate of tourist victimization identified by Mawby, Brunt and Hambly (1999) but it still exceeds the rates for resident victims presented in the International Crime Victim Survey (ICVS), which found rates of acquisitive crimes were generally no more than 6 per cent per annum (van Dijk *et al.* 2007).

The impact of crime against tourists can affect not only the individual but also the location where the incident happened. Florida, Bali and Egypt, among other locations, have suffered in the aftermath of victimization. In the first instance, following a number of violent crimes including murders in tourist areas in Florida, a number of changes took place including changing the appearance of car registration plates on hire cars[7] and an expansion of the tourist policing service. The reputations of Bali and Egypt as being top tourist destinations suffered greatly after terrorist attacks killed and maimed large numbers of visitors as well as residents. Airlines, hotels and other commercial businesses in these countries felt the economic fall-out from such offences (Benghiat 2008; Hall and O'Sullivan 1996) with a dramatic fall in bookings and income.

Supporting tourist victims in England and Wales

In view of the acknowledged importance of tourism to an increasing number of destinations, it is somewhat surprising that there is so little research into tourism and crime and particularly the experiences of tourist as victims of crime. In 1987, Cohen provided a relatively optimistic view of the development of tourist victim support services suggesting that, as tourism became increasingly important to the economy of the host region, governments would provide services specific to the tourist, including tourist police (Cohen 1987b). However that early optimism has not been sustained. In 1999, Brunt and Hambly suggested that 'within the tourism industry generally, agreement over where the responsibility for tourist safety lies, is unclear' (Brunt and Hambly 1999: 31). The significance of the role of the police in preventing tourist-related crime was posited by Muehsam and Tarlow (1995) and revisited by Pizam and colleagues (1997) and by Brunt and Hambly (1999) and, while police tourist victim support services have been developed in some locations, contributions by other agencies are generally absent.

The effectiveness of tourist victim support services is debateable. Whereas Mawby (2000) argued that tourists who had been victims of crime were no less likely to revisit the location where the incident had taken place, other research suggests otherwise (Hall and O'Sullivan 1996). As reactions to the issues surrounding tourist victimization vary in the academic literature, it is not surprising that different countries around the world choose to address the problem differently. The policing of tourist locations varies, as do the levels of support for those who have been victimized in such areas. This is illustrated by the following accounts of the victimization experiences of tourists in the UK, the Republic of Ireland and the USA. In all three countries, specialist victim assistance programmes exist to help crime victims. In the UK, these programmes are generic: Victim Support caters for tourist victims incidentally and only as part of its more general programmes. In the Republic of Ireland, although Victim Support also exists and is similar to the UK model, a separate and specialist agency is dedicated to helping tourists. In the USA, as in the UK, victim assistance programmes encompass tourist victims but do not provide specialist services for them. However, specialist Tourist Police units have been formed in many parts of the country, with a brief that may include providing help for victims alongside their more preventive remit.

Police working in Cornwall, in the southwest of England, are responsible for a largely rural environment of coastal villages and market towns with relatively low levels of crime compared with more urban areas. However, in summer, the arrival of many thousands of visitors changes the demography of the county into a large number of heavily populated centres with high crime levels. Reactions by the police to these seasonal variations vary, with some officers being sympathetic and supportive of visitors whereas others see the influx as troublesome and aggravating. In the extreme case there are officers who regard some crime victims as responsible for their own victimization. For example, in a case when a 17-year-old girl camping with friends in Newquay (a popular surfing area among young people) had a number of expensive items taken from her tent, the officer in charge of the case, who was a sergeant of many years' service, commented:

> By the time she rang us it was the following day and when I asked her why she had waited to report the loss she said that she was too wasted the night before and hadn't really realized. I have a daughter of a similar age and if she got into the state that that young lady was in she would hear about it from me.

In contrast, there are other officers who feel sympathy for victims but their response may be more to do with the identity of the victim rather than the process of victimization itself (Rock 2008), as the following case study demonstrates.

Case study 1

In 2001 a middle-aged woman and her elderly mother parked their hatch-back car in a beauty spot car park prior to taking a walk. Not only was there no closed-circuit television (CCTV) or similar security but the car park (owned by the National Trust) required purchase of a parking ticket which, in common with such machines around the country, clearly identified how long the car was being left for. (The lack of CCTV and the clear indication of the time the occupants of the car are likely to be absent increase the likelihood of theft.) On their return some two hours later they found that the car had been broken into and the elderly lady's handbag stolen from the boot of the car. The incident devastated her and left her feeling both emotionally traumatized and physically unwell (Jones 2008).

In the above case, a coordinator at Victim Support[8] was advised (informally) of this incident by a police officer whom she knew. The case had been reported to the police and, although Victim Support would not routinely make contact with victims of car crime given the volume of such crime and the shortage of volunteers, in this case she did and found both women to be severely traumatized by the event. The losses amounted to the theft of not only the handbag but more importantly some items of sentimental value, including the older woman's late husband's watch and photographs. It was this aspect of the crime that had the greatest impact.

Although the loss in material terms was negligible, both women reported a sense of isolation as they were far from home and supportive family members and friends. Neither had experienced such an event before and the fact that it happened in what they perceived to be a safe environment increased the sense of shock and bewilderment. They cut short their holiday and returned home the following day.

Devon and Cornwall Constabulary acknowledged some of the problems that arose during the holiday periods and took some steps to alleviate some of the risks. Among these were flyers issued to motorists about leaving valuables on view when parked at isolated car parks. However, in this case (as in many other similar instances) thieves took advantage of the remoteness of the car park. It was serendipitous that the officer contacted the victim support worker as, under normal circumstances, these women would not have been identified as being in need of care and support.

In face-to-face interviews with coordinators[9] of Victim Support in the County of Cornwall (Jones 2008), some coordinators acknowledged that tourist victims vary greatly in their experiences of crime and in the way they react to and cope with crime. Therefore, it might be presumed that these coordinators would see a need for a specialist victim assistance service for tourists. However none of the coordinators believed that was necessary and reasons given included that:

> Victim Support should be treating all victims equally.
>
> (Jones 2008: 286)

> We strive to offer the same high standard to all victims regardless of where they come from. We tailor our service to their needs and wishes.
>
> (Jones 2008: 287)

Supporting tourist victims in the Republic of Ireland

In 1994 a specialist tourist support organization was established which drew on the linguistic and cultural expertise of a number of volunteers. The organization was supported by the Irish police (the Gardai) and the Ministry of Tourism among other government departments. Material support was provided by a broad range of commercial enterprises that derived much of their income from tourists.

Case study 2

Two young German men arrived in Ireland for a two-week camping holiday. They intended to stay in a hostel in Dublin for the first night. However, as it was late on a Saturday evening there were no vacancies so they made their way to the outskirts of Dublin. They set up camp in a field for the night, during which they were attacked and robbed. One of them was assaulted with an iron bar, resulting in 10 days' hospitalization and surgery for a fractured jaw.

Although more serious than many of the cases of tourist victimization reported in Ireland, this case is not untypical of the problems that are referred to the Irish Tourist Assistance Service (ITAS) and exemplifies the practical, cultural and emotional demands made on the organization.

Following the attack, the Gardai escorted the second tourist, who was not injured, to the ITAS office. Even though he spoke good English, a native German-speaking volunteer was called to offer support in his native language. Free accommodation was organized by the volunteer for as long as needed. Phone calls were made to both sets of parents to explain what had happened and to organize money transfers. As all their belongings had been stolen, department store vouchers were offered for essentials – underwear and toiletries – until money became available.

The ITAS office was frequently visited by the second young man during the 10-day wait to make and receive phone calls to and from anxious parents and to organize the flights and airline tickets home through their insurance company. A native German-speaking volunteer regularly visited the injured tourist in hospital and also assisted the investigating detective with translation.

Compared with the British example, the Irish case shows the importance given to a formalized system of support for tourists by both the government and commercial concerns. Although the Irish Tourist Assistance Service preceded the Council Framework Decision from the European Commission (Council of the European Union 2001) on the standing of victims in criminal proceedings, it conformed to many of its most important features, namely:

> Each Member State shall encourage action taken in proceedings by such personnel or by victim support organizations, particularly as regards to providing victims with information and assisting victims according to their immediate needs.[10]

Article 2 of the framework is most relevant to the visitor victim:

> Each Member State shall ensure that victims who are particularly vulnerable can benefit from specific treatment best suited to their circumstances.[11]

Supporting tourist victims in Orange County, Florida, USA

In Florida in the USA, the picture differs somewhat from both the UK and Irish examples. In the early 1990s Florida experienced a number of violent crimes against tourists and, following adverse international media attention, bookings to the state declined. To rectify the situation, tourist police services were established in 'at risk' areas. Visible uniform patrols were increased, a problem-oriented approach to improve the area was adopted and, with support from local businesses and other government agencies, a law enforcement tourist support program was introduced to provide safety information.

By 2010, the Orange County Sheriff's Office (OCSO) programme had become formalized.[12] Police officers who had experience and skills in working with tourists and visitors to the area were encouraged to apply to join that arm of the service, which polices the 'at risk' areas in and around the Disney theme parks and International Drive at the heart of the tourist area of Orlando.[13] Policing in these Tourist Oriented Policing Sectors is publicized as an assistance service rather than a law enforcement provision.[14]

In 2004/5 the OCSO entered into a contract with the Reedy Creek Improvement District, commonly known as 'Disney'. In return for policing the locations covered by the Disney theme parks and surrounding area, Reedy Creek provides a building for the deputies and support staff with office equipment, salaries for 61 personnel, a new vehicle (marked or unmarked) every three years, weapons and any training as deemed necessary and agreed upon between Orange County and Disney Security. In addition, a separate agreement exists wherein off-duty officers are paid to police the main gate styles at the theme parks and also the Downtown Disney complex, which is a popular location for residents and tourists in the evenings.

Unlike the Republic of Ireland, Orange County does not offer victim assistance services, although the Office of the Attorney General manages a victims compensation scheme. Furthermore, although the Office for Victims of Crime and the National Organization for Victim Assistance represent victims of crime, neither appears to have any specialist assistance for victims of crime who are on holiday.

Discussion

According to the World Travel and Tourism Council in 2006, travel and tourism was set to account for 10.3 per cent of global gross domestic product, providing employment for an ever-growing number as traditional skills give way to the more profitable income from foreign currency. Studies indicate that tourists are more likely to be victimized than residents and the impact can be greater, with the loss of property having a significant and troublesome effect. Even among visitors who are victimized in their country of domicile, the effects can be devastating and result in negative impressions about the location. However, it would appear that, with a few exceptions, tourist victims of crime do not readily receive specialist support, as identified by the Irish Tourist Assistance Service.

In 2002, the European Council framework decision on the standing of victims in criminal proceedings highlighted the importance of the rights of victims across the European Union and the need to rationalize service provision so that all citizens of the Union may expect to receive a level of support corresponding to that which is available in their country of domicile. In spite of this coming into effect in March 2002, there is scant evidence of such provision among many of the partner states, including England and Wales.

With regard to the police, there is evidence to suggest that in some locations there is acknowledgement of the special problems experienced by tourist victims of crime who lack the linguistic and cultural knowledge of a particular place. There is a belief that tourist-oriented police can perform an important role for visitors who fall victim of crime, but it does raise a number of concerns. First, a visitor victim may not know how to recognize a police officer or the location of the police station in order to make contact with police. Second, there is an assumption that all tourists 'see' the police as helpful and non-threatening.

Other 'practical' support services can also be problematic. Visitors to other countries are often advised to contact their embassy or consulate in the event of criminal activity, particularly when the loss of passports or other documents is involved. However, such advice is generally provided on websites and there is no knowledge about how many people access this information prior to travelling. Tourism organizations and government websites also provide information relating to customs and legislation which may relate to visitors but again many potential tourists may not be able to access such material.

Although Victim Support, police and commercial organizations in tourist areas in England and Wales acknowledge the problems relating to tourist victimization, there is little evidence to suggest that there are few efforts in place to address them. Any success that is achieved is based on informal networks, serendipitous interventions and individual acts of kindness. Little attention is paid to the needs of tourists, nor the value of such services to the industry. In contrast, a survey undertaken in 2002 on behalf of tourist victim services in Ireland found that, because of the systematic intervention of a formal organization, over 90 per cent of visitor victims were happy to return to Ireland and would recommend it to others and, more importantly, identified ITAS as a positive experience (Campbell 2002).

In the case of Orange County, the Reedy Creek Improvement Area suggests that considerable resources are provided to sustain an adequate tourist support service. However, there is little evidence that this image is adopted by the tourist consumer.

The examples above demonstrate the variety of service provision available to tourist victims of crime. It is clear that, although the intent of some agencies is apparent, recognition of the problems experienced by tourist victims and appropriate responses to these problems do not necessarily follow. In themselves the examples are merely illustrative, but they do reveal important dimensions of the three systems they represent, which can be 'measured' to allow comparisons to be made. The three examples to a greater or lesser extent can be seen to be proactive/reactive, statutory/voluntary, uniform/civilian and partial/total.

By locating each of the three examples on these dimensions the underlying properties of each tourist support service can be assessed. For example, the service provided by the Republic of Ireland can be seen to be largely proactive, a mixture of statutory and voluntary elements, involving both uniform and civilian personnel and, overall, a comprehensive service with a humanistic rather than a legalistic orientation. In contrast the service offered in Florida, although having elements of proactivity, is statutory, uniform, partial and legalistic. The UK service suggests one that is somewhat more reactive and, although it can involve both statutory and volunteer agencies, the problems of reporting to Victim Support may potentially leave many victims with a sense of loss and dissatisfaction.

The analysis also allows services to be compared. Figure 14.1 provides a tentative description and comparison of service provision in the three locations identified in this chapter.

The comparison between the three locations illustrates that England and Wales has a reactive, generally statutory service largely delivered by the police. Victim

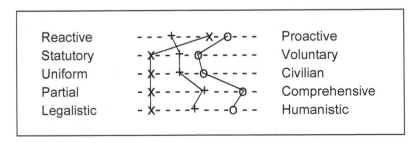

Figure 14.1 A preliminary model of tourist service provision. o, Republic of Ireland, x, Florida, USA, +, England and Wales.

Support, the largest victim assistance body in the UK, provides a range of services although there is no specialist provision for tourist victims. In the example of Cornwall, volunteers working within the Victim Support facility saw little need to amend their services. Identifying and accessing victims who may benefit from their service is dependent upon the discretion of the police officer who attends and/or records the incident. Access to Victim Support is largely dependent on the police. Victim Support would be mobilized only at their discretion and would offer only a general victim support service, not one specifically designed to meet the needs of tourists. In general the service is seen as legalistic – serving the needs of the criminal justice system rather than the specific needs of the victim.[15]

The nature of service provision in the Republic of Ireland is very different. The Gardai have, over a number of years, been made aware of the needs of tourist victims by ITAS. As a result, the reporting of a crime by a tourist victim brings into play set procedures whereby separate documentation is available if the victim has been the victim of an acquisitive crime. The ITAS is contacted to assist with language issues or if the victim has practical needs which require intervention by embassies or commercial organizations or to make contact with relatives of the victim at home. Hence the service provision available to tourist victims in Ireland is far more proactive than in the UK. In addition, a collaborative partnership exists between the Gardai and ITAS and with the organizations that support the service. The tourist victim is hence provided with an extensive service marred only occasionally, such as when a Garda may fail to use the facility. It is the interactivity and cohesion which, while addressing the legal paradigm, provides a humanistic service to victims at their time of need.

The third example, Orange County, Florida, indicates a generally reactive response to tourist victimization through the provision of the tourist-policing sector, which provides an assistance service and is visible in the most populated tourist areas. Officers provide a statutory service which is not supported by a victim assistance programme. Because of their employment status, the service is legalistic and provided by a uniformed agency with no formal civilian input. Therefore, this support network is partial in that there is no immediate access to a victim assistance programme.

In all three case studies, residents who are victims of crime while overseas can access advice through government websites. For example in the USA, citizens who require assistance in Spain can access details of an English-language telephone number to report an incident to the police. Many of the US websites offer assistance on compensation claims or victimization from terrorist incidents. For residents of the UK, the Foreign and Commonwealth Office provides information on its website advising victims of crime of the services that it may offer, although practical assistance is provided only in exceptional circumstances. Similarly, residents of the Republic of Ireland can, if victimized overseas, contact the embassy, which will provide a range of services similar to those available from the US agency. It may be speculated that few people will have this information to hand before travelling to their destination, and access after the event is dependent upon the availability of a computer.

The model provides a description of the parameters that determine the nature of existing services, allowing a comparison of service provision and the ability to evaluate the services from a victim perspective. However, using the Weberian analogy, although these parameters are a necessary part of the description of such services, they are not sufficient in that they do not explore other dimensions that would appear to be part of a more complete description of a tourist victim support service. A more comprehensive analysis can be established if the recommendations of the European Council Framework Decision (Council of the European Union 2001) are included. When this is done the profile of the three services is greatly enhanced and dimensions appear – such as safety, rights and specialist orientation – that could form the basis of an evaluation of the service from a tourist point of view.

Parameters identified in the European Council Framework can hypothetically expand upon the first model and, although there is insufficient space to fully explore these issues, it is important to note that as well as describing and comparing the qualities of different tourist support systems it enables us to consider more systematically the perceived needs of victims and an ideal type system that would meet their needs.

Conclusion

The issues identified and explored in this chapter result in a provisional model relating to systems that more or less address the needs of tourist victims of crime. It is clear that cultural norms and values as well as economic weight influence the levels of engagement by the various agencies. Such a model can provide the basis for an easy and illustrative template in which tourism is influential in the economic strength of the location.

Notes

1 In fieldwork by the author undertaken in 2010.
2 Respondents to a tourist survey distributed in 2001 to victims of crime in Cornwall who had reported the incident to the police.
3 http://www.thisiscornwall.co.uk/news/Crime-stats-reduction-crime-Cornwall/article-1124434-detail/article.html
4 Report by an officer of the Orange County Sheriff's Office, Florida, working in tourist locations.
5 Information provided by the proprietor of a UK-based insurance company.
6 http://www.telegraph.co.uk/travel/travelnews/2403709/One-in-10-British-tourists-have-been-crime-victims
7 http://www.miamibeach411.com/news/index.php?/news/comments/dead-german-tourist/
8 At the time of the incident, reports of crimes were routinely sent to Victim Support via the internet. Since the interpretation and implementation of the Data Protection Act (1998) this practice has been abolished.
9 Since the interviews, the co-ordinator role no longer exists.
10 http://eur-lex.europa.eu/LexUriServ/LexUriServ.do?uri=OJ:L:2001:082:0001:0004:EN:PDF; 82/4 (Article 13.2).

11 Ibid. 82/2 (Article 2.2).
12 http://www.ocso.com/TouristTips/tabid/141/Default.aspx
13 Other tourist-focused locations such as Universal Studios are 'policed' by other jurisdictions.
14 http://www.ocso.com/TouristTips/tabid/141/Default.aspx
15 This similarly impacts upon the legalistic/humanistic dimension of the service provision. In the case of Cornwall tourist victims, the majority were not offered the intervention of Victim Support (Jones 2008) and therefore the level of support can be seen to be more legalistic than humanistic.

Bibliography

Abane, M., Awusabo-Asare, K. and Kissi, M. (1999) 'In whose interest? Individual and societal needs in the creation of forest reserves: the case of Kakum in Ghana', *Bulletin of the Ghana Geographical Association*, (21): 12–19.

ABS (Australian Bureau of Statistics) (2006) *Agriculture in Focus: Farming Families, Australia, 2006,* Cat:7104.0.55.001. Canberra: Australian Bureau of Statistics.

ABS (2010) 8635.0 – Tourist Accommodation, Australia, Sep 2009. Canberra: Australian Bureau of Statistics.

Adamson, C. (2000) 'Defensive localism in white and black: a comparative history of European-American and African-American youth gangs', *Ethnic and Racial Studies*, 23(2): 272–298.

Advisory Council on the Misuse of Drugs (ACMD) (2005) *Khat (Qat): Assessment of Risk to the Individual and Communities in the UK.* London: Home Office.

ACMD (2009) *MDMA ('Ecstasy'): A Review of its Harms and Classification under the Misuse of Drugs Act 1971.* London: Home Office.

ACMD (2010a) *Anabolic Steroids.* London: Home Office.

ACMD (2010b) *Consideration of the Cathinones.* London: Home Office.

Agnew, R. (1992) 'Foundation for a general strain theory of crime and delinquency', *Criminology*, 30(1): 47–87.

Akyeampong, O. A. (1996) *Tourism and Regional Development in Sub-Saharan Africa: A Case Study of Ghana's Central Region.* PhD dissertation, University of Stockholm.

Alasuutari, P. (1992) *Desire and Craving: A Cultural Theory of Alcoholism.* New York: State University of New York Press.

de Albuquerque, K. and McElroy, J. (1999) 'Tourism and crime in the Caribbean', *Annals of Tourism Research*, 26(2): 968–984.

Allen, J. (1999) Crime against International Tourists. NSW Bureau of Crime Statistics and Research Bulletin No. 43.

Alleyne, D. and Boxill, I. (2003) 'The impact of crime on tourist arrivals in Jamaica', *International Journal of Tourism Research*, 5(1): 381–391.

Altbeker, A. (2005) 'Is South Africa really the world's crime capital?', *Institute for Security Studies SA Crime Quarterly*, 1 (March): 1–8.

Amster, R. (2004) *Street People and the Contested Realms of Public Space.* New York: LFB Scholarly Publishing.

Anderson, D., Chenery, S. and Pease, K. (1995) *Biting Back: Tackling Repeat Burglary and Car Crime.* Crime Detection and Prevention Series, no. 58. London: Home Office.

Ankomah, P. and Crompton, J. (1990) 'Unrealised tourism potential: the case of sub-Saharan Africa', *Tourism Management*, 11(3): 11–28.

APN (2009) 'Rape shuts down camp', *New Zealand Herald* [online]. Available at: http://www.nzherald.co.nz/news/print.cfm?objectid=10552401

APR Consultants (2009) *Rotorua District Perceptions of Safety Survey*. Rotorua District Council, New Zealand.

Ashton, M. (ed.) (1992) *The Ecstasy Papers: A Collection of ISDD's Publications on the Dance Drugs Phenomenon*. London: ISDD.

Aziz, H. (1995) 'Understanding attacks on tourists in Egypt', *Tourism Management*, 16: 91–95.

Barak, G. (1992) *Gimme Shelter: A Social History of Homelessness in Contemporary America*. New York: Praeger.

Barak, G. (1994) 'Between the waves: mass-mediated themes of crime and justice', *Social Justice*, 21(3): 133–147.

Barclay, E. and Donnermeyer, J. F. (2002) 'Property crime and crime prevention on farms in Australia', *Crime Prevention and Community Safety: An International Journal*, 4(2): 47–61.

Barclay, E. M., Donnermeyer, J. F., Doyle, B. D. and Talary, D. (2001) *Property Crime Victimisation and Crime Prevention on Farms*, report to the NSW Attorney General's Crime Prevention Division, Armidale, Institute for Rural Futures, University of New England, Armidale, NSW.

Barclay, E. M., Donnermeyer, J. F. and Jobes, P. C. (2004) 'The dark side of gemeinschaft: criminality within rural communities', *Crime Prevention and Community Safety: An International Journal*, 6(3): 7–22.

Barker, M., Page, S. J. and Meyer, D. (2002) 'Modeling tourism crime: the 2000 Americas Cup', *Annals of Tourism Research*, 29(3): 762–782.

Barker, M., Page, S. J. and Meyer, D. (2003) 'Urban visitor perceptions of safety during a special event', *Journal of Travel Research*, 41(4): 355–361.

Barter, C. (2009) 'In the name of love: partner abuse and violence in teenage relationships', *British Journal of Social Work*, 39(2): 211–233.

Barton, A. and James, Z. (2003) 'Run to the sun: policing contested perceptions of risk', *Policing and Society*, 13(3): 259–270.

Bauman, Z. (1998a) *Work, Consumerism and the New Poor*. Maidenhead: Open University Press.

Bauman, Z. (1998b) *Globalization: The Human Consequences*. New York: Columbia University Press.

BBC (2009) 'Karen Aim murder sentencing date' [online]. Available at: http://news.bbc.co.uk/2/hi/uk_news/scotland/north_east/7924635.stml

Beck, U. (1992) *Risk Society: Towards a New Modernity*. Sage Publications: London.

Becker, H. (1963) *Outsiders: Studies in the Sociology of Deviance*. New York: Free Press.

Becker, H. (1997) *Outsiders: Studies in the Sociology of Deviance* (2nd edn). New York: Free Press.

Bell, C. (2008) '100% pure New Zealand: branding for back-packers', *Journal of Vacation Marketing*, 14(4): 345–355.

Bell, D. (1997) 'Anti-idyll: rural horror', in P. Cloke and J. Little (eds) *Contested Countryside Cultures*. London: Routledge.

Bell, D. (2006a) 'Bodies, technologies, spaces: on "dogging"', *Sexualities*, 9(4): 387–407.

Bell, D. (2006b) 'Variations on the rural idyll', in P. Cloke, T. Marsden and P. H. Mooney (eds) *Handbook of Rural Studies*. London: Sage.

Bellis, M. A., Hale, G., Bennett, A., Chaudry, M. and Kilfoyle, M. (2000) 'Ibiza uncovered: changes in substance use and sexual behaviour among young people visiting an international night-life resort', *International Journal of Drug Policy*, 11, 235–244.

Bendelow, G. and Williams, S. (1998) *Emotions in Social Life: Critical Themes and Contemporary Issues*. London: Routledge.

Benghiat L. (2008) 'Crime in SA is a real threat to tourism', *Travelwires* [online]. Available at: http://www.travelwires.com/wp/2008/07/crime-in-sa-is-a-real-threat-to-tourism/

Bengry-Howell, A. and Griffin, C. (2007) 'Self-made motormen: the material construction of working-class masculine identity through car modification', *Journal of Youth Studies*, 10(4): 439–458.

Benson, D. E. (2001) 'Survey of state programs for habitat, hunting, and non-game management on private lands in the Unites States', *Wildlife Society Bulletin*, 29(1): 354–358.

Bentley, T. and Page, S. (2001) 'Scoping the extent of adventure tourism accidents in New Zealand', *Annals of Tourism Research*, 28(3): 705–726.

Blackwell, R. D., Miniard, P. W. and Engel, J. F. (2006) *Consumer Behaviour* (10th edn). Cincinnati, OH: South Western.

Bloom, J. (1996) 'A South Africa perspective of the effects of crime and violence on the tourism industry', in A. Pizam and Y. Mansfeld (eds) *Tourism, Crime and International Security Issues*. Chichester: Wiley & Sons.

Boakye, K. A. (2008) *An Empirical Investigation into Tourism Oriented Crimes: Focus on Cape Coast, Kumasi and Accra*. PhD dissertation, University of Cape Coast.

Boakye, K. A. (2009) 'Exploring tourists' vulnerability to crime: a travel behavior approach', *Oguaa Journal of Social Sciences*, 5(1): 1–20.

Boakye, K. A. (2010) 'Studying tourists' suitability as crime targets', *Annals of Tourism Research*, 37(3): 727–743.

Booth Davies, J. (1997) *Drugspeak: The Analysis of Drug Discourse*. Amsterdam: Harwood Academic Press.

Borochowitz, D. and Eisikovitz, Z. (2002) 'To love violently: strategies for reconciling love and violence', *Violence against Women*, 8(4): 476–494.

Boutellier, J. C. J. (1991) 'Prostitution, criminal law and morality in the Netherlands', *Crime, Law and Social Change*, 15: 201–211.

Box Office Mojo (2009) 'Saw V' [online]. Available at: http://boxofficemojo.com/movies/?id=saw5.htm

Brain, K. (2000) *Youth, Alcohol, and the Emergence of the Post-Modern Alcohol Order*. Occasional Paper no. 1. London: Institute of Alcohol Studies. Available at: http://www.ias.org.uk/resources/papers/brainpaper.pdf

Brandth, B. and Haugen, M. S. (1995) 'Rural masculinity in transition', *Journal of Rural Studies*, 11(2): 44–45.

Brandt, S., Sumnall, H., Measham, F. and Cole, J. (2010) 'Second generation mephedrone: the confusing case of NRG-1', *British Medical Journal*, 341: c3564.

Brandt, S., Freeman, S., Sumnall, H., Measham, F., and Cole, J. (2011) 'Analysis of NRG "legal highs" in the UK: identification and formulation of novel cathinones', *Drug Testing and Analysis*, early view. Available at: http://onlinelibrary.wiley.com/doi/10.1002/dta.204/pdf

Brants, C. (1998) 'The fine art of regulated tolerance: prostitution in Amsterdam', *Journal of Law and Society*, 25(4): 621–635.

Brayshaw, D. (1995) 'Negative publicity about tourism destinations: a Florida case study', *Travel and Tourism Analyst*, 5: 62–71.

Breda, Z. and Costa, C. (2006) 'Safety and security issues affecting inbound tourism in the People's Republic of China', in A. Pizam, and Y. Mansfeld (eds) *Tourism Security and Safety: From Theory to Practice*. New York: Butterworth Heinemann.

Briscoe, S. and Donnelly, N. (2001) 'Temporal and regional aspects of alcohol-related violence and disorder', *Alcohol Studies Bulletin no. 1*. Produced by the NSW Bureau of Crime Statistics and Research and the National Drug Research Institute of Curtin University.

Brown, O. (2000) 'Tourism and foreign investment in Africa', in P. Dieke (ed.) *The Political Economy of Tourism Development in Africa*. New York: Cognizant.

Brown, R. I. (1986) 'Arousal and sensation-seeking components in the general explanation of gambling and gambling addictions', *International Journal of the Addictions*, 21: 1001–1016.

Brunt, P. and Hambly, Z. (1999) 'Tourism and crime: a research agenda', *Crime Prevention and Community Safety: An International Journal*, 21: 417–424.

Brunt, P. and Hooton, N. (2010) 'Community responses to tourism and crime', *Crime Prevention and Community Safety: An International Journal*, 12(1): 42–57.

Brunt, P., Mawby, R. and Hambly, Z. (2000) 'Tourist victimisation and the fear of crime on holiday', *Tourism Management*, 21(4): 417–424.

Buchmann, A., Moore, K. and Fisher, D. (2010) 'Experiencing film tourism: authenticity and fellowship', *Annals of Tourism Research*, 37(1): 220–248.

Buckland, F. (2002) *Impossible Dance: Club Culture and Queer World-Making*. Middletown: Wesleyan University Press.

Burton, B. (2007) 'Need to curb a PR industry spinning out of control', *Sydney Morning Herald*, 7 August. Available at: http://www.smh.com.au/news/opinion/need-to-curb-a-pr-industry-spinning-out-of-control/2007/08/06/1186252624551.html

Butler, R. (1998) 'Rural recreation and tourism', in B. Ilbery (ed.) *The Geography of Rural Change*. Harlow: Longman.

Buttle, J. W. (2006) *What Is Known about Policing Rural Crime: Reviewing the Contemporary Literature*, report to the New Zealand Police Rural Liaison, New Zealand Police, Wellington.

Cabinet Office (2010) *The Coalition: Our Programme for Government*. London: Cabinet Office. Available at: http://www.cabinetoffice.gov.uk/media/409088/pfg_Coalition.pdf

Campbell, L. (2002) *Tourist Victim Support Services: Victim Impact Survey Report Dublin*. Dublin: Tourism Research Centre, Dublin Institute of Technology.

Campion, R. and Stephenson, J. (2010) 'The right to roam: lessons for New Zealand from Sweden's allemanstratt', *Australasian Journal of Environmental Management*, 17: 18–26.

Caplan, P. (2005) *The Myth of Women's Masochism*. Lincoln, NE: iUniverse.

Capraro, R. L. (2000) 'Why college men drink: alcohol, adventure, and the paradox of masculinity', *Journal of American College Health*, 48(6): 307–315.

Caputi, J. (1987) *The Age of Sex Crime*. London: Women's Press.

Carr, N. (2001) 'An exploratory study of gendered differences in young tourists' perception of danger within London', *Tourism Management*, 22(5): 565–570.

Carrabine, E. and Longhurst, B. (2002) 'Consuming the car: anticipation, use and meaning in contemporary youth culture', *Sociological Review*, 50(2): 181–196.

Carter, C. (2000) 'Sex in the tourist city: the development of commercial sex as part of the provision of tourist services', in S. Clift and S. Carter (eds) *Tourism and Sex: Culture, Commerce and Coercion*. London: Pinter.

Carter, S. (1998) 'Tourists and traveller's social construction of Africa and Asia as risky locations', *Tourism Management*, 19: 349–358.

Cavlek, N. (2002) 'Tour operators and destination safety', *Annals of Tourism Research*, 29(2): 478–496.

CBS News (2006) ' "CSI effect" adds drama to real-life crime solving', *CBS News Online*, 27 February. Available at: http://wwww.cbc.ca

CCIA (Caravan and Camping Industry Association of NSW) (2010) *Caravan and Camping Industry Profile* [online]. Available at: http://www.caravancamping.com.au/files/media-kits/Caravan%20and%20Camping%20Industry%20Profile%20S.pdf

Center for Business and Economic Research (2010) *Metropolitan Las Vegas Tourism Statistics*. University of Nevada, Las Vegas [online]. Available at: http://cber.unlv.edu/tour.html

Chan, J. B. L. (1997) *Changing Police Culture: Policing in a Multicultural Society*. Cambridge: Cambridge University Press.

Chan, S. (1999) 'Bubbling acid: Sydney's techno underground', in R. White (ed.) *Australian Youth Subcultures: On the Margins and in the Mainstream*. Hobart: Australian Clearinghouse for Youth Studies.

Channell, W. T. (1994) 'Fun, sun and security', *Security Management*, 38(9): 52.

Chatterton, P. and Hollands, R. (2003) *Urban Nightscapes: Youth Cultures, Pleasure Spaces and Corporate Power*. London: Routledge.

Chen, J. S. and Gursoy, D. (2001) 'An investigation of tourists' destination loyalty and preferences', *International Journal of Contemporary Hospitality Management*, 13(2): 79–85.

Chesney-Lind, M. and Lind, I. (1986) 'Visitors as victims: crimes against tourists in Hawaii', *Annals of Tourism Research*, 13(3): 167–191.

Chesney-Lind, M., Lind, I. Y. and Schaafsma, H. (1983) *Salient Factors in Hawaii's Crime Rate*, report no. 286, University of Hawaii-Manoa, Youth Development and Research Center.

Chibnall, S. (1977) *Law-and-Order News: An Analysis of Crime Reporting in the British Press*. London: Tavistock Publications.

Chikritzhs, T., Catalano, P., Pascal, R., and Henrickson, N. (2007) *Predicting Alcohol-Related Harms from Licensed Outlet Density: A Feasibility Study*. Hobart: National Drug Law Enforcement Research Fund, Commonwealth of Australia.

Chioji, W. (2004) *ASIS/CFHMA Law Enforcement Officer Awards*. Presentation of the American Society of Industrial Security and the Central Florida Hotel and Motel Association, Orlando, FL.

Cloke, P. and Little, J. (1997) 'Introduction: other countrysides?', in P. Cloke and J. Little (eds) *Contested Countryside Cultures*. London: Routledge.

Clover, C. (1992) *Men, Women and Chainsaws: Gender in the Modern Horror Film*. Princeton, NJ: Princeton University Press.

Cloward, R. and Ohlin, L. (1960) *Delinquency and Opportunity*. Chicago: Free Press.

Coffield, F. and Gofton, L. (1994) *Drugs and Young People*. London: Institute for Public Policy Research.

Cohen, E. (1972) 'Towards a sociology of international tourism', *Social Research*, (39)2: 164–182.

Cohen, E. (1987a) 'The tourist as victim and protégé of law enforcing agencies', *Leisure Studies*, (6)2: 181–198.

Cohen E. (1987b) 'Tourism-related crime: towards a sociology of crime', *Visions in Leisure and Business*, 16(1): 4–14

Cohen, L. and Felson, M. (1979) 'Social change and crime rate trends: a routine activities approach', *American Sociological Review*, 44(4): 588–608.

Cohen, L. and Cantor, D. (1981) 'Residential burglary in the United States: life-style and demographic factors associated with the probability of victimization', *Journal of Research in Crime and Delinquency*, 18, 113–127.

Cohen, S. (1980) *Folk Devils and Moral Panics* (new edn). Oxford: Martin Robertson.

Cohen, S. (2002) *Folk Devils and Moral Panics* (3rd edn), Abingdon: Routledge.

Cohen, S. and Young, J. (1973) *The Manufacture of News: Social Problems, Deviance and the Mass Media*. London: Constable.

Cole, S. A. and Dioso-Villa, R. (2007) 'CSI and its effects: media, juries, and the burden of proof', *New England Law Review*, 41(3), 435–470.

Coleman, C. and Moynihan, J. (1996) *Understanding Crime Data: Haunted by the Dark Figure*. Buckingham: Open University Press.

Collins, J., Noble, G., Poynting, S. and Tabar, P. (2000) *Kebabs, Kids, Cops, and Crime: Youth, Ethnicity and Crime*. Annandale: Pluto Press.

Connell, R. W. (2003) *Masculinities*. New South Wales: Allen and Unwin.

Cook, A. (2009) *Jack the Ripper*. Stroud: Amberley.

Cook, R. L. and McCleary, K. W. (1983) 'Redefining vacation distances in consumer minds', *Journal of Travel Research*, 22(2): 31–33.

Cordner, G. and Sheehan, R. (1999) *Police Administration*. Cincinatti, OH: Anderson Publishing.

Cordner, G. and Biebel, E. P. (2005) 'Problem-oriented policing in practice', *Criminology & Public Policy*, 4(2): 155–180.

Cottle, S. (2003) *News, Public Relations and Power*. London: Sage Publications.

Council of the European Union (2001) 'Council framework decision on the standing of victims in criminal proceedings', *Official Journal of the European Commission*, 2001/220/JHA.

Crime Prevention and Community Safety: An International Journal (2009) Special issue on alcohol and disorder, 11(3).

Cromwell, P. F., Olson, J. N. and Avary, D. A. W. (1991) *Breaking and Entering*. Newbury Park, CA: Sage.

Crompton, J. L. (1977) *A Systems Model of the Tourist's Destination Selection Process with Particular Reference to the Role of Image and Perceived Constraints*. Doctoral dissertation, Texas A & M University.

Crotts, J. (1996) 'Theoretical perspectives on tourist criminal victimisation', *Journal of Tourism Studies*, 7(1): 2–9.

Crouch, D. (2000) 'Places around us: embodied lay geographies in leisure and tourism', *Leisure Studies*, 19(2): 63–76.

Cunneen, C. (2007) 'Riot, resistance and moral panic: demonising the colonial other', in S. Poynting and G. Morgan (eds) *Outrageous! Moral Panics in Australia*. Hobart: ACYS Publishing.

Dahles, H. (1998) 'Redefining Amsterdam as a tourist destination', *Annals of Tourism Research*, 25(1): 55–69.

Daily Express (2010) '"Meddling" Labour accused over drug tragedies', 18 March. Available at: http://www.express.co.uk/posts/view/163595/-Meddling-Labour-accused-over-drug-tragedies

Daily Telegraph (2008) 'NSW Police Force profits as TV crime pays up', 29 December. Available at: http://www.news.com.au/entertainment/story/0,28383,24850251–5016681,00.html

Daily Telegraph (2010) 'Mephedrone ban comes into force', 16 April. Available at: http://www.telegraph.co.uk/health/healthnews/7596347/Mephedrone-ban-comes-into-force.html

D'Andrea, A. (2007) *Global Nomads: Techno and New Age as Transnational Countercultures in Ibiza and Goa*. London: Routledge.

Davidson, J. and Bondi, L. (2004) 'Spatialising affect; affecting space: an introduction', *Gender, Place and Culture*, 11(3): 373–374.

Davidson, J. and Milligan, C. (2004) 'Editorial: embodying emotion, sensing space, introducing emotional geographies', *Social and Cultural Geography*, 5(4): 523–532.

Davis, D., Allen, J. and Cosenza, R. M. (1988) 'Segmenting local residents by their attitudes, interests and opinions toward tourism', *Journal of Travel Research*, 27(2): 2–8.

Davis, M. (1990) *City of Quartz: Excavating the Future in Los Angeles*. London: Vintage.

Deacon, D. and Golding, P. (1994) *Taxation and Representation: The Media, Political Communication and the Poll Tax*. London: John Libbey.

Decker, S., van Gemert, F. and Pyrooz, D. (2009) 'Gangs, migration, and crime: the changing landscape in Europe and the USA', *International Migration and Integration*, 10: 393–408.

Deehan, A. and Saville, E. (2003) *Calculating the Risk: Recreational Drug Use among Clubbers in the South East of England*, Home Office Online Report 43/03. London: Home Office.

DEFRA (Department for Environment, Food and Rural Affairs UK) (2010) *Why Have the CROW Act?* [online]. Available at: http://www.defra.gov.uk/rural/countryside/crow/about.htm

Demos, E. (1992) 'Concern for safety: a potential problem in the tourist industry', *Journal of Travel and Tourism Marketing*, 1(1): 81–88.

Denholm, M. and Dalton, R. (2005) 'Dark side of the hoon', *The Australian*, 20 April.

Department of Health (2010) *Speeches: Anne Milton's Speech to the Westminster Hall*. London: Department of Health. Available at: http://www.dh.gov.uk/en/MediaCentre/Speeches/DH_117299

van Dijk, J., van Kesteren, J. and Smit, P. (2007) *Criminal Victimization in International Perspective: Key Findings from the 2004–2005 ICVS and EUICS*. The Hague: WODC.

Dimanche, F. and Lepetic, A. (1999) 'New Orleans tourism and crime: a case study', *Journal of Travel Research*, 38(August): 19–23.

Dittmar, H. (1998) *The Social Psychology of Material Possessions: To Have Is to Be*. London: Harvester-Wheatsheaf.

Ditton, J. and Chadee, D. (2005) 'People's perceptions of their likely future risk of criminal victimization', *British Journal of Criminology*, 46(3): 505–518.

Dobash, R. E. and Dobash, R. P. (2002) *Women, Violence and Social Change* (4th edn). London: Routledge.

Dowling, G. and Staelin, R. (1994) 'A model of perceived risk and intended risk-handling activity', *Journal of Consumer Research*, 21(June): 119–134.

Downes, D. H. (1966) *The Delinquent Solution: A Study in Subcultural Theory*. London: Routledge.

Doyle, A. (1998) ' "Cops": television policing as policing reality', in M. Fishman and G. Cavender (eds) *Entertaining Crime: Television Reality Programs*. New York: Aldine de Gruyter.

Doyle, A. C. (2006) *A Study in Scarlet*. London: Headline Review.

Duff, C. (2008) 'The pleasure in context', *International Journal of Drug Policy*, 19(5): 384–392.

Duruz, J. (1999) 'Cuisine nostalgie? Tourisms romance with the rural', *Communal/Plural*, 7(1): 97–109.

DutchNews (2009) 'Ministry warns tourists to New Zealand' [online]. Available at: http://www.dutchnews.nl/news/archives/2009/01/ministry_warns_tourists_to_new_zealand.htm

Edwards, C. (2005) *Changing Policing Theories for 21st Century Societies*. Sydney: Federation Press.

Ellickson, R. C. (1996) 'Controlling chronic misconduct in city spaces: of panhandlers, skid rows, and public-space zoning', *Yale Law Journal*, 105(5): 1165–1248.

Elliot, L. and Ryan, C. (1993) 'The impact of crime on Corsican tourism: a descriptive assessment', *World Travel and Tourism Review*, 3: 287–293.

Emerson, C. D. (2009) 'Merging public and private governance: how Disney's Reedy Creek Improvement District "re-imagined" the traditional division of local regulatory powers', *Florida State University Law Review*, 36: 177–214.

Emsley, C. (2005) *Crime and Society in England 1750–1900*. UK: Pearson Education.

Engineer, R., Phillips, A., Thompson, J. and Nicholls, J. (2003) *Drunk and Disorderly: A Qualitative Study of Binge Drinking among 18 to 24 year olds*, Home Office Research Study no. 262. London: Home Office.

Epley, N. and Caruso, E. M. (2004) 'Egocentric ethics', *Social Justice Research*, 17(2): 171–187.

Ericson, R. V. (1995) *Crime and the Media*. USA: Dartmouth Publishing.

Eriksen, A. M. (2009) 'Karen Aim's killer jailed for at least 12.5 years', *New Zealand Herald* [online]. Available at: http://www.nzherald.co.nz/youth/news/article. cfm?c_id=107&objectid=10563738

Ettorre, E. (1992) *Women and Substance Use*. Basingstoke: Macmillan.

Faulkner, B. and Vikulov, S. (2001) 'Katherine, washed out one day, back on track the next: a post-mortem of a tourism disaster', *Tourism Management*, 22: 331–344.

Federal Bureau of Investigation (2001) *Crime in the United States, 2001: Uniform Crime Reports*. USA: United States Department of Justice.

Felson, M. and Cohen, L. (1979) 'Social change and crime rate trends: a routine activities approach', *American Sociological Review*, 44: 588–608.

Felson, R. B., Messner, S. F., Hoskin, A. W. and Deane, G. (2002) 'Reasons for reporting and not reporting domestic violence to the police', *Criminology*, 40(3): 617–648.

Ferrell, J. (1997) 'Youth, crime and cultural space', *Social Justice*, 24(4): 21–38.

Ferrell, J. (1999) 'Cultural criminology', *American Review of Sociology*, 25: 395–418.

Ferrell, J., Hayward, K., and Young, J. (2008) *Cultural Criminology: An Invitation*. Los Angeles: Sage.

Fickling, D. (2003) 'Police on the beach poop schoolies party in Surfers Paradise', *Guardian*, 29 November. Available at: http://www.guardian.co.uk/world/2003/nov/29/ australia.internationaleducationnews

Finch, L. (1993) 'On the streets: working class youth culture in the nineteenth century', in R. White (ed.) *Youth Subcultures: Theory, History and the Australian Experience*. Hobart: National Clearinghouse for Youth Studies.

Finnane, M. (1987) 'Introduction: writing about police in Australia', in M. Finnane (ed.) *Policing in Australia: Historical Perspectives*. Kensington: New South Wales University Press.

Finnane, M. (1990) 'Police and politics in Australia: the case for historical revision', *Australian and New Zealand Journal of Criminology*, 23: 218–228.

Finnane, M. (1994a) *Police and Government: Histories of Policing in Australia*. Melbourne: Oxford University Press.

Finnane, M. (1994b) 'Larrikins, delinquents and cops: police and young people in Australian history', in R. White and C. Alder (eds) *The Police and Young People in Australia*. Melbourne: Cambridge University Press.

Fitzgerald, J. (2002) 'A political economy of doves', *Contemporary Drug Problems*, 29(1): 201–239.

Fodness, D. and Murray, B. (1998) 'A typology of tourist information search strategies', *Journal of Travel Research*, 37: 108–119.

Forrester, J. (1986) 'Rape, seduction and psychoanalysis', in S. Tomaselli and R. Porter (eds) *Rape*. London: Basil Blackwell.

Forrester, L. (1999) 'Street machiners and "showing off" ' in R. White (ed.) *Australian Youth Subcultures: On the Margins and in the Mainstream*. Hobart: Australian Clearinghouse for Youth Studies.

Foucault, M. (1998) *The Will to Knowledge: The History of Sexuality: Volume 1*, trans. Robert Hurley. London: Penguin Books.

Four Wheel Drive NSW and ACT (2010) *Join Us: 4 Wheel Drive NSW & ACT Inc.* [online]. Available at: http://www.4wdnsw-act.asn.au/

France, A. (2007) *Understanding Youth in Late Modernity*. Maidenhead: Open University Press.

Franzen, R. (2002) 'CSI effect on potential jurors has some prosecutors worried', *San Diego Union-Tribune*, 16 December. Available at: www.signonsandiego.com/index. html

Frayling, C. (1986) 'The house that Jack built', in S. Tomaselli and R. Porter (eds) *Rape*. UK: Basil Blackwell.

Frey, J. H., Reichert, L. R. and Russell, K. V. (1981) 'Prostitution, business, and police: the maintenance of an illegal economy', *Police Journal*, 54(3): 239–249.

Friedman, S. R., de Jong, W., Rossi, D., Touzé, G., Rockwell, R., Des Jarlais, D. C. and Elovich, R. (2007) 'Harm reduction theory: users' culture, micro-social harm reduction, and the self-organization and outside-organizing of users' groups', *International Journal of Drug Policy*, 18(2): 107–117.

Fuchs, G. and Reichel, A. (2004) 'Cultural differences in tourist destination risk perception: an explanatory study', *Tourism*, 52(4): 7–20.

Fujii, E. T. and Mak, J. (1979) 'The impact of alternative regional development strategies on crime rates: tourism vs. agriculture in Hawaii', *Annals of Regional Science*, 13(3): 42–56.

Fujii, E. T. and Mak, J. (1980) 'Tourism and crime: implications for regional development policy', *Regional Studies*, 14(1): 27–36.

Fukunaga, L. (1975) 'A new sun in Kohala: the socio-economic impact of tourism and resort development on a rural community in Hawaii', in W. Finney and F. Watson (eds) *A New Kind of Sugar: Tourism in the Pacific*. Honolulu: East West Center.

Furlong, A. and Cartmel, F. (1997) *Young People and Social Change: Individualism and Late Modernity*. Buckingham: Open University Press.

Garland, D. (2001) *The Culture of Control: Crime and Social Order in Contemporary Society*. Oxford: Oxford University Press.

Garofalo, J. (1981) 'Crime and the mass media: a selective review of research', *Journal of Research in Crime and Delinquency*, 18 (2): 319–350.

Gartman, D. (1994) *Auto Opium: A Social History of American Automobile Design*. London: Routledge.

Gartner, W. and Shen, J. (1992) 'The impact of Tiananmen Square on China's tourism image', *Journal of Travel Research*, 30(4): 47–52.

Gay, E. (2009a) 'Negative press putting Dutch off NZ holiday', *New Zealand Herald* [online]. Available at: http://www.nzherald.co.nz/nz/news/print. cfm?c_id=1&objectid=10553981&pnum=0

Gay, E. (2009b) 'Dutch government warns tourists of NZ crime', *New Zealand Herald* [online]. Available at: http://www.nzherald.co.nz/netherlands/news/article. cfm?1_id=69

Gee, C., Choy, D. and Mackens, C. (1989) *The Travel Industry*. New York: Cole and Sons.

Gefou-Madianou, D. (ed.) (1992) *Alcohol, Gender, and Culture*. London: Routledge.

van Gemert, F. and Verbraeck, H. (1994) 'Snacks, sex and smack: the ecology of the drug trade in the inner city of Amsterdam', in E. Leuw and L. H. Marshall (eds) *Between Prohibition and Legalisation: The Dutch Experiment in Drug Policy*. Amsterdam: Kugler.

van Gemert, F., Peterson, D. and Lien, I.-L. (eds) (2008) *Youth Gangs, Migration, and Ethnicity*. Cullompton, Devon: Willan Publishing.

George, R. (2001) 'The impact of crime on international tourist numbers to Cape Town', *Crime Prevention and Community Safety: An International Journal*, 3(3): 19–29.

George, R. (2003) 'Tourists' perceptions of safety and security while visiting Cape Town', *Tourism Management*, 24(October): 575–585.

Ghana Tourist Board (2009) *Fact Sheet, 2008*. Accra: author.

Ghoshray, S. (2007) 'Untangling the CSI effect in criminal jurisprudence: circumstantial evidence, reasonable doubt, and jury manipulation', *New England Law Review*, 41(3): 533–562.

Gibson, H. and Jordan, F. (1998) 'Travelling solo: a cross-cultural study of British and American women aged 30–50', paper presented at the Fourth International Conference of the Leisure Studies Association, Leeds, UK.

Gibson, H. and Yiannakis, A. (2002) 'Tourist roles: needs and the adult life course', *Annals of Tourism Research*, 2: 358–383.

Gillan, A. (2002) 'Erotic Emma: drunk and at risk', *Guardian*, 22 June, 13.

Glensor, R. and Peak, K. (2004) 'Crimes against tourists', in *Problem-Oriented Guides for Police: Problem Specific Guide*, No. 26 [online]. Available at: http://www.popcenter. org/problems/crimes_against_tourists/1

Glensor, R. W., Correia, M. E. and Peak, K. J. (2000) *Policing Communities: Understanding Crime and Solving Problems*. California: Roxbury Publishing.

Goehner, A. L., Lofaro, L. and Novack, K. (2004) 'Ripple effect: where CSI meets real law and order', *Time*. Available at: http://www.time.com/time/printout/0,8816,749437,00. html

Goldsmith, A. (2010) 'Policing's new visibility', *British Journal of Criminology*, 50(5): 914–934.

Gonzales, V. (2005) 'Prosecutors feel the "CSI effect"', *CBS News*, 10 February. Available at: http://www.cbsnews.com/stories/2005/02/10/eveningnews/main673060.shtml

Goodrich, J. N. (1978) 'The relationship between preferences for and perceptions of vacation destinations: application of a choice model', *Journal of Travel Research*, 17(3): 44–46.

Goudriaan, H., Wittebrood, K. and Nieuwbeerta, P. (2005) 'Neighbourhood characteristics and reporting crime: effects of social cohesion, confidence in police effectiveness and socio-economic disadvantage', *British Journal of Criminology*, 46(7): 719–742.

Graham, H. and White, R. (2007) 'Young people, dangerous driving and car culture', *Youth Studies Australia*, 26(3): 28–35.

Graham, K. and Homel, R. (2008) *Raising the Bar: Preventing Aggression in and around Bars, Pubs and Clubs*. Cullompton, Devon: Willan Publishing.

Green, R. (2007) 'Forensic investigation in the UK', in T. Newburn, T. Williamson and A. Wright (eds) *Handbook of Criminal Investigation*. Cullompton, Devon: Willan Publishing.

Green, R. and Moore, D. (2009) ' "Kiddie drugs" and controlled pleasure: recreational use of dexamphetamine in a social network of young Australians', *International Journal of Drug Policy*, 20(5): 402–408.

Grey, C. and Mentor, S. (1995) 'The cyborg body politic and the new world order', in G. Brahm and M. Driscoll (eds) *Prosthetic Territories: Politics and Hypertechnologies*. California: Westview Press

Hacking, I. (1986) 'Making up people', reprinted in M. Biagiolo (ed.) *The Science Studies Reader*. London: Routledge, 1999.

Hadfield, P. (2008) 'From threat to promise: nightclub "security", governance and consumer elites', *British Journal of Criminology*, 48: 429–447.

Hadfield, P. and Measham, F. (2010) *Lost Orders? Law Enforcement and Alcohol in England and Wales*, final report. London: Portman Group.

Hagedorn, J. (ed.) (2007) *Gangs in the Global City: Alternatives to Traditional Criminology*. Urbana: University of Illinois Press.

Hagedorn, J. (2008) *A World of Gangs: Armed Young Men and Gangsta Culture*. Minneapolis: University of Minnesota Press.

Halfacree, H. K. (1996) 'Out of place in the country: travellers and the "rural idyll"', *Antipode*, 28 (1): 42–72.

Hall, C. M. and O'Sullivan, V. (1996) 'Tourism, political stability and violence', in A. Pizam and Y. Mansfeld (eds) *Tourism, Crime and International Security Issue*. Chichester: Wiley.

Hall, J. and Pretty, J. (2008) 'Unwritten, unspoken: how norms of rural conduct affect public good provision', proceedings of the Rural Futures: Dreams, Dilemmas, Dangers Conference, 1–4 April, University of Plymouth, UK.

Hall, S. and Winlow, S. (2005) 'Night-time leisure violence and the break-down of the pseudo-pacification process', *Probation Journal*, 52(4): 367–389.

Halpern, J. H., Sherwood, A. R., Hudson, J. I., Gruber, S., Kozin, D. and Harrison, G. P. (2011) 'Residual neurocognitive features of long-term ecstasy users with minimal exposure to other drugs', *Addiction*, 106(4): 777–786.

Halsey, M. and Young, A. (2002) 'The meanings of graffiti and municipal administration', *Australian and New Zealand Journal of Criminology*, 35(2): 165–186.

Halsey, M. and Young, A. (2006) ' "Our desires are ungovernable": writing graffiti in urban space', *Theoretical Criminology*, 10(3): 275–306.

Hansard (2010) HC Deb, 21 January, c148WH.

Haralambopoulos, N. and Pizam, A. (1996) 'Perceived impact of tourism: the case of Samos', *Annals of Tourism Research*, 23: 503–526.

Hardin, G. (1968) 'The tragedy of the commons', *Science*, 162: 1243–1248.

Harper, D. W. (2001) 'Comparing tourists crime victimization', *Annals of Tourism Research*, 28(4): 1053–1056.

Harper, D. (2006) 'The tourist and his criminal: patterns in street robbery', in Y. Mansfeld and A. Pizam (eds) *Tourism Security and Safety: From Theory to Practice*. New York: Butterworth-Heinemann.

Harper, J. (2004) *Legacy of Blood: A Comprehensive Guide to Slasher Movies*. Manchester: Critical Vision.

Haskell, M. (1987) *From Reverence to Rape: Treatment of Women in the Movies*. London: University of Chicago Press.

Hattersley, G. (2004) 'Welcome to Sin on Sea', *Sunday Times*, 18 July (News Review), 1–2.

Hatton, Z. (2007) *The Tarmac Cowboys; An Ethnographic Study of the Cultural World of Boy Racers*. PhD dissertation, University of Plymouth.

Hayward, K. (2002) 'The vilification and pleasures of youthful transgression', in J. Muncie, G. Hughes and E. McLaughlin (eds) *Youth Justice: Critical Readings*. London: Sage.

Hayward, K. and Hobbs, D. (2007) 'Beyond the binge in "Booze Britain": market-led liminalization and the spectacle of binge drinking', *British Journal of Sociology*, 58(3): 437–456.

Hill, A. (2002) 'Acid house and Thatcherism: noise, the mob and the English countryside', *British Journal of Sociology*, 53(1): 89–105.

HM Government (2007) *Safe, Sensible, Social: The Next Steps in the National Alcohol Strategy*. London: TSO.

HMSO (2006) *The Government Reply to the Fifth Report from the House of Commons Science and Technology Committee Session 2005–2006*. London: HMSO.

Hoare, J. and Moon, D. (eds) (2010) *Drug Misuse Declared: Findings from the 2009/10 British Crime Survey England and Wales*, Home Office Statistical Bulletin 13/10. London: Home Office.

Hofstede, G. (2005) *Cultures and Organizations: Software of the Mind*. New York: McGraw-Hill.

Hogg, R. and Brown, D. (1998) *Rethinking Law and Order*. Annandale, NSW: Pluto Press.

Holcomb, J. and Pizam, A. (2006) 'Do incidents of theft at tourist destinations have a negative effect on tourists' decisions to travel to affected destinations?', in Y. Mansfeld and A. Pizam (eds) *Tourism, Security and Safety: From Theory to Practice*. Oxford: Elsevier Butterworth-Heinemann.

Homel, R., Haurtitz, M., McIllwain, G., Wortley, R. and Carvolth, R. (1997) 'Preventing drunkenness and violence around nightclubs in a tourist resort', in R. V. Clarke (ed.) *Situational Crime Prevention: Successful Case Studies* (2nd edn). Guilderland, NY: Harrow and Heston.

Home Office (2010a) *Drug Strategy 2010 Reducing Demand, Restricting Supply, Building Recovery: Supporting People to Live a Drug Free Life*. London: Home Office.

Home Office (2010b) *Rebalancing the Licensing Act: A Consultation on Empowering Individuals, Families and Local Communities to Shape and Determine Local Licensing*. London: Home Office.

Home Office (2010c) *2010 Drug Strategy Consultation Paper*. London: Home Office.

Home Office (2010d) 'Decriminalisation the wrong approach', 17 August [online]. Available at: http://www.homeoffice.gov.uk/media-centre/news/decriminalisation-wrong

Hooper, R. (2005) 'Television shows scramble forensic evidence', *New Scientist Tech*, 9 September.

Horsfield, P. (1997) 'Moral panic or moral action? The appropriateness of moral panics in the exercise of social control', *Media International Australia*, 85: 32–39.

Horstink-von Meyenfeldt, L. (1996) 'The Netherlands: tightening up of the cafes policy', in N. Dorn, J. Jepsen and E. Savona (eds) *European Drug Policies and Enforcement*. Basingstoke: Macmillan.

House of Commons (2010) *Control of Legal Highs* debate, Westminster Hall, House of Commons, London, Thursday 9 September. Available at: http://www.publications.parliament.uk/pa/cm201011/cmhansrd/cm100909/halltext/100909h0001.htm

House of Commons Science and Technology Committee (2006) *Drug Classification: Making a Hash of It?* Fifth Report of Session 2005–06, HC 1031. London: The Stationery Office. Available at: http://www.publications.parliament.uk/pa/cm200506/cmselect/cmsctech/1031/103102.htm

House of Commons Transport Committee (2010) *Drink and Drug Driving Law: First Report of Session 2010* (volume 1), Drug Driving Law. Available at http://www.publications.parliament.uk/pa/cm201011/cmselect/cmtran/460/460.pdf

Howitt, W. (1971) *The Rural Life of England*. Shannon: Irish University Press.

Hozic, A. A. (2002) 'Zoning, or, how to govern (cultural) violence', *Cultural Values*, 6(1–2): 183–195.

Hubbard, P. (2005) 'The geographies of "going out": emotion and embodiment in the evening economy', in J. Davidson, L. Bondi and M. Smith (eds) *Emotional Geographies*. Aldershot: Ashgate.

Hudson, S. and Ritchie, J. R. B. (2006) 'Promoting destinations via film tourism: an empirical identification of supporting marketing initiatives', *Journal of Travel Research*, 44(3): 387–396.

Huey, L. (2010) ' "I've seen this on CSI": criminal investigators' perceptions about the management of public expectations in the field', *Crime, Media, Culture*, 6(1): 49–68.

Hughes, K., Anderson, Z., Morleo, M. and Bellis, M. (2007) 'Alcohol, nightlife and violence: the relative contributions of drinking before and during nights out to negative health and criminal justice outcomes', *Addiction*, 103: 60–65.

Hunt, G. and Evans, K. (2008) ' "The great unmentionable": exploring the pleasures and benefits of ecstasy from the perspectives of drug users', *Drugs: Education, Prevention and Policy*, 15(4): 329–349.

Hunt, G., Evans, K. and Kares, F. (2007) 'Drug use and meanings of risk and pleasure', *Journal of Youth Studies*, 10(1): 73–96.

Hunt, G., Moloney, M. and Evans, K. (2010) *Youth, Drugs and Nightlife*. Abingdon: Routledge.

Hyde, J. (2003) 'The folly of Faliraki', *The Observer*, 24 August. Available at: http://observer.guardian.co.uk/travel/story/0,6903,1028229,00.html

Ingram D. (2000) *Impact of Crime on Victims: Findings from the 2000 Crime Survey*. Edinburgh: Scottish Executive Central Research Unit.

Innes, M. (1999) 'Media as an investigative source in police murder enquiries', *British Journal of Criminology*, 39(2): 268–286.

Innes, M. (2003) 'Signal crimes: detective work, mass media and constructing collective memory', in P. Mason (ed.) *Criminal Visions: Media Representations of Crime and Justice*. Cullompton, Devon: Willan Publishing.

Innes, M. (2004a) 'Signal crimes and signal disorders: notes on deviance as communicative action', *British Journal of Sociology*, 55(3): 336–355.

Innes, M. (2004b) 'Crime as a signal, crime as a memory', *Journal for Crime, Conflict and the Media*, 1(2): 15–22.

Innes, M. and Fielding, N. (2002) 'From community to communicative policing: "signal crimes" and the problem of public reassurance', *Sociological Research Online*, 7(2). Available at: http://www.socresonline.org.uk/7/2/innes.html

International Journal of Drug Policy (2008) Special Issue: Pleasure and Drugs, 19(5).

Jackson, J. (2006) 'Introducing fear of crime to risk research', *Risk Analysis*, 26(1): 253–264.

Jackson, P. (2004) *Inside Clubbing: Sensual Experiments in the Art of Being Human*. London: Berg.

James, V. and Gabe, J. (1996) *Health and the Sociology of Emotions*. Cambridge, MA: Blackwell Publishers.

Jansen, A. C. M. (1994) 'The development of a "legal" consumers' market for cannabis: the "coffee shop" phenomenon', in E. Leuw and I. H. Marshall (eds) *Between Prohibition and Legalization: The Dutch Experiment in Drug Policy*. Amsterdam: Kugler.

Jarrel, S and Howsen, R. (1990) 'Transient crowding and crime', *American Journal of Economics and Sociology*, 49(4): 483–494.

Jayne, M., Valentine, G. and Holloway, S. (2008) 'Fluid boundaries – British binge drinking and European civility: alcohol and the production and consumption of public space', *Space and Polity*, 12(1): 81–100.

Jefferson, T. and Holloway, W. (2000) 'The role of anxiety in fear of crime', in T. Hope and R. Sparks (eds) *Crime, Risk and Insecurity*. London: Routledge.

Jenkins, P. (1994) *Using Murder: The Social Construction of Serial Homicide*. New York: De Gruyter.

Jewkes, Y. (2004) *Media and Crime*. London: Sage Publications.

Jiggins, S. (2007) 'The news media', in M. Mitchell and J. Casey (eds) *Police Leadership and Management*. Sydney: Federation Press.

'Jobing' (2006) *Company Profile, Walt Disney World; Disney Reservation Center* [online]. Available at: http://orlando.jobing.com

Johnson, S. and Muhlhausen, D. (2005) 'North American transnational youth gangs: breaking the chain of violence', *Backgrounder*, no. 1834, 21 March. Washington, DC: Heritage Foundation.

Jones C. (2008) *Tourism and Crime, Whose Problem? A Cornish Perspective*. Doctoral dissertation, University of Plymouth.

Jones, J. (1998) 'Challenging the myth of the "rural idyll": a review essay of rural crime, disorder and social control in England and Wales', *Menai Papers*, 1(1): 10–27.

Jordan, L. A. and Workman, J. P. (1990) *Survey of Fee Hunting for Deer and Elk on Private Land in Utah*, Cooperative Extension Service Bulletin REC439, Utah State University, Logan, UT.

Jud, G. (1975) 'Tourism and crime in Mexico', *Social Sciences*, 56: 324–330.

Kaplan, E. A. (2000) 'Is the gaze male?', in E. A. Kaplan (ed.) *Feminism and Film*. Oxford: Oxford University Press.

Katz, J. (1988) *Seductions of Crime: Moral and Sensual Attractions in Doing Evil*. New York: Basic Books.

Kazmierow, B. J., Cessford, G. R., Wilson, C. H., Mayhew, P. and Morrison, B. I. (2009) *Vehicle Crime at Outdoor Recreation and Tourist Destinations: Prevalence, Impact and Solutions*. Wellington: Department of Conservation.

Katznelson, I. (1993 *Marxism and the City*. Oxford: Clarendon Press.

Kelly, I. (1993) 'Tourist destination crime rates: an examination of Cairns and the Gold Coast, Australia', *Journal of Tourism Studies*, 4(2): 2–11.

Kershaw, C., Nicholas, S. and Walker, A. (2008) *Crime in England and Wales 2007/08: Findings from the British Crime Survey and Police Recorded Crime*. London: Home Office.

Kidd, R. and Chayet, E. (1984) 'Why do victims fail to report? The psychology of criminal victimization', *Journal of Social Issues*, 40(1): 39–50.

Kinnaird, V. and Hall, D. (1996) 'Understanding tourism processes: a gender awareness framework', *Tourism Management*, 17: 95–102.

Knowles, D. (2004) 'Shocking violence in mall prompts call for tough response from authorities', *Sunday Mail*, 27 June, 4–5.

Koehler, J. J. (2001) 'When are people persuaded by DNA match statistics?', *Law and Human Behavior*, 25(5): 493–513.

Kohler, A. (2009) 'Attack hits NZ's safe image', *New Zealand Herald* [online]. Available at: http://www.nzherald.co.nz/nz/news/article.cfm?c_id=1&objectid=10592595&pnum=1

Kohn, M. (1997) 'The chemical generation and its ancestors: dance crazes and drug panics across eight decades', *International Journal of Drug Policy*, 8(3): 137–142.

Korf, D. J. (1994) 'Drug tourists and drug refugees', in E. Leuw and I. H. Marshall (eds) *Between Prohibition and Legalization: The Dutch Experiment in Drug Policy*. Amsterdam: Kugler.

Koubaridis, A. (2007) 'Police operation gears up for New Year's Eve revellers', *New Zealand Herald* [online]. Available at: http://www.nzherald.co.nz/coromandel/news/article.cfm?l_id=123&objectid=10484599

Kozak, M., Crotts, J. C. and Law, R. (2007) 'The impact of the perception of risk on international travellers', *International Journal of Tourism Research*, 9: 233–242.

Kruttschnitt, C. and Carbone-Lopez, K. (2009) 'Customer satisfaction: crime victims' willingness to call the police', *Ideas in American Policing* [online]. Available at: http://www.policefoundation.org/pdf/Ideas_12.pdf

Larcombe, W. (2005) *Compelling Engagements: Feminism, Rape Law and Romance Fiction*. Sydney: Federation Press.

Las Vegas Zoning Code (1997) [online]. Available at: http://www.lasvegasnevada.gov/files/Chapter_19.04.pdf

Lawrence, K. and Bissett, K. (2009) '$1m paid to police for TV ratings', *Daily Telegraph*, 2 February. Available at: http://www.news.com.au/dailytelegraph/story/0,22049,24992707-5001021,00.html

Lee, M. (2005) '"Fields of fire": crime, dissent and social isolation in south-western Sydney', in R. Julian, R. Rottier and R. White (eds) *TASA Conference 2005 Proceedings*. Hobart: University of Tasmania.

Lee, M. (2007) *Inventing Fear of Crime: Criminology and the Politics of Anxiety*. Cullompton, Devon: Willan Publishing.

Lees, J. (1997) 'The origins of the legacy', in J. Lees (ed.) *A Legacy under Threat*. Armidale, NSW: University of New England Press,.

Leishman, F. and Mason, P. (2003) *Policing and the Media: Facts, Fictions and Factions*. Cullompton, Devon: Willan Publishing.

Lemieux, A. L. (2011) 'Policing poaching and protecting pachyderms: lessons learned from Africa's elephants', in R. I. Mawby and R. Yarwood (eds) *Rural Policing and Policing the Rural: A Constable Countryside?* Aldershot: Ashgate.

Lemmens, P. H. H. M. and Garretsen, H. F. L. (1998) 'Unstable pragmatism: Dutch drug policy under national and international pressure', *Addiction*, 93(2): 157–162.

Lepp, A. and Gibson, H. (2003) 'Tourist roles, perceived risk and international tourism', *Annals of Tourism Research*, 30(3): 606–624.

Leuw, E. and Marshall, I. H. (eds) (1994) *Between Prohibition and Legalization: The Dutch Experiment in Drug Policy*. Amsterdam: Kugler.

Levantis, T. and Gani, A. (2000) 'Tourism demand and the nuisance of crime', *International Journal of Social Economics*, 27(7/8/9/10): 959–967.

Lewis, J., Cushion, S. and Thomas, J. (2005) 'Immediacy, convenience or engagement? An analysis of 24-hour news channels in the UK', *Journalism Studies*, 6(4): 461–477.

Lewis, R. and Gilespie, K. (2008) 'Text message halts "sickening attack" on teen tourists', *New Zealand Herald* [online]. Available at: http://www.nzherald.co.nz/nz/news/article.cfm?c_id=1&objectid=10529842

Lifeline (2010) *Mephedrone: Frequently Asked Questions*. Manchester: Lifeline.

Lin, V. L. and Loeb, P. D. (1977) 'Tourism and crime in Mexico: some comments', *Social Science Quarterly*, 58: 164–167.

Little, J., Panelli, R., Kraack, A. (2005) 'Women's fear of crime: a rural perspective', *Journal of Rural Studies*, 21(2): 151–163.

Loeb, P. D. and Lin, V. L. (1981) 'The economics of tourism and crime: a specific error approach', *Resource Management and Optimization*, 1(4): 315–331.

Lovgren, S. (2004) '"CSI effect" is mixed blessing for real crime labs', *National Geographic News*, 23 September.

Low, S. (2004) *Behind the Gates: Life, Security and the Pursuit of Happiness in Fortress America*. New York: Routledge.

Lumsden, K. (2009) 'Do we look like boy racers? The role of the folk devil in contemporary moral panics', *Sociological Research Online*, 14(1). Available at: www.socresonline. org.uk/14/1/2

Lupton, D. (1998) *The Emotional Self*. London: Sage.

Lurigio A. (1987) 'Are all victims alike? The adverse, generalized, and differential impact of crime', *Crime Delinquency*, 33(4): 452–467.

LVCVA (2010) *Only Vegas*. [online]. Available at: http://www.visitlasvegas.com/vegas/ index.jsp

Lynch, J. P. and Cantor, D. (1992) 'Ecological and behavioral influences on property victimization at home: implications for opportunity theory', *Journal of Research in Crime and Delinquency*, 29(3): 335–362.

Lyng, S. (1990) 'Edgework: a social psychological analysis of voluntary risk taking', *American Journal of Sociology*, 95(4): 851–886.

Lyng, S. (ed.) (2005) *Edgework: The Sociology of Risk-Taking*. London: Routledge.

MacCoun, R. and Reuter, P. (2001) *Drug War Heresies, Learning from Other Vices, Times and Place*. Cambridge: Cambridge University Press.

McDonald, K. (1999) *Struggles for Subjectivity: Identity, Action and Youth Experience*. Cambridge: Cambridge University Press.

McGovern, A. (2009) 'The best police force money can buy: the rise of police PR', in M. Segrave (ed.) *Proceedings of the Critical Criminology Conference*. Melbourne: Australian and New Zealand Crime and Justice Research Network Monash University.

McGovern, A. and Lee, M. (2010) 'Cop[ying] it sweet: police media units and the making of news', *Australian and New Zealand Journal of Criminology*, 43(3).

McLaughlin, E. (2005) 'Forcing the issue: new Labour, new localism and the democratic renewal of police accountability', *Howard Journal of Social Justice*, 44(5): 473–489.

McPheters, L. R. and Stronge, W. B. (1974) 'Crime as an environmental externality in tourism', *Land Economics*, 50(1): 350–381.

Macrae, F. (2010) 'Movies that scare for life: viewers left with fears for years', *Daily Mail*, 26 June. Available at: http://tinyurl.com/3ywuphw

McRobbie, A. and Thornton, S. L. (1995) 'Rethinking "moral panic" for multi-mediated social worlds', *British Journal of Sociology*, 46(4): 559–574.

McVeigh, K. (2003) 'Faliraki: a Greek tragedy', *The Scotsman*, 23 August.

Mail Online (2010) 'Drug addicts to have benefits cut unless they seek treatment', 21 August. Available at: http://www.dailymail.co.uk/news/article-1304650/Drug-addicts-benefits-cut-unless-seek-treatment.html

Makkai, T. (1998) 'Alcohol and disorder in the Australian community: Part 11 – perpetrators', *Trends and Issues in Crime and Criminal Justice*, No. 77. Canberra: Australian Institute of Criminology.

Malbon, B. (1999) *Clubbing: Dancing, Ecstasy and Vitality*. London: Routledge.

Manning, P. (1996) 'Dramaturgy, politics and the axial media event', *Sociological Quarterly*, 37(2): 261–278.

Mansfeld, Y. and Pizam, A. (eds) (2006) *Tourism, Security and Safety: from Theory to Practice*. Oxford: Elsevier Butterworth-Heinemann.

Manson, P. (2003) *Criminal Visions: Media Representations of Crime and Justice.* Cullompton, Devon: Willan Publishing.

Marsh, I. and Melville, G. (2009) *Crime, Justice and the Media.* London: Routledge.

Marsh, P. and Collett, P. (1986) *Driving Passions: The Psychology of the Car.* London: Jonathan Cape.

Martinic, M. and Measham, F. (eds) (2008) *Swimming with Crocodiles: Extreme Drinking and Young People*, ICAP Series on Alcohol in Society, Volume 8. New York: Routledge.

Mason, P. (2002) 'The thin blurred line: reality TV and policing', *The British Criminology Conference: Selected Proceedings Vol. 5. Papers from the British Society of Criminology Conference, July* [online]. Available at: http://www.britsoccrim.org/volume5/003.pdf

Mason, P. (2003) *Criminal Visions: Media Representations of Crime and Justice.* Cullompton, Devon: Willan Publishing.

Mawby, R. C. (2002) 'Continuity and change, convergence and divergence: the policy and practice of police–media relations', *Criminal Justice*, 2(3): 303–324.

Mawby, R. C. (2007) 'Criminal investigation and the media', in T. Newburn, T. Williamson and A. Wright (eds) *Handbook of Criminal Investigation.* Cullompton, Devon: Willan Publishing.

Mawby, R. C. (2010) 'Police corporate communications, crime reporting and the shaping of crime news', *Policing and Society*, Vol. 20, No. 1, pp. 124–139.

Mawby R. I. (2000) 'Tourists perceptions of security: the risk fear paradox', *Tourism Economics*, 6(2): 109–121.

Mawby, R. I. (2006) 'Commercial burglary', in M. Gill (ed.) *The Handbook of Security.* London: Macmillan/Pergamon.

Mawby, R. I. (2007) 'Crime, place and explaining rural hotspots', *International Journal of Rural Crime*, 1: 21–43. Available at: http://www.ruralfutures.une.edu.au/rurcrime/IJRC/ijrcv1.htm#3

Mawby, R. I. (2008) 'Understanding and responding to crime and disorder: ensuring a local dimension', *Crime Prevention and Community Safety: An International Journal*, 10(3): 158–173.

Mawby, R. I. (2009) 'Perceptions of police and policing in a rural county of England', *International Journal of Police Science and Management*, 11(1): 39–53.

Mawby, R. I. (2010) 'Property crime and tourists', in D. Botterill and T. Jones (eds) *Tourism and Crime: Key Themes.* Oxford: Goodfellow.

Mawby, R. I. and Walklate, S. (1994) *Critical Victimology: International Perspectives.* London: Sage.

Mawby, R. I. and Gorgenyi, I. (1997) 'Break-ins to weekend homes: research in a Hungarian city', in E. Raska and J. Saar (eds) *Crime and Criminology at the End of the Century.* Tallinn: Estonian National Defence and Public Service Academy.

Mawby, R. I., Brunt, P. and Hambly, Z. (1999) 'Victimisation on holiday: a British survey', *International Review of Victimology*, 6: 201–211.

Mawby, R. I., Brunt, P. and Hambly, Z. (2000) 'Fear of crime among British holidaymakers', *British Journal of Criminology*, 40: 468–479.

Mawby, R. I., McIntosh, W. and Barclay, E. (2008) 'Burglary geographies: applying theories from domestic burglary to caravan park crime', paper presented to British Society of Criminology Conference, Huddersfield, July.

Mawby, R. I., Barclay, E. and Jones, C. (2010) 'Tourism and victimization', in S. G. Shoham, P. Knepper and M. Kett (eds) *International Handbook of Victimology.* Boca Raton, FL: Taylor and Francis.

Maxfield, M. G. (1987) 'Household composition, routine activity and victimization: a comparative analysis', *Journal of Quantitative Criminology*, 3(4): 301–320.

Mazursky, D. (1989) 'Past experience and future tourism decisions', *Annals of Tourism Research*, 16: 333–344.

Meadows, R. J. (2001) *Understanding Violence and Victimization* (2nd edn). New Jersey: Prentice Hall.

Measham, F. (2002) ' "Doing gender" – "doing drugs": conceptualising the gendering of drugs cultures', *Contemporary Drug Problems*, 29(2): 335–373.

Measham, F. (2004a) 'Drug and alcohol research: the case for cultural criminology', in J. Ferrell, K. Haywood, B. Morrison and M. Presdee (eds) *Cultural Criminology Unleashed*. London: GlassHouse Press.

Measham, F. (2004b) 'The decline of ecstasy, the rise of "binge drinking" and the persistence of pleasure', *Probation Journal, Special Edition: Rethinking Drugs and Crime*, 51(4): 309–326.

Measham, F. (2004c) 'Play space: historical and socio-cultural reflections on drugs, licensed leisure locations, commercialization and control', *International Journal of Drug Policy*, 15(5): 337–345.

Measham, F. (2006) 'The new policy mix: alcohol, harm minimization, and determined drunkenness in contemporary society', *International Journal of Drug Policy*, 17(4): 258–268.

Measham, F. (2010) 'Drunkenness – a historical and contemporary cross-cultural perspective: "a voluntary madness" ', in A. Fox and M. MacAvoy (eds) *Expressions of Drunkenness (Four Hundred Rabbits)*. New York: Routledge.

Measham, F. and Brain, K. (2005) ' "Binge" drinking, British alcohol policy and the new culture of intoxication', *Crime, Media, Culture*, 1(3): 262–283.

Measham, F. and Moore, K. (2006) 'Reluctant reflexivity, implicit insider knowledge and the development of club studies', in B. Sanders (ed.) *Drugs, Clubs and Young People: Sociological and Public Health Perspectives*. Aldershot: Ashgate.

Measham, F. and Moore, K. (2008) 'The criminalization of intoxication', in P. Squires (ed.) *ASBO Nation: The Criminalisation of Nuisance*. London: Polity.

Measham, F. and Hadfield, P. (2009) 'Everything starts with an "E": exclusion, ethnicity and elite formation in contemporary English clubland', *Adicciones*, 21(4): 363–386.

Measham, F. and Moore, K. (2009) 'Repertoires of distinction: exploring patterns of weekend polydrug use within local leisure scenes across the English night time economy', *Criminology and Criminal Justice*, 9(4): 437–464.

Measham, F. and Østergaard, J. (2009) 'The public face of binge drinking: British and Danish young women, recent trends in alcohol consumption and the European binge drinking debate', *Probation Journal*, Special Issue, 56(4): 415–434.

Measham, F., Aldridge, J. and Parker, H. (2001) *Dancing on Drugs: Risk, Health and Hedonism in the British Club Scene*. London: Free Association Books.

Measham, F., Moore, K., Newcombe, R., and Welch, Z. (2010) 'Tweaking, bombing, dabbing and stockpiling: the emergence of mephedrone and the perversity of prohibition', *Drugs and Alcohol Today*, 10(1): 14–21.

Measham, F., Wood, D., Dargan, P. and Moore, K. (2011) 'The rise in legal highs: prevalence and patterns in the use of illegal drugs and first- and second-generation "legal highs" in South London gay dance clubs', *Journal of Substance Use*, 16(4): 263–272.

Meithe, T. D. and Meier, R. F. (1990) 'Opportunity, choice and criminal victimisation: a test of a theoretical model', *Journal of Research in Crime and Delinquency*, 27(1): 243–266.

Merton, R. (1938) 'Social structure and anomie', *American Sociological Review*, 3: 672–682.

Michalkó, G. (2003) 'Tourism eclipsed by crime: the vulnerability of foreign tourists in Hungary', *Journal of Travel and Tourism Marketing*, 15(2/3): 159–172.

Miles, S. (1998) *Consumerism as a Way of Life*. London: Sage.

Miller, D. (2002) *Car Cultures*. Oxford: Berg.

Miller, L. S. and Hess, K. M. (2002) *The Police in the Community: Strategies for the 21st Century*. California: Wadsworth Publishing.

Milligen, S. (2006) *Better to Reign in Hell: Serial Killers, Media Panics and the FBI*. London: Headpress.

Mingay, G. E. (1989) 'Introduction', in G. E. Mingay (ed.) *The Rural Idyll*. London: Routledge.

Ministry of Tourism: Te Manatu Tapoi (2009) *Key Tourism Statistics*. Wellington: New Zealand Government.

Mirrlees-Black, C. and Aye Maung, N. (1994) *Fear of Crime: Findings from the 1992 British Crime Survey*, HORS Research Paper 9. London: Home Office.

Mirrlees-Black, C., Mayhew, P. and Percy, A. (1996) *The 1996 British Crime Survey: England and Wales*, Home Office Statistical Bulletin 1996. London: HMSO.

Mixmag (2007) 'VIP: Q&A with the Chemical Brothers', July, 44.

Mixmag (2009) 'Mixmag drugs survey', February, 44–53.

Monaghan, L. (2002) 'Opportunity, pleasure and risk: an ethnography of urban male heterosexualities', *Journal of Contemporary Ethnography*, 31(4): 440–477.

Monckton Smith, J. (2010) *Relating Rape and Murder: Narratives of Sex, Death and Gender*. Hampshire: Palgrave Macmillan.

Moore, D. (1994) *The Lads in Action: Social Process in an Urban Youth Subculture*. Aldershot: Arena.

Moore, D. (2008) 'Erasing pleasure from public discourse on illicit drugs: on the creation and reproduction of an absence', *International Journal of Drug Policy*, 19(5): 353–358.

Moore, D. A. and Loewenstein, G. (2004) 'Self-interest, automaticity, and the psychology of conflict of interest', *Social Justice Research*, 17(2): 189–202.

Moore, K. (2010) 'The British "mainstream" post-rave trance scene: exploring emotional and spiritual expression amongst "crasher clubbers"', in S. Collins-Mayo and B. Pink-Dandelion (eds) *Religion and Youth*. Aldershot: Ashgate.

Moore, K. and Measham, F. (2008) '"It's the most fun you can have for £20": motivations, meanings and consequences of British ketamine use', *Addiction Research and Theory*, 16(3): 231–244.

Moore, K. and Miles, S. (2004) 'Young people, dance and the sub-cultural consumption of drugs', *Addiction Research and Theory*, 12(6): 507–523.

Morgan, C. J., Muetzelfeldt, L., Nutt, D. J. and Curran, H. V. (2010) 'Harms associated with psychoactive substances: findings of the UK National Drug Survey', *Journal of Psychopharmacology*, 24(2): 147–153.

Morgan, C. J., Curran, H. V. and the Independent Scientific Committee on Drugs (ISCD) (2011) 'Ketamine use: a review', *Addiction*, doi: 10.1111/j.1360–0443.2011.03576.x.

Morley, N. J., Ball, L. J. and Ormerod, T. C. (2006) 'How the detection of insurance fraud succeeds and fails', *Psychology, Crime & Law*, 12(2): 163–180.

Moutinho, L. (1987) 'Consumer behaviour in tourism', *European Journal of Marketing*, 21(10): 1–44.

Muehsam, M. and Tarlow, P. (1995) 'Involving the police in tourism', *Tourism Management*, 16(1): 9–14.

Mulvey, L. (1991) 'Visual pleasure and narrative cinema', in M. Durham and D. Kellner (eds) *Media and Cultural Studies: Keyworks*. London: Blackwell Publishing.

Murray, J. (1973) *Larrikins: 19th Century Outrage*. Melbourne: Lansdowne Press.

Ned Kelly GPS Tour website (2010) Available at: http://www.nedkellygpstour.com.au/

Nelson, A. L., Bromley, R. D. F. and Thomas, C. J. (2001) 'Identifying micro-spatial and temporal patterns of violent crime and disorder in the British city centre', *Applied Geography*, 21: 249–274.

New Zealand Herald (2006) 'Thugs stopped mother and baby leaving camp ground' [online]. Available at: http://www.nzherald.co.nz/topic/print.cfm?c_id=124&objectid=10362185

New Zealand Herald (2008) 'Tourists told New Zealand not "safe country"' [online]. Available at: http://www.odt.co.nz/news/national/11766/tourists-told-new-zealand-not-039-safe-country039

Newbold, G. (2000) *Crime in New Zealand*. Palmerston North: Dunmore Press.

Nicholas, R. (2008) *Understanding and Responding to Alcohol-Related Social Harms in Australia: Options for Policing*. Hobart: National Drug Law Enforcement Research Fund, Commonwealth of Australia.

Nicholls, L. L. (1976) 'Tourism and crime', *Annals of Tourism Research*, 3(4): 176–182.

Nijman, J. (1999) 'Cultural globalization and the identity of place: the reconstruction of Amsterdam', *Cultural Geographies*, 6(2): 146–164.

Noble, G. (ed.) (2009) *Lines in the Sand: The Cronulla Riots, Multiculturalism and National Belonging*. Sydney: Federation Press.

Nolan, J. J., Conti, N. and McDevitt, J. (2005) 'Situational policing', *FBI Law Enforcement Bulletin*, 74(11): 1–9.

Nolan, T. W. (2007) 'Depiction of the "CSI effect" in popular culture: portrait in domination and effective affectation', *New England Law Review*, 41(3): 575–590.

Norris, P. and Williams, D. (2008) ' "Binge drinking", anti-social behaviour and alcohol-related disorder: examining the 2003 Licensing Act', in P. Squires (ed.) *ASBO Nation: The Criminalisation of Nuisance*. London: Polity.

Nutt, D., King, L. and Phillips, D (2010) 'Drug harms in the UK: a multicriteria decision analysis', *The Lancet*, 376(9752): 1558–1565.

NZPA (2007) 'Attackers posed as police to abduct Dutch tourists, says Crown' [online]. Available at: http://www.nzherald.co.nz/nz/news/article.cfm?c_id=1&objectid=10425250.

NZPA (2008) 'Man arrested for tourist attacks' [online]. Available at: http://tvnz.co.nz/view/page/1318360/2050069

NZPA (2009) 'Karen Aim's father vows to fight to keep killer in jail' [online]. Available at: http://www.nzherald.co.nz/nz/news/article.cfm?c_id=1&objectid=10564466

NZPA (2010) 'Nelson, Coromandel take "worst-behaved" awards' [online]. Available at: http://www.nzherald.co.nz/nz/news/article.cfm?c_id=1&objectid=10618037&pnum=2

O'Brien, N. (2008) 'PR for police spins to \$10m', *Australian Online Edition*, 28 August [online]. Available at: http://www.theaustralian.news.com.au/story/0,25197,23979270–2702,00.html

Oliver, M. and Sanders, M. (2004) 'The appeal of horror and suspense', in S. Prince (ed.) *The Horror Film*. New Jersey: Rutgers.

O'Malley, P. (1998) 'Consuming risks: harm minimization and the government of "drug users" ', in R. Smandych (ed.) *Governable Places: Readings in Governmentality and Crime Control*. Aldershot: Dartmouth.

O'Malley, P. and Valverde, M. (2004) 'Pleasure, freedom and drugs: the uses of "pleasure" in liberal governance of drug and alcohol consumption', *Sociology*, 38(1): 25–42.

Orange County Code (2010) [Online]. Available at: http://library.municode.com/index.aspx?clientId=10182&stateId=9&stateName=Florida

Orlando/Orange County Convention Visitor's Bureau (2010a) *Orlando Makes Me Smile* [online]. Available at: http://www.orlandoinfo.com/cvb/orlando-makes-me-smilecampaign.cfm

Orlando/Orange County Convention Visitor's Bureau (2010b) *State of the Market* [online]. Available at: http://www.orlandoinfo.com/research/market/index.cfm

Pantazis, C. (2000) '"Fear of crime", vulnerability and poverty', *British Journal of Criminology*, 40(3): 414–436.

Papayanis, M. A. (2000) 'Sex and the revanchist city: zoning out pornography in New York', *Environment and Planning D: Society and Space*, 18(3): 341–354.

Parker, H., Aldridge, J. and Measham, F. (1998) *Illegal Leisure: The Normalization of Adolescent Recreational Drug Use*. London: Routledge.

Peel, V. and Steen, A. (2007) 'Victims, hooligans and cash-cows: media representations of the international backpacker in Australia', *Tourism Management*, 28: 1057–1067.

Pelfrey, W. V. (1998) 'Tourism and crime: a preliminary assessment of the relationship of crime to the number of visitors at selected sites', *International Journal of Comparative and Applied Criminal Justice*, 22(2): 293–304.

Peralta, R. (2007) 'College alcohol use and the embodiment of hegemonic masculinity among European American men', *Sex Roles*, 56(11–12): 741–756.

Perdue, R. R. (1985) 'Segmenting state information inquirers by timing of destination decision and previous experience', *Journal of Travel Research*, 23(Spring): 6–11.

Perrone, D. (2006) 'New York City club kids: a contextual understanding of club drug use', in B. Sanders (ed.) *Drugs, Clubs and Young People: Sociological and Public Health Perspectives*. Aldershot: Ashgate.

Phillips, H. and Lawton, G. (2004) 'The intoxication instinct', *New Scientist*, 184(2473), 13 November: 32.

Pigram, J. J. (1981) 'Outdoor recreation and access to countryside: focus on the Australian experience', *Natural Resources Journal*, 21(1): 107–123.

Pigram, J. J. and Jenkins, J. M. (1999) *Outdoor Recreation Management*. London: Routledge.

Pinedo, I. C. (1997) *Recreational Terror: Women and the Pleasures of Viewing Horror Film*. New York: SUNY Press.

Pinhey, T. K. and Iverson, T. J. (1994) 'Safety concerns of Japanese visitors to Guam', *Journal of Travel and Tourism Marketing*, 3(2): 87–94.

Pini, M. (2001) *Club Cultures and Female Subjectivity: The Move from Home to House*. Basingstoke: Palgrave.

Pizam, A. (1982) 'Tourism and crime: is there a relationship?', *Journal of Travel Research*, 20(3): 7–10.

Pizam, A. (1999) 'A comprehensive approach to classifying acts of crime and violence at tourism destinations', *Journal of Travel Research*, 38(1): 5–12.

Pizam, A. and Mansfeld, Y. (eds) (1996) *Tourism Crime and International Security Issues*. Chichester: Wiley.

Pizam, A. and Mansfield, Y. (2006) (eds) *Tourism Security and Safety: From Theory to Practice*. New York: Butterworth Heinemann.

Pizam, A., Tarlow, P. and Bloom, J. (1997) 'Making tourists feel safe: whose responsibility is it?', *Journal of Travel Research*, 36(1): 23–28.

Podlas, K. (2006) '"The CSI effect": exposing the media myth', *Fordham Intell. Prop. Media & Ent. L. J.*, 16: 429–465.

Police Foundation (1999) *Drugs and the Law: Report of the Independent Inquiry into the Misuse of Drugs Act 1971*. London: Police Foundation. (Also known as the Runciman

Report.) Available at: http://www.druglibrary.org/schaffer/Library/studies/runciman/default.htm

Polvi, N., Looman, T., Humphries, C. and Pease, K. (1991) 'The time course of repeat burglary victimisation', *British Journal of Criminology*, 31: 411–414.

Porteous, D. (2009) 'Dutch tourists attacked', *Otago Daily Times* [online]. Available at: http://www.odt.co.nz/the-regions/southland/39558/dutch-tourists-attacked

Potter, G. W. and Kappeler, V. E. (1998) *Constructing Crime: Perspectives on Making News and Social Problems*. Prospect Heights: Waveland Press.

Potter, R. H. (1996) *Pornography: Group Pressures and Individual Rights*. Annandale (Sydney): Federation Press.

Poynting, S. and Morgan, G. (eds) (2007) *Outrageous!: Moral Panics in Australia*. Hobart: ACYS Publishing.

Poynting, S., Noble, G., Tabar, P. and Collins, J. (2004) *Bin Laden in the Suburbs: Criminalising the Arab Other*. Sydney: Sydney Institute of Criminology, University of Sydney.

Presdee, M. (2000) *Cultural Criminology and the Carnival of Crime*. London: Routledge.

Presdee, M. (2004) 'Cultural criminology: the long and winding road', *Theoretical Criminology*, 8(3): 275–285.

Presdee, M. (2005) 'The story of crime: biography and the excavation of transgression', in J. Ferrell, K. Hayward, W. Morrison and M. Presdee (eds) *Cultural Criminology Unleashed*. London: Glasshouse Press.

The Press (2009a) 'Dutch tourists warned after rape', *Stuff* [online]. Available at: http://www.stuff.co.nz/national/807496

The Press (2009b) 'Tourists warned about South Island danger spots', *Stuff* [online]. Available at: http://www.stuff.co.nz/the-press/802244

Prideaux, B. (1996) 'The tourism crime cycle: a beach destination case study', in A. Pizam and Y. Mansfield (eds) *Tourism, Crime and International Security Issues*. New York: John Wiley.

Prideaux, B. and Dunn, A. (1995) 'Tourism and crime: how can the tourism industry respond? The Gold Coast experience', *Australian Journal of Hospitality Management*, 2(1): 7–15.

Pritchard, D. and Hughes, K. D. (1997) 'Patterns of deviance in crime news', *Journal of Communication*, 47(3): 49–67.

Purpura, P. P. (2001) *Police and the Community: Concepts and Cases*. Massachusetts: Allyn and Bacon.

van Raaij, W. F. and Francken, D. A. (1984) 'Vacation decisions, activities, and satisfactions', *Annals of Tourism Research*, 11: 101–112.

Race, K. (2007) 'Engaging in a culture of barebacking: gay men and the risk of HIV prevention', in K. Hannah-Moffat and Pat O'Malley (eds) *Gendered Risks*. London: Routledge.

Race, K. (2009) *Pleasure Consuming Medicine: The Queer Politics of Drugs*. Durham, NC: Duke University Press.

Ratcliffe, J. and McCullagh, M. (1998) 'Aoristic crime analysis', *International journal of Geographical Information Science*, 12(7): 751–764.

Reeve, I. (2002) *Property Rights and Natural Resource Management*, Institute for Rural Futures Occasional Paper 2002/1, University of New England, Armidale, NSW.

Reinarman, C., Cohen, P. and Kaal, H. (2004) 'The limited relevance of drug policy: Cannabis in Amsterdam and in San Francisco', *American Journal of Public Health*, 94(5): 836–842.

Reiner, R. (2000) *The Politics of Police*. Oxford: Oxford University Press.

Reiner, R. (2007) 'Media-made criminality: the representation of crime in the mass media', in M. Maguire and R. Morgan (eds) *The Oxford Handbook of Criminology* (4th edn). London: Oxford University Press.

Reisinger, Y. and Mavondo, F. (2005) 'Travel anxiety and intentions to travel internationally: implications of travel risk perceptions', *Journal of Travel Research*, 43(3): 212–225.

Reisinger, Y. and Mavondo, F. (2006) 'Cultural differences in travel risk perception', *Journal of Travel and Tourism Marketing*, 20(1): 13–31.

Reynolds, S. (1998) *Energy Flash*. London: Picador.

Rhodes, T. (2002) 'The "risk environment"; a framework for understanding and reducing drug-related harm', *International Journal of Drug Policy*, 13(2): 85–94.

Richardson, A. and Budd, T. (2003) *Alcohol, Crime and Disorder: A Study of Young Adults*. London: Home Office Research, Development and Statistics Directorate.

Richardson, S. and Crompton, J. (1988) 'Vacation patterns of French and English Canadians', *Annals of Tourism Research*, 15(3): 430–545.

Richter, L. K. and Waugh, W. L. (1986) 'Terrorism and tourism as logical companions', *Tourism Management*, 7: 230–238.

Roane, K. R. (2005) 'The CSI effect: on TV, it's all slam-dunk evidence and quick convictions. Now juries expect the same thing – and that's a big problem', *US News*, 17 April. Available at: http://www.usnews.com/usnews/culture/articles/050425/25csi.htm

Robinson, K. (2003) 'The passion and the pleasure: Foucault's art of not being oneself', *Theory, Culture and Society*, 20(2): 119–144.

Robinson, M. B. (1998) 'Burglary revictimisation: the time period of heightened risk', *British Journal of Criminology*, 38, 78–87.

Roche, A., Bywood, P., Borlagdan, J., Lunnay, B., Freeman, T., Lawton, L., Tovell, A. and Nicholas, R. (2008) *Young People and Alcohol: The Role of Cultural Influences*. Melbourne: DrinkWise Australia.

Rock, P. (2008) 'The treatment of victims in England and Wales', *Policing*, 2(1): 110–119.

Roehl, W. S. and Fesenmaier, D. R. (1992) 'Risk perceptions and pleasure travel: an exploratory analysis', *Journal of Travel Research*, 30(4): 17–26.

Rojek, C. (1997) 'Indexing, dragging and the social construction of tourist sites', in C. Rojek (ed.) *Touring Cultures: Transformations of Travel and Theory*. London: Routledge.

Romer, D., Hall Jamieson, K. and Aday, S. (2006) 'Television news and the cultivation of fear of crime', *Journal of Communication,* 53(1): 88–104.

Rose, N. (2000) 'Government and control', *British Journal of Criminology*, 40: 321–339.

Rose, N. and Miller, P. (2010) 'Political power beyond the state: problematics of government', *British Journal of Sociology*, 6(14): 271–303.

Roselius, T. (1971) 'Consumer rankings of risk reduction methods', *Journal of Marketing*, 35: 56–61.

Ross, G. F. (1992) 'Resident perceptions of the impact of tourism on an Australian city', *Journal of Travel Research*, (Winter): 13–17.

Rountree, P. W. and Land, K. C. (1996) 'Burglary victimization, perceptions of crime risk, and routine activities: a multilevel analysis across Seattle neighborhoods and census tracts', *Journal of Research in Crime and Delinquency*, 33(2): 147–180.

Royal Society of Arts Drugs Commission (2007) *Drugs-Facing Facts: The Report of the RSA Commission on Illegal Drugs, Communities and Public Policy*. London: RSA.

Ruback, R. B., Greenberg, M. S. and Westcott, D. R. (1984) 'Social influence and crime-victim decision making', *Journal of Social Issues*, 40(1): 51–76.

Ruggiero, V. (2000) *Crime and Markets: Essays in Anti-criminology*. Oxford: Oxford University Press.

Ryan, C. (1993a) 'Crime, violence, terrorism, and tourism: an accidental or intrinsic relationship?', *Tourism Management*, 14: 173–183.

Ryan, C. (1993b) *Recreational Tourism: A Social Science Perspective*. London: Routledge.

St John, G. (ed.) (2004) *Rave Culture and Religion*. London: Sage.

Sampson, R. J., Raudenbush, S. W. and Earls, F. (1997) 'Neighborhoods and violent crime: a multilevel study of collective efficacy', *Science*, 277: 918–924.

Sanchez, L. E. (2004) 'The global e-rotic subject, the ban, and the prostitute-free zone: sex work and the theory of differential exclusion', *Environment and Planning D: Society and Space*, 22(6): 861–883.

Sandercock, L. (1997) 'From main street to fortress: the future of malls as public spaces – OR – "Shut Up and Shop"', *Just Policy*, 9: 27–34.

Sanders, T. (2005) *Sex Work: A Risky Business*. Cullompton, Devon: Willan.

Saner, E. (2007) 'Everything but the ghoul', *The Guardian*, 6 April. Available at: http://www.guardian.co.uk/film/2007/apr/06/2

Sassen, S. (1993) 'Rebuilding the global city: economy, ethnicity and space', *Social Justice*, 20(3–4): 32–50.

Savage, J. (2007) 'Backpacker rape charges', *New Zealand Herald* [online]. Available at:http://www.nzherald.co.nz/nz/news/print.cfm?c_id=1objectid=10422368&pnum=0

Schiebler, S., Crotts, J. C. and Hollinger, R. (1996) 'Florida tourists' vulnerability to crime', in A. Pizam and Y. Mansfeld (eds) *Tourism, Crime and International Security Issues*. Chichester: John Wiley & Sons.

Schlesinger, P., Dobash, R. E., Dobash, R. P. and Weaver, C. K. (1992) *Women Viewing Violence*. London: BFI Publishing.

Schmid, D. (2005) *Natural Born Celebrities: Serial Killers in American Culture*. Chicago: University of Chicago Press.

Schweitzer, N. J. and Saks, M. J. (2007) 'The *CSI* effect: popular fiction about forensic science affects the public's expectations about real forensic science', *Jurimetrics*, (Spring): 357–364.

Seddighi, H., Nuttall, M. and Theocharous, A. (2001) 'Does cultural background of tourists influence the destination choice? An empirical study with special references to political instability', *Tourism Management*, 22(2): 181–191.

Sessa, B. and Nutt, D. (2007) 'MDMA, politics and medical research: have we thrown the baby out with the bathwater?', *Journal of Psychopharmacology*, 21(8): 787–791.

Shanklin, M. and Barker, T. (2001) 'Tourists grab thrills – locals ride same old economy', Series: Special Report One-Ticket Town: The Costs of a Tourism Economy Part 1 in a 5-part series, *The Orlando Sentinel*, 16 December: p. A1.

Shaw, C. R. and McKay, H. D. (1942) *Juvenile Delinquency and Urban Areas*. Chicago: University of Chicago Press.

Shaw, M. and Pease, K. (2000) *Research on Repeat Victimisation in Scotland.* Scottish Executive Central Research Unit [online]. Available at: http://www.scotland.gov.uk/cru/kd01/green/victim00.htm

Sherman, L. W., Gartin, P. and Beurger, M. (1989) 'Hot spots of predatory crime: routine activities and the criminology of place', *Criminology*, 27(1): 27–56.

Shifflet, D. K. and Associates (2010) 'U. S. Department of Commerce, Office of Travel & Tourism Industries', Orlando CVB Research Department.

Shiner, M. (2010) 'Flying without wings: drug tourism and the political economy of pleasure', in D. Botterill and T. Jones (eds) *Tourism and Crime: Key Concepts*. Oxford: Goodfellow.

Short, B. (2006) 'Idyllic ruralities', in P. Cloke, T. Marsden and P. H. Mooney (eds) *Handbook of Rural Studies*. London: Sage.

Short, J. and Hughes, L. (eds) (2006) *Studying Youth Gangs*. Walnut Creek, CA: AltaMira Press.

Simic, O. (2009) 'Remembering, visiting and placing the dead: law, authority and genocide in Srebrenica', *Law Text Culture*, 13: 273–310.

Simmons, J., Legg, C. and Hosking, R. (2003) *National Crime Recording Standard (NCRS): An Analysis of the Impact on Recorded Crime*, companion volume to *Crime in England and Wales 2002/2003*, On-Line Report 32/03. Available at: http://rds.homeoffice.gov.uk/rds/pdfs2/rdsolr3203intro.pdf

Sims, B., Hooper, M. and Peterson, S. A. (2002) 'Determinants of citizens' attitudes toward police: results of the Harrisburg Citizen Survey – 1999', *Policing*, 25(3): 457–471.

Sin City Chamber of Commerce (2010) *The Very Best of Sin City* [online]. Available at: http://www.sincitychamberofcommerce.com/index.html

Skogan, W. G. (1984) 'Reporting crimes to the police: the status of world research', *Journal of Research in Crime and Delinquency*, 21: 113–137.

Sky News (2008) 'Karen Aim murder in New Zealand: Briton's dad devastated' [online]. Available at: http://news.sky.com/skynews/home/Sky-News-Archive/Article/2008/Karen-Aim-Murder-In-New-Zealand-Briton's-Dad-Devastated

Smith A. (2006) *Crime Statistics: An Independent Review*. London: Home Office.

Snider, E. (2008) *Saw Is Now the Most Lucrative Horror Franchise in History* [online]. Available at: http://www.cinematical.com/2008/10/26/saw-is-now-the-most-lucrative-horror-franchise-in-history/

Snow, D. (1999) 'Skateboarders, streets and style', in R. White (ed.) *Australian Youth Subcultures: On the Margins and In the Mainstream*. Hobart: Australian Clearinghouse for Youth Studies.

Sönmez, S. F. and Graefe, A. R. (1998) 'International vacation decision and terrorism risk', *Annals of Tourism Research*, 25(1): 122–124

Sonmez, S. F., Apostolopoulos, Y. and Tarlow, P. (1999) 'Tourism in crisis: managing the effects of terrorism', *Journal of Travel Research*, 38: 13–18.

Soothill, K. (1993) 'The serial killer industry', *Journal of Forensic Psychiatry*, 4(2): 341–54.

South African National Parks (2008) http://www.sanparks.org/parks

South African Tourism (2008) *The Marketing Tourism Growth Strategy for South Africa 2008–2010*. Johannesburg: South African Tourism.

South African Tourism (2010) *2009 Annual Tourism Report*. Johannesburg: South African Tourism – Strategic Research Unit.

Spalek, B. (2006) *Crime Victims: Theory, Policy and Practice*. Hampshire: Palgrave Macmillan

Sparti, D. (2001) 'Making up people: on some looping effects of the human kind – institutional reflexivity or social control?', *European Journal of Social Theory*, 4(3): 331–349.

Statistics New Zealand (2006) *Crime in New Zealand: 1996–2005*. Wellington: Statistics New Zealand.

Stimpson, G. (2007) ' "Harm reduction – coming of age": a local movement with global impact', *International Journal of Drug Policy*, 18(2): 67–69.

Stangeland, P. (1998) 'Other targets or other locations?', *British Journal of Criminology*, 38: 61–77.

Stuff.co.nz (2009) 'Tourists warned about South Island danger spots' [online]. Available at: http://www.stuff.co.nz/the-press/802244

Sumnall, H., Bellis, M. A., Hughes, K., Calafat, A., Juan, M. and Mendes, F. (2010) 'A choice between fun and health? Relationships between nightlife substance use, happiness and mental well-being', *Journal of Substance Use*, 15(2): 89–104.

Sutton, A., Cherney, A. and White, R. (2008) *Crime Prevention: Principles, Perspectives and Practices*. Melbourne: Cambridge University Press.

Swaffield, S. and Fairweather, J. (1998) 'In search of Arcadia: the persistence of rural idyll in New Zealand rural subdivisions', *Journal of Environment Planning and Management*, 41 (1): 111–127.

Swedish Environmental Protection Agency (2009) *The Right of Public Access: The Freedom to Roam* [online]. Available at: http://www.swed-ishepa.se/en/In-English/Menu/Enjoying-nature/The-right-of-public-access/The-Right-of-Public-Access--the-freedom-to-roam/

Szmigin, I., Griffin, C., Mistral, W., Bengry-Howell, A., Weale, L. and Hackley, C. (2008) 'Re-framing "binge drinking" as calculated hedonism: empirical evidence from the UK', *International Journal of Drug Policy*, 19 (5): 359–366.

Tackett-Gibson, M. (2008) 'Constructions of risk and harm in online discussions of ketamine use', *Addiction Research and Theory*, 16(3): 245–257.

Tarlow, P. (2000) 'Creating safe and secure communities in economically challenging times', *Tourism Economics*, 6 (2): 139–149.

Tarlow P. (2006) 'A social theory of terrorism and tourism', in A. Pizam and Y. Mansfield (eds) *Tourism Security and Safety: From Theory to Practice*. New York: John Wiley.

Teye, V. B. (1988) 'Coup d'etats and African tourism: a study of Ghana', *Annals of Tourism Research*, 15(3): 329–356.

Teye, V., Sönmez, S. and Sirakaya, E. (2002) 'Resident attitudes toward tourism development', *Annals of Tourism Research*, 29(3): 668–688.

Thibault, E., Lynch, L. and McBride, R. (2001) *Proactive Police Management*. Upper Saddle River, NJ: Prentice Hall.

Thomas, M. and Butcher, M. (2003) 'Cruising', in M. Butcher and M. Thomas (eds) *Ingenious: Emerging Youth Cultures in Urban Australia*. Melbourne: Pluto Press.

Tolkien, J. R. R. (1982) *The Hobbit*. New York: Del Rey, Ballantine Books.

Tomsen, S. (1997a) 'A top night: social protest, masculinity and the culture of drinking violence', *British Journal of Criminology*, 37(1): 90–102.

Tomsen, S. (1997b) 'Youth violence and the limits of moral panic', *Youth Studies Australia*, 16(1): 25–30.

Toohey, P. (2003) 'Party animals', *Weekend Australian Magazine*, 12–13 July: 16–19.

Turner, L. and Ash, J. (1975) *The Golden Hordes: International Tourism and the Pleasure Periphery*. London: Constable.

Um, S. and Crompton, J. L. (1990) 'Attitude determinants in tourism destination choice', *Annals of Tourism Research*, 17: 432–448.

Ungar, S. (2001) 'Moral panic versus the risk society: the implications of the changing sites of social anxiety', *British Journal of Sociology*, 52(2): 271–291.

United Nations World Tourism Organisation (UNWTO) (2010) *Tourism Highlights 2009*. Madrid: UNWTO.

United States Bureau of Labor Statistics (2010) *Nonfarm Wage and Salary Employment* [online]. Available at: http://data.bls.gov/cgi-bin/print.pl/eag/eag.fl_orlando_msa.htm

United States Census Bureau (2008) *The 2008 Statistical Abstract: The National Data Book* [online]. Available at: http://www.census.gov/compendia/statab/2008/2008edition.html

United States Department of Justice (2009) 'Crime in the United States' [online]. Available at: http://www2.fbi.gov/ucr/cius2009/index.html

Urbanowicz, C. (1977) 'Integrating tourism with other industries in Tonga', in B. H. Farrel (ed.) *The Social and Economic Impact of Tourism on Pacific Communities*. Santa Cruz: University of Santa Cruz.

Uriely, N. and Belhassen, Y. (2005) 'Drugs and tourists' experiences', *Journal of Travel Research*, 43(3): 238–246.

Vaaranen, H. and Wieloch, N. (2002) 'Car crashes and dead end careers: leisure pursuits of the Finnish subculture of the Kortteliralli street racing', *Young: Nordic Journal of Youth Research*, 10: 42–59.

Valdez, A. and Sifaneck, S. J. (1997) 'Drug tourists and drug policy on the U.S.–Mexican border: an ethnographic investigation of the acquisition of prescribed drugs', *Journal of Drug Issues*, 27(4): 879–897.

Venditto, J. and Mouzos, J. (2006) 'The murder of overseas visitors in Australia', *Trends & Issues in Crime and Criminal Justice, no. 316*, Australian Institute of Criminology [online]. Available at: www.aic.gov.au/publications/tandi2/tandi316t.html

Vesselinov, E., Cazessus, M. and Falk, W. (2007) 'Gated communities and spatial inequality', *Journal of Urban Affairs*, 29(2): 109–127.

Visit Orlando (2011) 'Orlando visitor volume' [online]. Available at: http://www.orlandoinfo.com/research/market/index.cfmhttp://www.visitorlando.com/research/visitors/volume.cfm

Vronsky, P. (2004) *Serial Killers. The Method and Madness of Monsters*. New York: Berkley Publishing Group Penguin.

Walker, A., Flatley, J., Kershaw, C. and Moon, D. (2009) *Crime in England and Wales 2008/09*, HOSB 11/09. London: Home Office. Available at: http://www.homeoffice.gov.uk/rds/pdfs09/hosb1109vol1.pdf

Walker, L. and Page, S. J. (2007) 'The visitor experience of crime: the case of central Scotland', *Current Issues in Tourism*, 10(6): 505–542.

Walker, L., Butland, D. and Connell, R. (2000) 'Boys on the road: masculinities, car culture and road safety education', *Journal of Men's Studies*, 2(8): 153–166.

Walkowitz, J. (1992) *City of Dreadful Delight: Narratives of Sexual Danger in Late Victorian London*. London: Virago Press.

Wallace, A. (2008) 'Things like that don't happen here: crime, place and real estate in the news', *Crime Media Culture*, 4(3): 395–409.

Walmsley, D. J., Boskovic, R. M. and Pigram, J. J. (1983) 'Tourism and crime: an Australian perspective', *Journal of Leisure Research*, 15(2): 136–155.

Wang, Y. (2008) 'Collaborative destination marketing: roles and strategies of convention and visitors bureau', *Journal of Vacation Marketing*, 14(3): 191–209.

Warburton, H., May, T. and Hough, M (2005) 'Looking the other way: the impact of reclassifying cannabis on police warnings, arrests and informal action in England and Wales', *British Journal of Criminology*, 45(2): 113–128.

Ward Jouve, N. (1988) *'The Street-Cleaner': The Yorkshire Ripper Case on Trial*. London: Marion Boyers Publications.

Warren, I. and Palmer, D. (2010) 'Crime risks of three-dimensional virtual environments', *Trends and Issues in Crime and Criminal Justice*, No. 388. Canberra: Australian Institute of Criminology.

Waszkiewicz, P. (2007) 'Gated communities: effect of fear of crime', paper to 7th Annual Conference of the European Society of Criminology, Bologna, September.

Weber, E. U. and Bottom, W. P. (1989) 'Axiomatic measures of perceived risk: some tests and extensions', *Journal of Behavioral Decision-Making*, 2(2): 113–131.

Western Morning News (2006) 'Racers make life a misery, say residents', March.

White, C. (2006) 'The Spanner trials and the changing law on sadomasochism in the UK', *Journal of Homosexuality*, 50(2): 167–187.

White, R. (1990) *No Space of their Own: Young People and Social Control in Australia*. Melbourne: Cambridge University Press.

White, R. (ed.) (1993) *Youth Subcultures: Theory, History and the Australian Experience*. Hobart: National Clearinghouse for Youth Studies.

White, R. (ed.) (1999) *Australian Youth Subcultures: On the Margins and in the Mainstream*. Hobart: National Clearinghouse for Youth Studies.

White, R. (2001) 'Graffiti, crime prevention and cultural space', *Current Issues in Criminal Justice*, 12(3): 253–268.

White, R. (2002) 'Indigenous young Australians, criminal justice and offensive language', *Journal of Youth Studies*, 5(1): 21–34.

White, R. (2006a) 'Swarming and the social dynamics of group violence', *Trends and Issues in Crime and Criminal Justice*, No. 326. Canberra: Australian Institute of Criminology,

White, R. (2006b) 'Youth gang research in Australia', in J. Short and L. Hughes (eds) *Studying Youth Gangs*. Walnut Creek, CA: AltaMira Press.

White, R. (2007a) 'Public spaces, consumption, and the social regulation of young people', in S. Venkatesh and R. Kassimir (eds) *Youth, Globalization, and the Law*. Stanford, CA: Stanford University Press.

White, R. (2007b) 'Taking it to the streets: from the larrikins to the Lebanese', in S. Ponyting and G. Morgan (eds) *Outrageous!: Moral Panics in Australia*. Hobart: ACYS Publishing.

White, R. (2008a) 'Disputed definitions and fluid identities: the limitations of social profiling in relation to ethnic youth gangs', *Youth Justice: An International Journal*, 8(2): 149–161.

White, R. (2008b) 'Australian youth gangs and the social dynamics of ethnicity', in F. van Gemert, D. Peterson and I.-L. Lien (eds) *Youth Gangs, Migration, and Ethnicity*. Cullompton, Devon: Willan Publishing.

White, R. (2009) 'Indigenous youth and gangs as family', *Youth Studies Australia*, 28(3): 47–56.

White, R. and Mason, R. (2006) 'Youth gangs and youth violence: charting the key dimensions', *Australian and New Zealand Journal of Criminology*, 39(1): 54–70.

White, R. and Sutton, A. (1995) 'Crime prevention, urban space and social exclusion', *Australian and New Zealand Journal of Sociology*, 31(1): 82–99.

White, R. and Wyn, J. (2008) *Youth and Society: Exploring the Social Dynamics of Youth Experience*. Melbourne: Oxford University Press.

Whyte, W. (1964) *Street Corner Society*. Chicago: University of Chicago Press.

Wilbert, C. and Hansen, R. (2009) 'Walks in spectral space: East London crime scene tourism', in A. Jansson and A. Lagerkvist (eds) *Strange Spaces: Explorations into Mediated Obscurity*. Surrey: Ashgate Publishing.

Williams, S. (2000) *Emotion and Social Theory: Corporeal Reflections on the Ir(rational)*. London: Sage.

Willing, R. (2004) ' "CSI effect" has juries wanting more evidence', *USA Today* [online]. Available at: http://www.usatoday.com/news/nation/2004–08–05-csi-effect_x.htm

Wilson, J. Q. and Kelling, G. L. (1982) 'Broken windows: the police and neighbourhood safety', *Atlantic Monthly*, 249: 29–38.

Winstock, A., Mitchenson, L. and Marsden, J. (2010) 'Mephedrone: still available and twice the price', *The Lancet*, 376(9752): 1537.

Wise, J. (2009) *The New Scientific Eyewitness: The Role of DNA Profiling in Shaping Criminal Justice*. Saarbrücken, Germany: VDM Verlag.

Wise, J. (2010) 'Providing the CSI treatment: criminal justice practitioners and the CSI effect', *Current Issues in Criminal Justice*, 21(3): 383–399.

Witt, S. F. and Moutinho, L. (eds) (1989) *Tourism Marketing and Management Handbook*. Upper Saddle River, NJ: Prentice Hall.

Wolf, R. (2002) 'Proactive change toward a tourism-oriented police in Saint Lucia', *Caribbean Journal of Criminology and Social Psychology*, 7(1–2): 235–244.

Wolf, R. (2008) 'Tourism oriented policing: an examination of a Florida/Caribbean partnership for police training', *International Journal of Police Science and Management*, 10(4): 402–416.

Wonders, N. A. and Michalowski, R. (2001) 'Bodies, borders and sex tourism in a globalized world: a tale of two cities – Amsterdam and Havana', *Social Problems*, 48(4): 545–571.

Wood, D., Warren-Gash, C., Ashraf, T., Greene, S. L., Sather, Z., Trivedy, C., Clarke, S., Ramsey, J., Holt, D. and Dargen, P. (2008) 'Medical and legal confusion surrounding gamma-hydroxybutrate (GHB) and its precursors gamma-butyrolactone (GBL) and 1,4-butanediol (1,4BD)', *Quarterly Journal of Medicine*, 101: 23–29.

Woods, M. (2011) 'Policing rural protest', in Mawby, R. I. and Yarwood, R. (eds) *Rural Policing and Policing the Rural: A Constable Countryside*. Surrey: Ashgate.

Worpole, K. and Greenhalgh, L. (1996) *The Freedom of the City*. London: Demos.

Woulfe, C., Erwin, M. and Longmore, M. (2006) 'Honeymooners in kidnap and rape ordeal', *New Zealand Herald* [online]. Available at: http://www.nzherald.co.nz/miles-erwin/news/article.cfm?a_id=297&objectid=10410342

Wyatt, T. (2009) 'Exploring the organization of Russia far east's illegal wildlife trade: two case studies of the illegal fur and illegal falcon trades', *Global Crime*, 10(1–2): 144–154.

Zajdow, G. (2010) '"It blasted me into space": intoxication and an ethics of pleasure', *Health Sociology Review*, 19(2): 218–229.

Index